The "honorable men" who ruled the Old South had a language all their own, one comprised of many apparently outlandish features yet revealing much about the lives of masters and the nature of slavery. When we examine Jefferson Davis's explanation as to why he was wearing women's clothes when caught by Union soldiers, or when we consider the story of Virginia statesman John Randolph, who stood on his doorstep declaring to an unwanted dinner guest that he was "not at home," we see that conveying empirical truths was not the goal of their speech. As Kenneth Greenberg so skillfully demonstrates, the language of honor embraced a complex system of phrases, gestures, and behaviors that centered on deep-rooted values: asserting authority and maintaining respect. How these values were encoded in such acts as nose-pulling, outright lying, dueling, and gift-giving is a matter that Greenberg takes up in a fascinating and original way.

(CONTINUED ON BACK FLAP)

Honor & Slavery

Honor & Slavery

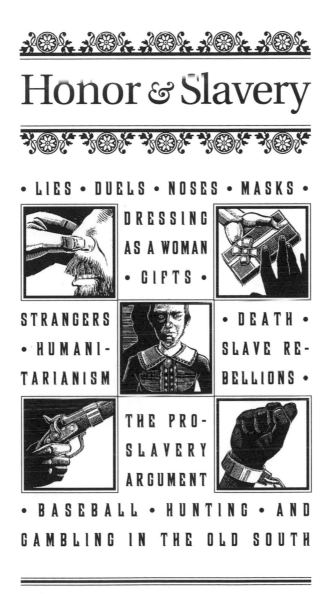

· LIES · DUELS · NOSES · MASKS ·
DRESSING AS A WOMAN · GIFTS · STRANGERS · HUMANI- TARIANISM · DEATH · SLAVE RE- BELLIONS · THE PRO- SLAVERY ARGUMENT · BASEBALL · HUNTING · AND GAMBLING IN THE OLD SOUTH

KENNETH S. GREENBERG

PRINCETON UNIVERSITY PRESS · PRINCETON, NEW JERSEY

LIBRARY OF CONGRESS CATALOGING-IN-PUBLICATION DATA

GREENBERG, KENNETH S.

HONOR & SLAVERY : LIES, DUELS, NOSES, MASKS, DRESSING AS A WOMAN,

GIFTS, STRANGERS, HUMANITARIANISM, DEATH, SLAVE REBELLIONS,

THE PROSLAVERY ARGUMENT, BASEBALL, HUNTING, AND GAMBLING

IN THE OLD SOUTH /KENNETH S. GREENBERG.

P. CM.

INCLUDES INDEX.

ISBN 0-691-02734-X (CL : ALK. PAPER)

1. SOUTHERN STATES—CIVILIZATION—1775–1865.

2. SOUTHERN STATES—SOCIAL LIFE AND CUSTOMS—1775–1865.

3. HONOR—SOUTHERN STATES—HISTORY—19TH CENTURY.

4. SLAVERY—SOUTHERN STATES.   I. TITLE.

F213.G793   1996

306.3′62′0975—DC20   95-43051

THIS BOOK HAS BEEN COMPOSED IN UTOPIA

PRINCETON UNIVERSITY PRESS BOOKS ARE PRINTED
ON ACID-FREE PAPER AND MEET THE GUIDELINES FOR
PERMANENCE AND DURABILITY OF THE COMMITTEE ON
PRODUCTION GUIDELINES FOR BOOK LONGEVITY
OF THE COUNCIL ON LIBRARY RESOURCES

PRINTED IN THE UNITED STATES OF AMERICA
BY PRINCETON ACADEMIC PRESS

3 5 7 9 10 8 6 4 2

For Judi
and for Laura, Amy, and Lisa

CONTENTS

ILLUSTRATIONS

PREFACE

THIS BOOK is a work of translation. It is a reconstruction and inter- pretation of a "dead" language—the language of the "honorable gentlemen" who ruled the Old South. Such an approach may strike a modern reader as peculiar. After all, antebellum Southern men of honor spoke and wrote in English. What is the nature and purpose of a transla- tion from English into English?

Actually, the use of English by men of honor makes them more difficult to understand than they would be if they had spoken in a more obviously foreign tongue. It is easy to assume that their communications do not require translation—that when they used words and gestures that resem- ble ones we still use, they meant what we mean. But words and gestures are merely components of a language system; they achieve their meaning in relation to other parts of that system. Meaning varies with the sur- rounding culture and context. Most significantly, the language of honor used by Southern gentlemen was embedded in a slave society. Hence, Southern men of honor spoke a language as alien to a modern English speaker as any more conventional foreign tongue. Since the language of honor was the dominant language of the men who ruled the slave South, we will never understand masters, the nature of slavery, or the Civil War without first understanding that language.

The reconstruction of a language is a messy business—as is suggested by the sprawling subtitle of this volume. Such a reconstruction cannot be accomplished in dictionary form, since dictionaries usually reduce con- text: they isolate words and connect them to other isolated words. My approach has been to search the language of Southern men of honor for phrases, gestures, values, and behaviors that seem remote and unusually difficult to understand. I have then recreated the appropriate contexts and associations that made them comprehensible to men of honor. Each chapter contains several puzzles involving actions or words that do not make obvious sense to a modern mind. Some of these puzzles may seem trivial at first glance. But in explaining a "sign" by placing it in context, each chapter moves to a deep description of a worldview and a culture. As one might expect in a language system, each sign points toward larger connections and associations; the themes of each chapter move outward and ultimately cross and recross each other.

Who spoke the language of honor? At an early stage in the writing of this book, I thought that the extent of dueling activity would be a good indicator of the spread of the language in space and time. The duel, after all, embodied the core values of honor.[1] However, when I attempted to apply the duel as a measure, I realized it was not a useful device. At first I thought it would be informative to count all Southern men who exchanged shots on dueling grounds. Then I discovered that most "dueling encounters" never involved bullets. Every time Southern men exchanged harsh words in a certain form, they were involved in a confrontation that demonstrated their adherence to the same set of values as men who exchanged shots. I also realized that the formal duel of upper-class gentlemen was only one version of a duel; lower-class men who fought with their fists or who tried to gouge out each other's eyes also were involved in a type of dueling encounter. And what about the many men who never became directly involved in any of these deadly encounters, but who looked on them with favor? Were they not also duelists—at least for the purpose of using the duel as a measure of the language of honor? Ultimately, I recognized that the values of honor as expressed in the duel could even be advocated by people who opposed the duel. This was the case with the many state legislators who passed statutes outlawing the duel all over the South.

The duel, however one may choose to define it, was just one ritual that embodied the values of the language of honor.[2] Those same values could be expressed in many other ways. They were articulated when masters called slaves liars and whipped them, when gentlemen gave gifts, when they gambled for high stakes, when they hunted, when they refused to play baseball, when they extended hospitality, when they died, when they rejected a humanitarian concern for strangers, when they expressed an appreciation for their noses, when they fought the Civil War—and in countless other ways. In other words, the language of honor was spoken almost universally by the white men of the South. It was connected to slavery, but it was spoken by many men who did not actually own slaves.

The search for meaning in the language of honor has led me to ask numerous questions rarely posed by other students of the South. Why did Lieutenant Robert Beverly Randolph pull President Andrew Jackson's nose? Why did United States Senator John Randolph give so many gifts during his dueling encounter with Secretary of State Henry Clay? Why did Southerners dissect Nat Turner's body? Why did Southern gentlemen *not* invent and play baseball? The answers to these kinds of questions require links to other parts of the language of honor. For example, in order to understand nose pulling, it is necessary to explore the attitudes of men of honor toward lying, science, market activities, slaves, and much more. The gifts John Randolph gave during his dueling encounter relate to the meaning of gift exchange in the master-slave relation, to the proslavery argument, to attitudes toward strangers, to humanitarianism, and to the loans gentlemen extended to each other. The dissection of Nat Turner's body connects to the way Southern gentlemen hoped to die, to their proslavery argument, and to their ideas on the nature of slavery and slave rebellions.

Since this book covers a broad range of associations, it portrays a landscape viewed without the constraints of space and time. While I largely confine the analysis to the antebellum South, I freely move within those limits. Moreover, characters keep popping up and disappearing. P. T. Barnum sends his mermaid to Charleston early in the book, later requests the women's clothing worn by Jefferson Davis at his capture, and finally comments on gambling. J. Marion Sims, the "father" of American gynecology, pulls the chair out from under a friend in one place and dresses as a woman in another. James Henry Hammond learns to live with the petty thievery of his slaves in one chapter, gives loans to friends in another, and dies in a third. Similarly, themes keep reappearing in unexpected places. A discussion of nose pulling turns to conceptions of lying, but so do analyses of masks and of gambling. The chapter on gift exchange leads to a new understanding of the proslavery argument, and so does the chapter on death. The connection between death and slavery emerges as a theme in discussions of Nat Turner, baseball, hunting, and gambling. The duel is central to every chapter in the book.

I have portrayed a world in which events, gestures, and words are related, a discourse in which meanings are often homologous. Repeatedly, discussions that head down one path end up returning to paths already taken. Every puzzling action or statement analyzed in the book relates to honor, and since Southern gentlemen defined a slave as a person without honor, all issues of honor relate to slavery. Each chapter sets out in a new direction and ends up returning to the same place—the place where slavery and honor intersect. I have concentrated on three ways in which men of honor distinguished themselves from slaves: they would never allow anyone to call them liars; they gave gifts; and they did not fear death. Every path in the book leads back to these themes; these themes, in turn, lead back to one another, for they all involve different aspects of the ritual of the duel. The components of the language of honor echoed each other in countless variations within a complex, interrelated system.

Since the focus of this volume is on the reconstruction of a language, it does not deal with issues of linear or dialectical causation. The book makes no claim that the language of honor caused slavery, that slavery caused the language of honor, or that either caused the Civil War. I do not argue that events or structures in a real or material world caused language, or that language caused a real world to change. In fact, my method involves the collapse of these categories. Since we must interpret the world through language, it is not possible to separate one from the other. Overall, my goal has been the goal of a translator: to understand the language of Southern men of honor. To understand their language is to enter the fluid world of the past—a world where a conversation about base-ball is a conversation about death and slavery, where an election is a gift exchange, where a concern for noses conveys attitudes about lies. To understand the language of the men who ruled the Old South is to know them as deeply as it is possible to know other humans. It is to compre-hend a world rather than its pieces.

It would have been impossible to reconstruct the world of honor and slavery if others had not pointed the way. This book builds on the work of a number of scholars who have appreciated the importance of honor in the culture of the antebellum South. John Hope Franklin, Edward L. Ayers, and Steven M. Stowe have all written important books with South-ern honor as a central theme. Bertram Wyatt-Brown's classic *Southern Honor: Ethics and Behavior in the Old South* enlightened and inspired me when I first read it. It remains the place to begin any study of honor in the Old South.[3] My intention in *Honor and Slavery* has been to move the discussion of honor in directions not fully explored in the works of my colleagues in the field. My hope is that readers of this volume will be stimulated to extend the analysis even further.

ACKNOWLEDGMENTS

SUPPORT for this book was supplied by the National Endowment for the Humanities, the Charles Warren Center at Harvard University, Harvard Law School's program in Law and Humanities, and Suffolk University. Together, these institutions provided the financial backing, as well as the physical space and intellectual environments, that made it possible to complete the volume.

I delivered talks based on versions of several chapters of the book at a variety of institutions. Questions, comments, and conversations generated by these lectures allowed me to clarify and to improve the manuscript in numerous ways. I deeply appreciate the invitations to speak at the Boston University School of Law, Harvard Law School, the Charles Warren Center at Harvard University, Brandeis University, Suffolk University, and Alfred University.

A version of chapter 1 was published as "The Nose, the Lie, and the Duel in the Antebellum South," *American Historical Review* 95, no. 1 (February 1990): 57–74.

Many readers have commented on part or all of the manuscript of this book. I am grateful that the members of the community of scholars to which I belong never hesitated to point out my mistakes. Nor did they hold back on the praise that every scholar needs in order to avoid discouragement. I cannot imagine a more conscientious and helpful group of readers. I am especially grateful to Edward L. Ayers, Bernard Bailyn, Catherine Clinton, Eugene D. Genovese, Peter Kolchin, Stuart A. Marks, Louis P. Masur, Martha Minow, Daniel T. Rodgers, Steven M. Stowe, and Bertram Wyatt-Brown.

My community at Suffolk University provided the kind of intellectual and social environment that makes scholarly work enjoyable. Dean Michael Ronayne, a professor of chemistry who appreciates a good nose-pulling story, always generously supported my work. The Integrated Studies Faculty Seminar provided a forum for the airing of many ideas in the manuscript. Robert Hannigan, Fred Marchant, and Alexandra Todd offered the kind of criticism and encouragement one can expect from friends. Susan Keefe and Sharon Lenzie gave generously of their time and energy on many occasions.

Several of my friends from the community of legal scholars provided a model of political commitment, intellectual innovation, and scholarly rigor that has inspired my work. I owe a great debt to Gerald Frug, Morton Horwitz, Duncan Kennedy, Fran Olsen, Joe Singer, and Avi Soifer. Mary Joe Frug, a brilliant postmodern feminist legal scholar, was murdered shortly after I began work on this volume, but her ideas have assumed a life of their own through her friends and family, her publications, and the many works of scholarship she influenced. In this book, she helped dress Jefferson Davis as a woman.

I discussed virtually every page of the manuscript with Judi Greenberg. This volume would not have been possible without her intellectual and emotional support. Laura Greenberg, Amy Greenberg, and Lisa Greenberg provided help in countless ways—offering critical comments, telling me when I was boring, and patting me on the back when I needed it. Similar support came from Howard Greenberg, Jean Guttman, and Roslyn Marino. The various members of the Berwick family had much to say about honor and slavery—especially when we hiked together at high altitudes on narrow mountain trails. The Guttmans and Jacobsons generally offered their insights at a lower topographical location. Alan Guttman died just as I began work on this book. He was not a trained academic, but his love of ideas and his humane purposes continue to shape my scholarship.

Honor & Slavery

ONE

THE NOSE, THE LIE, AND THE DUEL

SOMETIMES, white men of the antebellum South pulled, or tweaked, one another's noses. Slaves never pulled anyone's nose; neither did white women. Nose pulling was a meaningful gesture that appeared almost exclusively in the active vocabulary of white men. To pull a nose was to communicate a complex set of meanings to an antagonist and an audience. What did the act mean to the men who performed it and witnessed it? For Southern white men, nose pulling was an action embedded in a larger system of signs—a "language" of honor.[1] One must reconstruct the system in order to understand the meaning of its parts.[2]

To understand the system of meanings that surrounded nose pulling in the South, it is necessary to interpret and to connect parts of white male language that may at first appear to be unrelated. En route to an analysis of nose pulling, this chapter explains why P. T. Barnum was less popular in the South than in the North; how scientific and market activities were connected to each other but not to the world of honor; why men of honor dueled over disagreements that people outside their tradition regarded as trivial; why practical jokes had a different meaning for men of honor than for men of trade; why many antidueling laws required the mutilation of men who dueled; why abolitionists and proslavery apologists read the meaning of scars on the backs of slaves differently; and why the nose was more important than the genitals to Southern gentlemen. One thread runs through and around each of these cultural phenomena. Each demonstrates that Southern men of honor were "superficial." They were concerned, to a degree we would consider unusual, with the surface of things—with the world of appearances.

I

One good way to approach the language of white men of honor is through an analysis of a dispute occasioned by the exhibition of the Feejee Mermaid to the people of Charleston, South Carolina, in early 1843. This

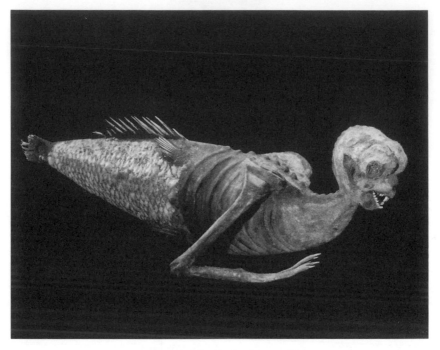

FIGURE 1. The Feejee Mermaid.

event contains no explicit mention of noses (or lies or duels), but it harbors many oblique references. The story begins with a collaboration between Moses Kimball of Boston, the owner of the mermaid, and P. T. Barnum, who arranged for its exhibition. Barnum, that quintessential Connecticut Yankee, that master of deceit, showmanship, and humbug in nineteenth-century America, undoubtedly was aware from the start that the mermaid was a fake—the upper torso of a dead monkey skillfully joined to the lower body of a fish. Nevertheless, he hired a manager to take it on tour and arranged for an elaborate publicity campaign to herald its arrival in Philadelphia and New York. The exhibit met with such an enthusiastic reception in these cities that Barnum decided on a tour of the South that began in Charleston, South Carolina, early in 1843.[3]

The mermaid stirred more than wonder upon its arrival in the South. It became the object of a controversy that threatened to break into violence. The disturbance began in the newspapers of Charleston just after the mermaid arrived. Richard Yeadon, a local lawyer and one of the three editors of the *Charleston Courier*, wrote an unsigned review of the exhibit, venturing his opinion that the mermaid was probably a natural object

and that he could detect no seam to indicate that it was an artificial combination of ape and fish. "We were permitted to handle and examine it as
closely as could be effected by touch and sight," he wrote, "and . . . if
there be any deception, it is beyond the discovery of both those senses."
But, at almost the same time, a very different article appeared in the rival
Charleston Mercury. Writing under the name "No Humbug," the respected naturalist and Lutheran minister John Bachman declared the
mermaid to be a fraud, "a fishes tail attached to the head and shoulders
of a Baboon," "a clumsy affair," "a smoke dried affair" created by "our
Yankee neighbors." He suggested that the naturalists of Charleston
should be allowed to examine it, and if they found it to be a hoax they
should "throw the creature into the fire" and the exhibitor should "clear
himself from the city as fast as his heels can carry him."[5] The debate
initiated by these notes led to the publication of more than two dozen
letters during the next few months—some of considerable length, occasionally occupying more than a quarter of all the article space in the
major South Carolina newspapers.

Among the dispute's many interesting features was Bachman's contention that the editors of the *Courier* had failed to treat him with respect.
He had originally gone to them with his letter denouncing the exhibit as
a fraud. They refused to publish it because they found the language of the
letter "too severe." He then brought it to the *Mercury*, whose editors
promptly printed it—only to discover that the *Courier* had not only rejected his letter but also published an editorial review in support of the
mermaid. "Who was the writer of this anonymous communication
[the editorial] I am not prepared to say," Bachman wrote with barely con-
cealed fury, "and I leave the public to judge both of the author and the
motives of its insertion in the very nick of time to serve as a foil to protect
an Impostor [the exhibitor of the mermaid] from public indignation."[6]

At the same time, Bachman raised the question of who was competent
to pass judgment on the mermaid. Joined by other South Carolina scientists, he wondered why the lawyer and editor, Yeadon, felt qualified to
make statements about matters scientific. Bachman had seen a seam at
the juncture of fish and monkey, and if Yeadon did not detect one, it was
only because he was "untrained in such observations."[7] Yeadon conceded that he was no scientist and emphasized that he had not made an
unequivocal claim about the authenticity of the mermaid—he had stated
only that, when he took it from the case, he could neither see nor feel a
seam. He cared "not a whit, not a stiver, whether the Mermaid is real or
not."[8] He only demanded that his observation be treated with respect.
"Mr. No Humbug," Yeadon claimed, had unfairly attacked him: "he has
assaulted us whip in hand, but we mean to take it from him and lay it, and
that smartly, on his own shoulders."[9]

Another theme in the dispute involved the use of names and pseudonyms. The original articles were either unsigned editorials or pieces signed with noms de plume such as "No Humbug" and "The Man Who Exhibits the Mermaid." But after February 6, the real names began to appear in print. This was an important transition. Yeadon apparently had long felt that, as editor of the *Courier*, he could not maintain anonymity as easily as could Bachman. An inequality had developed. He objected to his opponent's practice of addressing his letters to "the editor of the *Courier*." There were three editors, and it was offensive, Yeadon felt, to single out one by not using the plural form of address. The singular form of address had begun to move the dispute to a more dangerous and personal level. Moreover, Yeadon believed that Bachman had mentioned his name to other people, and he objected that "it [his name] was a common subject of conversation out of doors promiscuously," with the result that he had been "frequently met with the taunt that Mr. —— has given it to you well."[10]

In fact, the moment of transition from anonymity to names was so delicate that it required the intervention of "a mutual friend" to prevent the dispute from ending in an exchange of pistol shots. The mutual friend negotiated an agreement that allowed for the simultaneous public use of real names by each party. In the February 6 issue of the *Courier* Yeadon wrote that "an explanatory interview and consequent cessation of hostilities" had been effected, "the *amende honorable* has been made us, and mutual explanations were given."[11] Both men then began to sign their names to their articles. But the anonymity issue would not die. When Yeadon later reverted to signing his initials—a tactic that did not really hide his identity but indicated a slight movement away from the open assertion of names that had become characteristic of the dispute— Bachman complained to the editor of the *Courier* (who of course was Yeadon), "I trust I am not making an unfair request that when any of your correspondents undertake to correct my statements in your Journal, you require them to give their names in full. In these matters I prefer seeing something beyond initials."[12] Clearly, some important maneuvering was involved here.

What is most startling about the debate over the Feejee Mermaid is the remarkable lack of interest in the mermaid itself. While in another context the scientists might have had a desire to discover whether or not this was a natural mermaid, neither they nor Yeadon devoted much of their newspaper discussion to that topic. More important were such matters as whether Bachman had been handled with dignity by the *Courier*, whether Yeadon's observation that he could see no seam had been treated with proper respect by the scientists, and whether the parties had properly or improperly used and treated pseudonyms supplied by the writers. It was not a debate about whether the Feejee Mermaid was a real mermaid or a hoax. Yeadon himself had said so unequivocally. He "care[d] not a whit, not a stiver, whether the Mermaid is real or not."[13] Although the mermaid had left town by the end of January, the dispute continued to rage until late March. The central concern of these men was to have their words, names, and pseudonyms treated with respect. Honor was at stake. Penetration into the secrets of nature was of little interest.

II

If the dispute over the Feejee Mermaid had been an isolated event in antebellum Southern history, it could be dismissed as trivial, but it was not. The lack of interest in the Feejee Mermaid and in other secrets of nature was characteristic of the antebellum South. The incident may clarify why scientists and other intellectuals in this culture felt unappreciated. Historians have long been aware of the complaints of neglect by the intellectuals of the South.[14] Some have attributed the problem to the absence of cities and the consequent lack of a reading public concentrated in urban areas. Others have suggested that intellectuals play a marginal role in most societies. While these explanations offer some insight into the problems of Southern thinkers, the Feejee Mermaid episode points in another direction.

A central concern of nineteenth-century scientific and intellectual activity was to penetrate into the secrets of nature, to move from the level of superficial appearance to a deeper, hidden reality; it therefore may have involved a sensibility alien to antebellum Southern white male culture. Many cultures concerned with honor value appearance highly. Their members project themselves through how they look and what they say.[15] They are treated honorably when their projections are respected and accepted as true. The central issue of concern to men in such a culture is not the nature of some underlying reality but the acceptance of their projections. They "care not a whit" about the reality of the mermaid. The men who achieve the most honorable positions in such a culture are statesmen—men whose vision of themselves and their world is confirmed by popular acclamation.[16] Intellectuals, who conceive of their activity as exposing hidden levels of reality, are engaged in work of peripheral interest.[17]

The Feejee Mermaid episode also echoed the world of Southern dueling. This connection is significant because the duel was a central ritual of antebellum Southern life, embodying many core values of white society. Evidence of its centrality exists everywhere. Large numbers of public figures participated in duels as principals or seconds; the South maintained a tenacious attachment to the institution even as it died in the North. Even more revealing of its importance in Southern life are the many examples of men who achieved great political success after they dueled, and men who feared that to refuse a duel was to become an outcast in the culture, and the almost complete absence of any successful prosecution of the substantial number of men who killed others in duels.[18]

The Feejee Mermaid dispute resembled the duel in several striking ways. First, the form of the dispute was remarkably similar to the form of typical nineteenth-century dueling encounters. In both cases the conflict originated in insulting words or actions. Then came a carefully worded exchange of letters in which each party tried to describe how he had been injured—how he had not been treated with the kind of courtesy due him as a social equal. There was the intervention of another party whose job it was to bring about a reconciliation through a carefully constructed understanding in which each party explained his language and acknowledged his equality with the other. Even the publication of the details of the Feejee Mermaid dispute paralleled a practice typical of dueling encounters. A duel was a theatrical display for public consumption, and the parties expected descriptions of the events to be widely circulated. The Feejee Mermaid episode did not lead to an exchange of pistol shots, but neither did the vast majority of conflicts that were part of the world of dueling.[19]

Second, participants in dueling encounters and in the Feejee Mermaid case expressed similar conceptions of what constituted an insult. At the heart of both encounters was the accusation of lying. Consider the importance of lying as an insult in a typical dueling dispute. Although white men of the South came in conflict with each other over many issues, they did not always duel. Only certain kinds of insulting language and behavior led to duels. The central insult that could turn a disagreement into a duel involved a direct or indirect attack on someone's word—the accusation that a man was a liar. To "give someone the lie," as it was called, had always been an insult of great consequence among men of honor. As one early-seventeenth-century English writer noted, "It is reputed so great a shame to be accounted a lyer, that any other injury is canceled by giving the lie, and he that receiveth it standeth so charged in his honor and reputation, that he cannot disburden himself of that imputation, but by the striking of him that hath so given it, or by chalenging him the combat."[20]

It is easy to underestimate the importance of "giving the lie" as a reason for Southern duels without a broad understanding of what Southern white men had in mind by "lying." Sometimes, people would say it quite directly: "I hold Francis H. Welman a Liar, Coward and Poltroon," wrote John Moorehead in an 1809 issue of the *Savannah Republican*. But to

search for the actual word "liar" in Southern insults is to miss the pervasive presence of the charge. "Giving the lie" to someone meant announcing that his appearance differed from his true nature—proclaiming as
false his projection of himself. Thus the charge of being a coward or a
poltroon was another form of the charge of lying: the accuser unmasked
the accused. The goal of this unmasking was not to discover the real
character underneath but to expose and shame an opponent. It was to
identify an image as falsely projected and to show contempt for it. This
was a charge made not by a scientist in search of hidden truths but by a
gentleman intending to dishonor someone. For example, one man implicitly made the accusation of the lie as he pointed out his enemy to an
audience. "Citizens," he announced, "this is not the profile of a man; it is
the profile of a dog!" Similarly, when Charles A. Luzenberg woke up one
day in antebellum New Orleans, opened his morning newspaper, and
read a note accusing him of being a "puppy" who had "long humbugged
the community with false ideas of his courage," he understood that
someone was trying to unmask him—someone was accusing him of
lying.[21]

The Feejee Mermaid episode also involved the charge of lying. Yeadon
worried that his words in support of the mermaid had been discounted.
He had run his hands over the surface of the creature and detected no
seam. His projection of the truth and thereby of himself had become
connected to the appearance of the mermaid. Bachman, after having his
own words rejected for publication in Yeadon's paper, exposed the humbuggery of the mermaid as a "clumsy affair" and thus came close to accusing Yeadon of lying. The dispute over the use of pseudonyms was
actually another, even more complicated conversation about the relationship between asserted appearance and reality. The discussion
touched on the dangerous issue of the connection between a man's real
character and the character projected by a pseudonym. As the dispute
moved from pseudonyms to names, Yeadon and Bachman each had to
avoid the public perception that he had been unmasked and thereby
shamed by his opponent. To avoid a confrontation that could only end
in a duel, they had to move from pseudonyms to real names simultaneously; each had to unmask himself and have his new projection immediately accepted by his opponent.

Both the duel and the Feejee Mermaid episode evidence a world that
placed a high value on appearances as asserted and projected through
the words of honorable gentlemen. Many Northern men, the type who
shared the values of the mermaid-exhibitor P. T. Barnum, could never
fully understand this world. This is not to suggest that men like Barnum
failed to appreciate the value of self-promotion and the manipulation of
appearances. Barnum, after all, was the great showman of the nineteenth

FIGURE 2. Phineas T. Barnum.

century. He was the virtual founder of modern American print advertising. He transformed Joice Heth, an elderly and nearly blind black woman, into "the most astonishing and interesting curiosity in the world," the 161-year-old former nurse of George Washington; he turned Tom Thumb from a very short person into a world celebrity; he elevated a large mammal into Jumbo the Elephant and then used him to advertise thread and baking powder—how could such a man not value the world of appearances?[22] Yet it was precisely because he could manipulate such a world and simultaneously make money from it that he could never really see it as worthy of serious respect or disrespect. Words were his instruments in pursuit of gain; they were not linked to honor or dishonor. Perhaps nothing so clearly sums up Barnum's attitude toward the surface of images and language as his description of his first business experience in a Connecticut country store: "The customers cheated us in their fabrics, we cheated the customers with our goods. Each party expected to be cheated, if it was possible. Our eyes and not our ears, had to be our masters. We must believe little that we saw, and less that we heard."[23] No nineteenth-century merchant could have expressed the core assumptions of this worldview with greater clarity. The world of trade was a world full of liars. People constantly unmasked each other, but at stake were profit and loss rather than honor and dishonor. When Bachman called his mermaid a fake, Barnum did not reach for his gun but instead thought of ways to turn the charge to his profit.[24]

To recognize the connection between Barnum's experience of trade and his attitude toward appearance is not to make the reductive point that economic experience creates meaning. Economic experience does not exist prior to and outside a world of meaning, and therefore it cannot constitute such a world in any simple sense. Antebellum Americans did not first experience economics and then create meaning. Their experience of economic activity came to them already filtered through a system of meaning. Barnum and Bachman did not differ from each other simply because one traded and the other did not. In fact, many Southern men who spoke the language of honor were deeply involved in the market. But men who spoke the language of honor experienced trading and bargaining differently than did Barnum. To reconstruct their language is to reconstruct their different experience. Of course, to recognize that economic experience is filtered through language is not to make the equally reductive point that language creates experience; it only means that language and experience are not two separate categories.[25]

Just as one can connect Barnum's experience of trade to his ideas about appearance, one can relate the white Southern experience of slavery to the white Southern attitude toward the surface of the world. Masters and potential masters distinguished themselves from slaves in many ways, but one of the most important distinctions involved the issue of lying. The words of the master had to be accorded respect and accepted as true simply because they were the words of a man of honor. The words of the slave could never become objects of honor. Whites assumed that slaves lied all the time—and that their lies were intimately connected to their position as slaves. Masters articulated these beliefs when they argued that it was absurd for slaves to engage in duels and that the testimony of blacks could never be used in legal cases involving whites. Moreover, for many masters, the lie was at the heart of their problems with slave labor. Instead of engaging in the open confrontation expected of men of honor, slaves seemed to resist their masters by stealth and deceit. They stole food, ran away, burned buildings, broke tools, feigned illness or laziness, and sometimes even poisoned their masters' or mistresses' food. Masters repeatedly expressed exasperation about the deceitful behavior of their slaves. But in another sense, masters welcomed the chance to catch their slaves in lies. Their own honor and the respect accorded their words could then stand in favorable contrast to the dishonored condition of their slaves.[26]

III

The clash between the lie as expressed in the world of the duel and the lie in the world of P. T. Barnum recurred in other places in nineteenth-century American culture. For example, men of honor and Barnum reacted quite differently to lies as expressed in practical jokes, a form of play Barnum loved. In a way, his entire career was based on a series of practical jokes—lying to the public in order to make money. But Barnum also enjoyed practical jokes outside the world of show business. In an echo of many market transactions, he especially enjoyed tricking a man who was trying to trick him. In his autobiography, Barnum proudly told the story of the "whole shirt" trick. A noted joker named Darrow used to frequent the barroom of a Bridgeport hotel and prey on unsuspecting guests. A favorite trick of Darrow's was to taunt a man with the declaration that he was probably wearing tattered clothes and did not have a whole shirt on his back. Darrow would persuade the man to bet that he did have a whole shirt on his back and then triumphantly point out that all men wore only half their shirts on their backs. One day, Barnum deliberately allowed himself to be drawn into the bet, then produced a whole shirt that he had carefully folded onto his back beneath his vest. Darrow was furious, but he paid what he owed, and the entire barroom had a good laugh and a round of drinks. Like the tricks played in the marketplaces frequented by men of trade, this joke did not make Barnum feel his life was in danger. Barnum had tricked Darrow this time. Darrow would trick Barnum and others the next time. That was life in the world of the market.[27]

But a different set of meanings attended practical jokes among men of honor. J. Marion Sims describes one incident that parallels Barnum's joke except in its markedly different consequences. While he was at South Carolina College, Sims roomed with a group of other young Carolina gentlemen, including James Aiken and Boykin Witherspoon. One day at dinner, Aiken playfully pulled Sims's chair away just as Sims was about to be seated. Sims, however, seeing the motion out of the corner of his eye, did not sit down but reached over and pulled Witherspoon's chair away from him. Witherspoon fell on the floor. Unlike the men in the barroom with Barnum, however, no one thought this was funny. This was a moment of danger, not of laughter. One man had manipulated the world of appearances in order to humiliate another man. Sims immediately understood the seriousness of what had happened. As he later described it, "I apologized in the humblest manner that I possibly could. I assured him that I did not intend to throw him down, that I regretted it then, and that I was not ashamed to say that I was heartily sorry and should regret it always." Witherspoon said he was not satisfied. After dinner, he confronted Sims again. Sims repeated the abject apology, yet Witherspoon was still not satisfied. At this point, Sims believed he had humbled himself as much as was possible for a gentleman. "Now, Sir, help yourself," Sims finally blurted, meaning that he was willing to give Witherspoon satisfaction in a duel. Sims would apologize no more for fear that his friends, witnesses to the entire series of events, might think he was humbling himself in order to avoid risking his life in a duel.[28] Everyone understood that this kind of joke in South Carolina did not end in laughter and a round of drinks. It was likely to end in death.

Sims is an intriguing figure. After he left the South he came to reject the values of the world of honorable gentlemen. In his autobiography, written late in his life, he sometimes assumed the tone of an anthropologist describing early experiences in some strange and exotic culture. He recounted the Witherspoon episode along with a condemnation of the set of values that could lead to the loss of life over trivia. He also condemned several other instances of the dangerous consequences that accompanied practical jokes in South Carolina. For example, while Sims was at college, one student attempted to trick and shame another by appearing dressed as a ghost at his door on several occasions. The humiliated student took a shot at the head of this ghost one night.[29] Similarly, while in grade school Sims put a tack on a teacher's chair and lied about it when confronted. As a grown man, he met the teacher twenty-eight years later and confessed his foolish trick. Sims had long since left the culture of honor and was therefore surprised to discover that his confession was met not with a smile but with a chill. It ended their relationship.[30]

Conflicting conceptions of the lie between men inside and outside the culture of honor are apparent in the failure of many critics of the duel—frequently men outside Southern culture—to make sense of the world of the duelists. Benjamin Franklin, for example, wrote to a friend in 1784 that he could not understand the logic of the duel: "A man says something which another tells him is a lie. They fight, but whichever is killed the point in dispute remains unsettled." Franklin continued with an illustrative anecdote. A famous French duelist, St. Froix, was sitting at a cafe and turned to a stranger, asking him to move away because he smelled. "This is an affront," exclaimed the stranger. "You must fight me." "I will fight you if you insist on it," St. Froix replied, "but I do not see how that will mend the matter, for if you kill me I shall smell too, and if I kill you, you will smell, if possible, worse than you do at present."[31] Whether or not the anecdote is true, men of honor would not have gleaned from it the point made by Franklin. For him, the duel seemed a pointless activity because it could not determine whether a man had really lied or whether he really smelled; it had no practical result. If Franklin had been involved in the Feejee Mermaid dispute, he probably would have used the same logic to push for an internal examination of the mermaid, rather than lingering over seemingly trivial insults. But men of honor "care not a whit" about real mermaids or real lies or real smells. What is central to their disputes is that someone has given expression to an insult. When the man of honor is told that he smells, he does not draw a bath—he draws his pistol. The man of honor does not care if he stinks, but he does care that someone has accused him of stinking.

Timothy Dwight, in his famous antidueling sermon delivered at Yale after the Aaron Burr–Alexander Hamilton affair, misunderstood the duel in precisely the same way Franklin had. He could not figure out why someone would duel if he had been called a liar. "If the charge is just," he pointed out, "he is a liar still." For Dwight, the point was simple: "Truth and falsehood must, if evinced at all, be evinced by evidence; not by fighting." Neither man could understand the nature of an insult to a man of honor.[32]

Fifty years later, Lorenzo Sabine, an antebellum critic from the North and a historian of the duel, restated the point. He could not understand how a duel could be of any use in a dispute over a debt. The exchange of shots did not get the money back. But this time, the Southern novelist William Gilmore Simms immediately set Sabine straight, responding that the duelist "fights to maintain his position in society, to silence insult, to check brutality, prevent encroachment, avenge a wrong of some sort, and in obedience to fierce passions that will not let him sleep under the sense of injury and annoyance."[33] Getting his money back, in other words, was the least of his concerns.

Some critics of the duel did understand the causes of these encounters. One can see this in some of the laws designed to eliminate duels. No antidueling law ever worked to repress the institution; most people refused to treat men of honor in the ways demanded by such laws. But many of these laws at least show an understanding of the nature of the duel. For example, one law provided that the dead duelist should be "buried without a coffin, with a stake drove through the body." The survi-

vor should be executed and similarly buried. A later revision offered an
alternative to burial with a stake. The body could be delivered to "any
surgeon or surgeons to be dissected and anatomized."[34] Other laws
ordered gibbeting— hanging the dead bodies to rot in public. But in the
United States, by the nineteenth century the most common antidueling
penalty was a disqualification from holding office. This may seem a
rather strange development, a break from past punishment practices. But
there are similarities among the stake through the heart, the gibbet, and
the disqualification from office: all are ways of dishonoring a person in a
culture of honor. Moreover, all involve the same technique: they prevent
an individual from creating an image of himself that might become an
object of public honor. To withhold office from a statesman is to prevent
the public from confirming his vision of himself. To mutilate his dead
body is to turn his physical projection into an ugly object worthy of scorn
and shame.

The antidueling laws that struck at the body of the duelist show that
some legislators understood the nature of men of honor. What was important to a man of honor was respect for the parts of a man that were
visible to the public. These visible parts included his words and his version of the truth. They also included the visible surface of his body. This
concern for the body can be seen in many different contexts in the culture of honor. To gouge out an eye or otherwise mutilate the face of an
enemy was the most common objective of men involved in fistfights.[35]
With the possible exception of wounds received in battle, the mutilation
itself was a dishonor no matter how it was actually acquired. In a sense,
all mutilations were equal because men read the character of other men
through the external physical features of their faces and bodies.[36] This
attitude toward appearance was given expression in the many letters of
reference and descriptions of great men that mentioned their noble features. One can also see it in the way white Southerners used skin color as
a way of determining the character of a man.

The same attitude toward the external appears in the masters' interpretation of scars on the backs of their slaves. For white Southerners, the
mark of the whip on the back of a slave was a sign of the slave's bad
character and "vicious temper."[37] When the abolitionists disagreed, in-
terpreting the scars on a slave as a sign of the bad character of the master
or as an expression of the evils of enslavement, they were clashing with
white Southerners in a fundamental way. This dispute involved not simply a difference of interpretation over the sign of the scar but also a different conception of the nature of reading signs. The abolitionists read for
meaning beneath and beyond the surface. They found it important to
imagine the scene behind the scar, and they recreated it endless times in
word and woodcut. But men of honor did not linger over the scene that

gave rise to the scar; it was irrelevant. The scar, in a sense, spoke for itself—or rather spoke about the man whose body carried it—regardless of the process or the larger set of relations that brought it into existence. Men of honor "care not a whit" if the mermaid is real.

IV

This brings us to the nose. For Southern men of honor, the nose was the part of the face that preceded a man as he moved in the world. It was the most prominent physical projection of a man's character, and it was always exposed to the gaze of others. Little wonder that men of honor should regard the nose as the most important part of their bodies. As one antebellum Southern writer described it in a humorous, but also deadly serious, article on noses, "No organ of the body is so characteristic as the nose. A man may lose an eye or an ear without altering his features essentially. Not so with the nose." He went on to describe a man with "a most extravagantly protuberant nose"—a nose that "moved to and fro like a pendulum"—who had decided to have it trimmed by a doctor. "I saw him afterwards," he wrote, "and did not recognize him. I do not recognize him now, nor do I intend to. His individuality, his whole identity is lost. . . . The features do not fit; they become incongruous; he is himself no more; for, in truth, the individuality of a man is centred in his nose. Hence it is that nature, to indicate its great importance, has granted us but one nose, while all other organs are supplied in pairs."[38] That this writer had it wrong—not all organs come in pairs—is another illustration of the focus of a man of honor. Clearly, he was comparing the nose to the eyes and the ears. The liver, the heart, the penis, and the stomach were not even considered. A man's character was expressed in what could be publicly displayed, not in what was hidden under clothes or skin. And the man of honor demanded respect for this display. Men of honor do not trim their noses. If P. T. Barnum, a man outside the tradition of honor, had a nose that drew laughs, he might have charged admission; Cyrano de Bergerac, on the other hand, fought duels with those who mocked his protuberance.

One of the greatest insults for a man of honor, then, was to have his nose pulled or tweaked. Actually, nose pulling was just another, more aggressive form of accusing a man of lying. It was the ultimate act of contempt toward the most public part of a man's face, an extreme expression of disdain for a man's projected mask. The meaning of nose pulling for men of honor is clear in one well-documented incident of the 1830s: when Thomas Walker Gilmer pulled the nose of William C. Rives.

The pulling of Rives's nose had its origin in a friendship and political alliance gone sour. Rives and Gilmer had long been close associates in Virginia politics as well as neighbors who frequently met socially. During the 1820s, they worked together as opponents of the administration of John Quincy Adams, and Rives had hopes that Gilmer might one day succeed him in Congress. Rives helped advance Gilmer, and Gilmer did the same for Rives. With the enthusiastic support of Gilmer in the state legislature, Rives returned home in 1832 after serving as ambassador to France and was immediately elected to the United States Senate. When other legislators raised doubts about Rives's soundness on the tariff issue—they feared that he might not take the position that it was unconstitutional, and that he might not support South Carolina's attempt to nullify the law—Gilmer assured his skeptical colleagues that they could rely on his friend.[39]

But relations began to deteriorate within a few months when it became clear that Rives would not live up to the expectations created by Gilmer. Contrary to what Gilmer had indicated, Rives did not view the tariff law as unconstitutional. Moreover, he voted for the much hated Force Bill— Andrew Jackson's heavy-handed attempt to coerce the South Carolina nullifiers into submission. This betrayal became intertwined with more-specific grievances detailed in letters exchanged between the two men. Gilmer had several complaints. First, he had given his word to other men that Rives could be trusted on the tariff issue. Rives's vote on the Force Bill meant that these men had come to regard Gilmer as a liar. "I have been taunted more than once," Gilmer wrote Rives, "of having abused the confidence of those who listened to my appeal on your behalf." In fact, shortly after he pulled Rives's nose, Gilmer tried to show the public that he had legitimate grievances against Rives by publishing all the relevant correspondence. He included letters solicited from his colleagues in the legislature attesting that they "distrusted" him because his words about Rives had been shown to be false. In short, Gilmer stood in the same relation to Rives as Richard Yeadon did in relation to the Feejee Mermaid. Both men became identified with the object for which they spoke.[40]

Gilmer had a second major grievance. Rives himself, like his colleagues in the legislature, had begun to denounce Gilmer as a liar. Rives accused Gilmer of appearing to be a friend on the surface while actually working against him in devious and hidden ways. Rives believed (erroneously, it turns out) that Gilmer was the author of an anonymous and highly critical article sent to the *Richmond Enquirer*; that, writing under the name "Buckskin" in the *Charlottesville Advocate*, Gilmer had viciously attacked him in print; and that Gilmer was behind a legislative attempt in Virginia to instruct Rives on how to vote on the Force Bill when it came before the

Senate. Gilmer defended himself by acknowledging that he and Rives disagreed over the tariff issue but maintained that he had never tried to give any other impression. In other words, while Rives said that Gilmer's appearance differed from his reality, Gilmer argued that the two were in complete conformity. Gilmer claimed he had always been open and honest about their differences, and that these differences existed within the context of their friendship.[41]

Rives had parallel grievances against Gilmer. He was disturbed that Gilmer pretended friendship and yet betrayed him behind his back. Rives also objected to Gilmer's insinuation that it was Rives who was the liar in the dispute—that he had misled Gilmer about his position on the tariff issue in order to win his support in the Senate election, and that he had secretly joined with his brother in a conspiracy to destroy Gilmer's reputation and career. Rives singled out for special mention Gilmer's accusation that "he had betrayed the principles of the party to which he *falsely* professed to belong."

After months of festering distrust and hatred, the Rives-Gilmer dispute reached its climax at the courthouse in Charlottesville, Virginia, in early July 1833. The two men's deteriorating relations up to that point could be followed in the salutations Rives used in his letters to Gilmer: first "Dear Gilmer," then "Dear Sir," then "Sir." By the time Rives began to call Gilmer "Sir" it must have looked as if they were close to some violent outbreak—perhaps even on the edge of fighting a duel. In Virginia in the 1830s, a duel was a logical result of this kind of dispute. By shooting at each other, men accused of lying could show the world that they would rather die or kill than allow the charge to stand.

But the Rives-Gilmer dispute did not reach the stage of a duel. Instead, Gilmer approached Rives on the terrace of the tavern next to the courthouse in Charlottesville. They began to go over their charges and countercharges, deciding first to move into the public room of the tavern and then into a more private back room. They could agree on nothing. Words between the two men became increasingly heated. Gilmer called Rives a "hypocrite," and Rives retorted that Gilmer was a "scoundrel." There are two versions of what happened next. As Gilmer described it:

> I then applied my right hand gently to his nose. He instantly disengaged himself from me, either by drawing back or pushing me from him, and having a horsewhip in his hand, struck me several times with the butt end of it. While I parried these blows with my right arm, I attempted to catch him by the collar of his coat with my left hand, and in this effort the fore-finger of my left hand got into his mouth and was severely bitten. In the attempt to extricate it, my right thumb was painfully injured. While my finger was thus in his mouth I struck him two blows in the face with my right hand.

Gilmer then pulled the whip from Rives and used the "smaller end" to inflict "several stripes with it on his legs and shoulders and . . . one on his forehead." At that moment a crowd rushed in and separated the two struggling men.

The account of the fight offered by Rives and his supporters agreed with this description in all respects but one. The pro-Rives account emphasized that Rives was attacked completely by surprise and that he was seated while Gilmer stood and assaulted him. Gilmer denied this version of the attack. He preferred to portray himself and Rives as equals in combat. He also stressed that it was not his intent to draw blood or to hurt Rives in any way. He meant to apply his right hand "gently" to Rives's nose. The rest of the scuffle was in self-defense. As he stated, "My purpose throughout has been to vindicate myself—not to injure Mr. Rives."[42]

Several features of this nose-pulling incident are worthy of emphasis here. Just as in the Feejee Mermaid episode, the dispute that led up to the attack was essentially about the proper treatment to be accorded the word of a gentleman. At its heart were accusations of lying. It is easy to miss this point. One might be tempted to say that the conflict was really a disagreement about the tariff issue or nullification. In one sense this would be correct, because it is impossible to imagine this series of events without the political dispute that gave rise to it. Similarly, it is impossible to imagine the Feejee Mermaid incident without a mermaid. But it is also clear from the angry letters in both cases that, at least in this context, the men involved did not focus on the substance of the matter that gave rise to the dispute. In the same way that Yeadon "care[d] not a whit" about the mermaid, Gilmer and Rives never discussed the substance of the tariff issue or nullification in their correspondence that led to the nose pulling. Many men disagreed over the tariff and nullification, but those disagreements did not lead to nose pullings or duels unless a man's character came under attack. This point is essential if one is to understand why the pulling of a nose seemed the appropriate remedy here. Gilmer had been accused of lying—of putting forth a projection of himself that was false. He pulled Rives's nose to show his contempt for the projection of his accuser. It was his way of invalidating the words of his enemy. The nose pulling was not primarily part of a conversation about the merits of the tariff or nullification. It was part of a conversation about lying.

V

Another remarkable feature of this nose-pulling episode is the evidence it offers that the community seemed to regard the nose as a sacred object. In the newspaper reports, virtually the only person who uses the word "nose" is Gilmer. But his use of the word is a kind of extension of his pulling of it; it is part of the way he humiliates Rives. Newspaper editors found ways of avoiding direct reference to noses, or labeled the act of nose pulling a "Lieutenant Randolph outrage." The reference here, well understood by every Virginian of the time, was to another extraordinary nose-pulling incident, worth describing because it even more dramatically illustrates the symbolic nature of the nose. The "Lieutenant Randolph outrage" was an attack on perhaps the most highly venerated nose of the age—that of President Andrew Jackson.

Lieutenant Robert Beverly Randolph was a naval officer from Fredericksburg, Virginia, who had been dismissed in disgrace under direct orders from Jackson. His attack on Jackson had causes and consequences extending over nearly ten years and involving some of the most prominent political leaders and events of the Jacksonian era. In 1828, Randolph had been appointed purser aboard the U.S.S. *Constitution* after the sudden death of the former purser, John B. Timberlake. An auditor's report and subsequent investigation had found that Randolph's accounts did not balance and that he was in debt to the government, but that there was no evidence of intentional wrongdoing. However, on the strength of this investigation, Jackson dismissed Randolph from the navy, noting that "the facts which appear in this case, and the *conduct of Lieut. Randolph throughout the investigation*, prove him to be unworthy the Naval Service of this Republic, and *an unfit associate for those sons of chivalry, integrity, and honor, who adorn our Navy.*"[43]

Randolph felt himself unjustly treated by Jackson on several counts. He had interpreted the investigative report as a vindication of his conduct because it found no intentional wrongdoing. Moreover, he believed that the man who actually embezzled the money was his predecessor. He also believed that Timberlake had funneled some of that money to John H. Eaton, a man who had become the secretary of war by the time the controversy became a major public issue. Randolph probably suspected an even greater conspiracy, but was too discreet ever to describe it for the public record. The famous socialite Peggy O'Neale had been Timberlake's wife; upon his death she married John H. Eaton with the kind of unseemly haste that excited the Washington rumor mill. For complex reasons, probably rooted in associations with his own wife, Jackson felt some need to protect Peggy O'Neale. His dismissal of Randolph may have been part of a defense of the good name of O'Neale's first husband and thereby of her good name.

At any rate, by 1833 Randolph was a disgraced former naval officer who perceived Jackson's unjust actions as the cause of his misery. Since no sitting United States president would possibly condescend to fight a duel with a dismissed naval officer, Randolph saw only one route open for vindication—an attack on Jackson's nose. What better occasion for the assault than President Jackson's trip on May 6 to Randolph's hometown of Fredericksburg in order to lay the cornerstone at a monument to George Washington's mother? One can imagine Randolph's sense of outrage to have the very man who had humiliated him come to Randolph's own town to be honored. Jackson made the trip by boat. When the boat made a brief stopover in Alexandria, Randolph boarded, along with many others wishing to offer their greetings to the president. After most of the well-wishers had left, Randolph made his way into a cabin where Jackson was seated, surrounded by several members of his party.

There are two versions of what happened in the cabin. The version used in virtually all newspaper accounts of the assault was the one most favorable to the dignity of the president. According to this story, Randolph approached the aged Jackson with "timidity" and "humility." His hands trembled as he tried to draw off his glove, and the president, supposing that Randolph wished to shake his hand, said it was not necessary to remove the glove. The pro-Jackson accounts use several different expressions to describe what happened next. Most say that Randolph "thrust one hand violently into the President's face" or that Randolph "struck him in the face."[44] Hardly any account mentions Jackson's nose as the object of either the intended or the actual attack.

Descriptions of Jackson's reaction to the assault, however, clearly indicate that Jackson and all the bystanders understood that it was the president's honor, not just his body, that was under attack. Jackson immediately "thrust the dastardly assailant from him" and stood up. As men rushed in to restrain Randolph, the sixty-six-year-old Jackson grabbed his cane and demanded that everyone move away and leave him free to wreak vengeance on his attacker. "Let no man stand between me and the villain," an eyewitness reported Jackson saying.[45] Another witness, perhaps with a bit more embellishment, claimed that the president said "Let no man interfere between me and this personal insult; I am an old man, but fully capable of defending myself against, and punishing a dozen cowardly assassins."[46] Jackson himself later wrote Martin Van Buren that if he had been prepared for the assault he would have killed Randolph. He disliked the interference of friends who "interposed, closed the passage of the door, and held me, until I was oblige[d] to tell them if they did not open a passage I would open it with my cane."[47] In fact, when one friend offered to kill Randolph immediately, the president rejected the offer: "I want no man to stand between me and my assailants, and none to take revenge on my account."[48] Several years later, after Jackson had left office and Randolph was finally apprehended for the assault, Jackson also rejected the interference of the courts in what he regarded as an affair of honor. He asked President Van Buren to pardon Randolph. Such an act, he told Van Buren, would be in conformity with the wishes of his mother, who had long ago advised him to "indict no man for assault and battery or sue him for slander."[49] A personal attack on the body could only be countered by a return attack on the body.

There is another version of this episode that received virtually no mention in the newspapers. This account did not linger over Jackson's spirited reaction to the assault. It went to the heart of the matter and focused on the one event that overwhelmed all others in significance. Andrew Jackson had had his nose pulled. This is what Randolph understood he had intended and accomplished, for as Randolph approached Jackson, he announced "that he came to take his revenge of him for the disgrace imposed upon him, by pulling his nose."[50] A few months later, during the dispute between Rives and Gilmer, a "Lieutenant Randolph outrage" had become another name for a nose pulling. Jackson himself, although denying that he had actually been touched on the nose, certainly understood that his nose was the object of the assault. In her autobiography, Peggy O'Neale—a woman with an extraordinary understanding of the minds of men of honor—recounted Jackson's sensitivity on the subject of his nose:

> When the President was on visits to my father's, and I wished to tease him,— for I could take any of those childish liberties with him, as he regarded me only as a child—I would suddenly change whatever conversation was going on by looking upon the floor shaking my head mournfully, and saying, "Ah! General, it was very bad in you to let R. pull your nose." To this day I shake with laughter when I recall the violence with which he would always repel it. He invariably sprang to his feet, shook his fist, and said, "No; by the eternal God, madam, no man ever pulled my nose."[51]

Perhaps not. But certainly whether or not it actually happened, Jackson would not permit anyone to think that his nose had been pulled. He understood the full meaning of the act in the language of honor.

VI

Although men who cared about noses no doubt also dreamed about them, few recorded their nightmares. But one Southern man's nose nightmare did reach print in an 1835 issue of the *Southern Literary Messenger*.[52] It is the tale of a man who lay awake and restless, unable to sleep while crowded in with other bodies on a steamboat. Men with large noses snored loudly all around him as he pondered the prophecy of his aunt Deborah that unless he learned to practice prudence and economy "his nose must come to the grindstone." Suddenly two slaves (men he recognized as workers from a local tobacco factory) grabbed him by his arms and dragged him to the deck of the ship toward a grindstone being turned by a "black urchin." The slaves "forced my head downward, until my proboscis rooted upon the revolving stone, and I felt its horrid inroads upon that sensitive member."[53] While the wheel did its work the slaves began to sing:

> De man who hold his nose too high
> Mus' be brought low:
> Put him on de grinstone
> And grind him off slow.
>
> Wheel about, and turn about,
> And wheel about slow;
> And every time he wheel about
> De nose must go.[54]

The man of honor, held down by black slaves, slowly felt his nose disappear. "The friction of the stone upon my cheeks," he wrote, "gave fearful evidence that what had been a nose, existed no longer, and brought the horrid reflection that I was noseless! That the pride of my countenance was gone, and forever."[55] Here was a nightmare well understood by those who spoke the language of honor. It gave expression to their worst fears. To deprive a Southern man of honor of his nose (with the added humiliation of having it removed by slaves) was to threaten his appearance and thus his very self.

We who live in a post-Freudian age smile knowingly at these men who dreamed about the loss of their noses. We think we know what they really feared to lose. But if we are to explain why they acted as they did we must dig deeper and recognize the importance they attached to the most "superficial" and visible part of their bodies. We must move beyond their genitals—to their noses.

TWO

MASKS AND SLAVERY

ONCE, J. Marion Sims, the man destined to become the "father" of American gynecological surgery, dressed as a woman. It was during his years as a medical student in antebellum Charleston, South Carolina—years during which he still aspired to become an honorable Southern gentleman. His friend Dick Baker came to him one day and said, "See here, Marion, there's to be a masquerade ball at Fayall's ballroom next Saturday night, and I tell you I want you to go with me. I will go as a country wagoner just come to town, and you will go with me as my daughter." Sims hesitated at first; "it will be discovered." But Baker quieted his anxiety. "It is a masquerade," he pointed out, "and you have a right to do as you please, so long as it's a masquerade, and while they all have on masks. I will play my whip and flourish it around, and play that I am a country wagoner."[1] This satisfied Sims. Dick Baker's cousins supplied the dress and a set of dangling earrings to be attached by strings to his ears.

Despite his willingness to participate in the "fun," Sims was relieved to discover upon his arrival at the door of the ballroom that the gala had been indefinitely postponed because of heavy rains that afternoon. Mixed with his love of the adventure was a considerable fear of public exposure as a man who dressed as a woman. But Dick Baker was not to be so easily denied. "By George!" he announced, "I have an idea. Let's go to the theatre. That is the thing. We will certainly have this frolic out, for there is no telling if we will ever have another chance." Sims agreed to the proposal, although not without some concern that he might be humiliated. He insisted that they sit inconspicuously in the rear, for "it would sound rather bad to be carried before the police in the morning, and have it known that two young medical students were arrested, and one of them in women's clothes at that."[2] Still, Sims spent a tense few hours in the theater, thrust into a front seat by Southern gentlemen anxious to show their respect for a "lady," examined through opera glasses by nearly everyone in the brightly illuminated house, fearful that he would be "carried before the court the next day for appearing in public in women's clothes."[3] Luckily for Sims, the evening ended with his secret intact. He had dressed as a woman and avoided public humiliation.

At one level, when J. Marion Sims dressed as a woman he engaged in a typical college prank. Such pranks often involved the danger associated with breaking a sacred barrier in the culture—in this case, the barrier that separated the sexes. But a prank of this type, carried out in antebellum South Carolina by men who aspired to be thought of as honorable gentlemen, carries additional meanings. It stands as an illustration of the way Southern gentlemen thought of the wearing of a mask—the wearing of a constructed face into the public world. Neither Sims nor Baker thought he had compromised his honor by wearing a mask. For Sims, the danger to his honor came from the possibility that he might be "unmasked"— that he would lose face. To wear a mask was no shame for a man of honor; the horror was to be unmasked—to be publicly shamed and exposed as a man who dressed as a woman.

Southern gentlemen expected men of honor to wear masks, to display a crafted version of themselves through their voices, faces, noses, and a thousand other projections into the world.[4] Hence, when Sims agreed to wear the mask of a woman to a masquerade ball, it was only an odd variation on the wearing of masks in what was essentially a masquerade culture. Men of honor did not regularly dress as women, but they dressed. Dressing as a woman certainly was a risky activity for a gentleman. It was different from dressing with a whip because it was more likely to be exposed. Dressing as a woman invited undressing; the mask could easily be treated with contempt by any man who discovered it. The real danger, however, lay not in the dressing but in wearing a dress that could so easily be removed.

The Baker-Sims frolic illuminates the intimate relationship between honor and power in white male Southern culture. The difference between having and not having honor was the difference between having and not having power. The man of honor was the man who had the power to prevent his being unmasked. Anyone could unmask the dishonored. For those who aspired to honor, what you wore mattered less than whether you could and would risk your life to repel any man who tried to remove what you wore. A Southern gentleman could wear anything—even a dress or a lie—as long as he could prevent it from being removed.

I

Jefferson Davis, president of the Confederate States of America and symbolic bearer of its honor, actually lived through a version of the nightmare feared by Sims. His Northern enemies claimed that he was unmasked at the moment of his capture—that he was caught trying to escape from Union soldiers while wearing his wife's clothing as a disguise. Davis denied the charge, but with the collapse of the Confederacy he did not have the power to silence his accusers. The humiliation stung him deeply. Davis described the Northern version of the story of his capture as "the spawn of a malignity that shames the civilization of the age." One of his biographers concluded that the charge that he had been unmasked while dressed as a woman caused Davis more "anguish" than any other event in his life.[5] That is an extraordinary conclusion about a man who presided over the death of a nation.

In early April 1865, the Confederate government fled Richmond, Virginia, after the surrender of Robert E. Lee's army at the Appomattox courthouse. With enemy soldiers in hot pursuit, Jefferson Davis and an ever diminishing escort of military and government officials headed south. Finally, on May 10, Union troops caught up with him at his small camp in the woods just north of the Florida border. The scene at first was confused. Davis and his wife Varina remained in their tent, and the soldiers did not immediately discover the prize they had just caught. At the same time, a short distance away from the camp, two groups of Union soldiers approaching from opposite directions mistakenly began to fire at each other.

In various accounts of the event, Union soldiers on the scene stated their impression that Davis had dressed as a woman in order to avoid capture. One soldier, for example, said he saw two women emerge from the Davis tent. One had a pail and asked permission to go with her grandmother to wash in the brook. They were quickly joined by a servant girl. The "grandmother" of the group—who turned out to be Jefferson Davis— "had on a black morning gown, belted at the waist, and reaching to his ankles, a shawl over his head, beard and shoulders, and a black cloth under the shawl covering his forehead." But the soldier reported that the disguise did not fool him for long. He unmasked the Confederate leader. "I . . . saw," he later reported, "that the old woman had on boots." "See," he shouted to a friend, "that is Jeff himself! That is no woman."[6]

While the firsthand accounts of Union soldiers differ about some matters, they all agree that when they first saw Davis they thought they had seen a woman; that Davis had a shawl on his head and a long coat or dress on his body; that he (or a woman in his company) carried a pail, intending to make it appear that he was on his way to fetch water; that his boots betrayed him; and that once he was discovered, his feminine clothes were stripped from his body. They also reported that—in a reversal of the usual roles—Varina Davis saved her husband's life at the mo-

FIGURE 3. "The Last Ditch of the Chivalry, or a President in Petticoats."

ment of exposure. She threw her arms around his neck and begged the soldiers not to shoot.

Once these stories began to circulate they struck a responsive chord in the North. Even men outside the culture of honor understood that the act of unmasking was the worst humiliation one could inflict on a gentleman. And the unmasking of the leader of the Confederacy while he was dressed as a woman added a delicious layer of mockery that Davis's enemies could not resist lingering over and embellishing. The story eventually became a piece of merchandise to be bought and sold. News of the capture of Davis became a commodity of the popular culture of the North, with renditions eventually sold in the form of newspaper stories and prints suitable for framing. P. T. Barnum even created a version as an attraction for his American Museum. At first, the news spread by word of mouth among the soldiers. Then General James Harrison Wilson telegraphed Secretary of War Edwin M. Stanton about the extraordinary nature of the capture. Davis, he reported, "hastily put on one of Mrs. Davis's dresses and started for the woods, closely pursued by our men, who at first thought him a woman, but seeing his boots while running suspected his sex at once. The race was a short one, and the rebel President was soon brought to bay. He brandished a bowie-knife of elegant pattern and showed signs of battle, but yielded promptly to the persuasion of the Colt revolvers without compelling our men to fire."[7]

Stanton readily recognized the importance of this story. He rushed to create a visual image of the event that could be circulated to the Northern public. He bought a woman's dress, a hoopskirt, and a shawl to drape on a mannequin. Adding heavy army boots as the finishing touch, he posed the figure for the photographer Alexander Gardner and arranged for distribution of copies to the press. Soon, sketches of the mannequin began to appear in newspapers over the caption "The Clothes in Which Davis Disguised Himself."[8] But the mannequin was only of temporary interest. Stanton also ordered soldiers guarding Varina Davis to secure the actual clothing worn by her husband at the moment of capture. With the authentic clothing in hand he arranged for a massive news conference—including Washington news reporters, War Department staffers, United States senators, the governor of New York, and other dignitaries.[9]

Once in the hands of newspapers, the tale began to assume a life of its own. The initial stories consisted of copies of military dispatches from the scene, but they were framed by provocative headlines. For example, the *New York Herald* of May 15 greeted its readers with a long series of headlines and subheadlines, including such eye-catching phrases as "He Disguises Himself in His Wife's Clothing, and, Like His Accomplice Booth, Takes to the Woods."[10] The next day the *New York Herald* published a story entitled "The Farce of the Rebellion—Jeff Davis as Low Comedian," which contained such provocative statements as "He began the rebellion with a tragic strut, ended with a melodramatic exit, and was caught in his wife's petticoats, with spurs on his heels and a bowie knife in his red right hand."[11] On May 21, the story reappeared, fully embellished with a set of direct quotations that evoked images of Little Red Riding Hood confronting the wolf. In this version, Davis was a wolf dressed as a grandmother—but in a reversal of the usual story, he was a completely powerless wolf. The Union soldiers immediately disrobed and captured him. Davis at first appeared with a shawl over his head, along with his wife, who pleaded "Please let my old mother go to the spring for some water to wash in." But the guard "hoisted the old lady's dress with his sabre, and discovered a pair of number thirteen calfskins." " 'It strikes me your mother wears very big boots,' said the guard. 'And whiskers, too,' said the sergeant, as he pulled the hood from her face."[12]

The tale of Davis dressing as a woman could never achieve genuine mythic status in nineteenth-century American culture until it had been fully enshrined by P. T. Barnum. The instant he heard the story he recognized its potential as a moneymaker. He understood that people would pay to see a re-creation of the humiliation of the Confederate leader. Hopeful of a spectacular exhibition at his American Museum in New York, Barnum dashed off a note to Secretary of War Stanton, offering to "give five hundred dollars to Sanitary Commission of Freedman's Association for the petticoats in which Jeff Davis was caught."[13] Stanton would not sell to Barnum, so Barnum had to content himself with a life-size replica of Davis in a purchased petticoat surrounded by Union soldiers. Still, the tableau proved popular. When the American Museum burned to the ground shortly after the tableau's installation, Davis in petticoats was singled out for special attention. He was one of the few objects hurled to safety through a window. He was promptly picked up by onlookers and hung from a lamppost on Fulton Street.[14]

The press gave even wider circulation to visual depictions of the Davis story. At first, the imagery took its inspiration from the photo supplied by Edwin M. Stanton. But more-ambitious artists quickly re-created the entire scene of the capture. One modern trio of careful historians has uncovered no fewer than thirty-two independently published prints of the Davis capture. Many of these appeared in newspapers and magazines; many others were separately published cartoons intended for display on walls. We will never know how many saloons and homes contained images of Jefferson Davis in a dress, but there is considerable evidence that the work of supplying these wall ornaments was more than a minor industry. Currier and Ives alone published five separate prints of the capture.[15]

The cartoons shared many elements. In every picture, Davis was depicted in the dress of a woman; he was usually wearing a big hoopskirt. Some had him in a shawl, but many exchanged the shawl for a bonnet. He often had a pail in one hand and a bowie knife in the other. While some cartoons portrayed him as feminine in appearance, most showed his beard, and they all emphasized his boots peeking out from under the dress. Many of the cartoons delighted in puns. One caption noted Davis's "last shift"—referring both to his dress and to his capture. Another played on the words "chaste" and "chased" by using the label "The Chas-ed 'Old Lady' of the C.S.A." Still another awkwardly stretched the boundaries of both acceptable public language and the art of punning by referring to Davis's genitals and to his military powerlessness in the single caption, "How Jeff In His Extremity Put His Navel Affairs and Ram-Parts Under Petticoat Protection."[16]

Most importantly, the cartoons explicitly revealed a meaning that deeply disturbed Jefferson Davis. This was a story of a powerless man who was unmasked. Always, the Northern soldiers in these images were frozen in place, holding erect sabers or rifles or pistols. Always, they were

FIGURE 4. "Jeff's Last Shift."

lifting Davis's skirt to reveal his boots. Always, Davis was helpless in the dress of a woman—sometimes even with his legs spread open, suggesting a powerless woman about to be raped.[17]

Not surprisingly, Jefferson Davis had a very different interpretation of the events on that May morning. He wrote his version in letters to friends, in words later quoted in the memoirs of his wife Varina Davis, and in his monumental *Rise and Fall of the Confederate Government.*[18] When Davis told the story he began by explaining that he was only in camp with his wife in order to protect her. He could have escaped more rapidly, but he had heard that she was about to be attacked by marauders in search of a rumored Confederate treasure train. In describing his presence this way, he changed his image from a man in flight to a fearless man about to resist. He embellished the imagery; the night before his capture, he wrote, "My horse remained saddled and my pistols in the holsters, and I lay down fully dressed to sleep." Here was the image of a man not easily unmasked. Moreover, Davis noted that when the troops arrived on the scene, it was not his idea to run. It was Varina Davis who "implored" him to leave.

Davis also had a different version of the crucial act of dressing in his wife's clothing: "As it was quite dark in the tent, I picked up what was supposed to be my 'raglan,' a waterproof, light overcoat, without sleeves; it was subsequently found to be my wife's, so very like my own as to be mistaken for it; as I started, my wife thoughtfully threw over my head and shoulders a shawl." There was no hoopskirt. His wearing extra clothing was merely the result of an understandable mistake and his wife's loving care.

But what about the moment of his capture and unmasking—the moment when the cartoons depict his terror and the saber slipping under his dress? Davis gave a radically different portrait of that instant as well. He described his captor as galloping toward him on horseback. The cartoons always showed the Union soldiers on foot. Moreover, when the trooper ordered him to halt, he recalled,

> I gave a defiant answer, and dropping the shawl and raglan from my shoulders, advanced toward him; he leveled his carbine at me, but I expected if he fired, he would miss me, and my intention was in that event to put my hand under his foot, tumble him off on the other side, spring into his saddle and attempt to escape. My wife, who had been watching, when she saw the soldier aim his carbine at me, ran forward and threw her arms around me. Success depended on instantaneous action, and, recognizing that the opportunity had been lost, I turned back.

Here we have Davis far from terrified or submissive. He threw off his shawl and raglan as he moved toward the attack. Nobody undressed him. Like the anonymous writers in the Feejee Mermaid episode, Davis claimed he had unmasked himself. He was ready to have a bullet shot at him. He was unarmed and on foot and yet he shouted defiance to an armed man on horseback. Had it not been for Varina Davis throwing her arms around his neck, all would have been well. He could have been shot at, tumbled the trooper off his horse, and ridden away—perhaps to fight another day. In Jefferson Davis's version of the tale, his wife did not save his life; she crippled his ability to resist.

One of the most significant portions of Davis's account of his capture is his admission that he wore his wife's clothing. It was not intentional, but he had done it. Like J. Marion Sims, Jefferson Davis did not believe he had been dishonored by dressing as a woman. It was the removal of the clothes that concerned him. No man could be permitted to unmask a man of honor. Unfortunately for Davis, by the end of the Civil War he had lost the power to silence the people who mocked him.

The same fear of being unmasked is illustrated by a story that circulated about one of the most famous Southern duelists and men of honor—John Randolph of Roanoke, Virginia. One day he invited a man to dine with him and then promptly forgot he had extended the invitation.

When the guest arrived some time later, ready for his meal, Randolph personally greeted him and without hesitation announced "Sir, I am not at home."[19] This produced a brief, dangerous moment. It was just the kind of moment that might end in a duel. Randolph had clearly just lied, and the guest could have announced it. In the language of the duel, the guest could have "given him the lie" and provoked a challenge. Instead, the man turned on his heels and left the Randolph residence, never to return.

Whether or not this encounter really happened is of little consequence. Southern men told the story. But why? The point of the story was not to prove that John Randolph was a liar—that he had told a guest the falsehood that he was not at home. The story circulated because it confirmed Randolph's status as a man of honor. He had dressed himself as a man not at home, and he had the power to prevent another man from unmasking him. That he so obviously *was* at home only served to confirm the extraordinary power of his word. He could create a reality and have it honored even when it was clearly false.[20]

This interaction illuminates one meaning embedded in the idea of "giving the lie" in a culture of honor. The act of lying did not mean you actually *had* the lie. Someone had to "give it" to you—had to call you a liar. You did not own a lie until you were called a liar. As a man of honor, Randolph might sometimes lie, but he could never permit anyone to "give him the lie"; he could never permit anyone to unmask him. He would kill or be killed rather than accept the affront.

Although Southern gentlemen did place a positive value on acting in an open, truthful, and straightforward manner, they placed a higher value on not being called liars. In fact, there is no evidence that Southern men of honor were more truthful than members of any other segment of the antebellum population. Such a statement is not susceptible to rigorous proof because the concepts of truth telling and lying are virtually impossible to define and to apply with clarity. It would be silly to make the attempt in this context. But it is worth making the impressionistic point because so much has been written about the lies of white women and slaves in the antebellum South and so little has been said about the lies of men of honor.

Consider the issue of lies in the relationship between masters and slaves. We know a great deal about the way slaves undertook the activity of "puttin' on ole massa," but we have paid less attention to the way the master engaged in "puttin' on ole slave." Some slaves believed that masters generally told the truth, but most understood that masters were not always what they seemed. Sometimes, a slave was told he could purchase himself—only to discover that as his earnings accumulated, his purchase price rose. Such a slave could count himself lucky compared to others whose masters simply took their money while denying them their liberty.[21] Many slaves also learned not to rely on pledges of manumission from dying masters. The greedy heirs would sometimes not live up to the promises of their fathers or the state might intervene. Similarly, some slaves saw masters break their word not to split up families through sale.[22] Two of the most common circumstances in which slaves recognized the lies of their masters involved religion and sex. Although the preaching of some white ministers to black congregations seemed sincere, blacks often detected lies in the sermons of whites. The central message of many of these sermons seemed to be an admonition to "obey your master"—intentionally collapsing any distinction between a master in heaven and a master on earth.[23] Another common lie easily perceived by the slaves involved the master's refusal to acknowledge sexual involvement with black women. As one slave wrote of his master, "He used to have some Irishmen on the plantation, and he said these children were theirs, but everybody knew they were his. They were as much like him as himself."[24]

Some masters seem to have used stealth and deceit as a management technique. For example, Frederick Douglass described Edward Covey as a man who "seldom approached the spot where we were at work openly, if he could do it secretly. He always aimed at taking us by surprise." Douglass noted, "Such was his cunning, that we used to call him, among ourselves, 'the snake.' When we were at work in the cornfield, he would sometimes crawl on his hands and knees to avoid detection, and all at once he would rise nearly in our midst, and scream out, 'Ha ha! Come come! Dash on, dash on!'" Harriet Jacobs described her battle with her master as a "Competition in Cunning."[25]

The difference between masters and slaves arose not in the area of truthfulness, but in the area of power. Power enabled masters forcefully and publicly to dishonor their slaves by unmasking them and calling them liars. Both masters and slaves dressed up for the masquerade ball of slavery, but it was only masters who felt strong enough to walk around the ballroom pulling off the masks of their slaves. Any slave who sought to unmask his master could expect immediate and deadly retaliation.

II

The relationship between honor and power throws light on the way Southern gentlemen viewed their slaves. Slaves did not have the power to prevent themselves from being unmasked. Sometimes, kindly men of honor might indulge the masks of their slaves, especially if they were masks of subservience. But a mask worn at the indulgence of a master could never be a mask of honor. A Southern gentleman might just as easily treat the mask of a slave with contempt. The mask of a slave could never *command* the kind of honorable respect accorded to men of power.

In this context, we can understand the significance of masters denying their slaves the "privilege" of dueling. Not having the power to duel was one of the distinguishing features of enslavement. The slave was a person who did not have the power to risk his life in a confrontation with a man who tried to unmask him—with a man who "gave him the lie." The slave James Curry, for example, once came close to calling his master a liar until he recollected his relatively powerless position. He had married a free black woman against the wishes of his owner. As Curry described it, the master became furious and "told me she was a bad girl, and endeavored by his falsehoods to make me believe it. My indignation was roused, I forgot whom I was talking to, and was on the point of giving him the lie, when I recollected myself and smothered my feelings." Curry understood that if he attempted to unmask his master he would not be challenged to a duel. He would more likely be beaten, or perhaps killed on the spot. If he was to fight his master it would have to be by indirection.[26]

Slaves were deprived by masters of all the elements necessary for the formal duels of gentlemen of honor. They could not exchange notes because law and custom forbid their literacy. After all, a slave who could write a challenge note could also write a pass allowing him his freedom— or could read the abolitionist press. Slaves also had no guns or swords, since these weapons of the duel were also the weapons of insurrection. Furthermore, masters had a great stake in preventing slaves from exposing themselves to death in a duel. It was not simply that for a slave to risk his life was also to risk the investment of his master; it was also that to encourage a slave to risk his life in a duel might also encourage him to risk his life in a bid for freedom.

Some masters even seem to have taken pleasure in watching their slaves not duel. Although in one sense masters could look at all slave activities as "not-duels," they could best get the pleasure of watching a "not-duel" by having their slaves almost duel. Henry Bibb, in a narrative written after his escape from slavery, described the activity of one group of masters who enjoyed watching such a performance. They encouraged encounters by giving their slaves whiskey, "making bets on them; laying chips on one slave's head, and daring another to tip it off with his hand; and if he tipped it off, it would be called an insult, and cause a fight. Before fighting, the parties choose their seconds to stand by them while fighting; a ring or a circle is formed to fight in, and no one is allowed to enter the ring while they are fighting, but their seconds and the white gentleman." This was a duel except for two critical elements. First, the slaves were not in control. They were like marionettes whose reaction to insult was determined by their masters. Secondly, the slaves were not allowed to risk their lives by using weapons. "The blows are made by kicking, knocking, and butting with their heads; they grab each other by their ears, and jam their heads together like sheep. If they are likely to hurt each other very bad, their masters would rap them with their walking canes, and make them stop." Here, then, was an activity that duplicated the form of the duel without its substance. Masters determined when their slaves would feel insulted, and they would rap them with their canes when injury or death threatened. It pleased gentlemen of honor to witness the emptiness of such an encounter—an emptiness that confirmed their own fullness.[27]

Frederick Douglass understood the deep connection between slavery and the inability to duel. Douglass was one of the few slaves ever to engage in a duel. Historians have failed to recognize this because it was not exactly the formal duel of a gentleman of honor. Douglass and his opponent did not exchange notes or label their encounter a duel. Yet, at least in Douglass's mind, it had most of the major elements central to a duel between Southern gentlemen: it was triggered by language and behavior that degraded, humiliated, and unmasked Douglass; it involved a personal confrontation in which Douglass risked his life; and it resulted in the feeling (at least for Douglass) that the encounter had made him the equal of his adversary.

It is ironic that a man who hated slavery so passionately should define the moment of his emancipation through participation in a ritual deeply embedded in the ideology of Southern masters. Thomas Auld, Douglass's master, had leased Douglass for the year to Edward Covey, a man widely considered a "Negro breaker"—a man with the ability to transform slave resistance into docility.[28] From the moment of his arrival on Covey's farm, the sixteen-year-old Douglass was subjected to intense brutality. Repeatedly, Douglass was beaten and "unmasked" by being called a liar. Covey treated with contempt both the surface of Douglass's body and the projections of his character. Within a week of his arrival on the farm, Douglass received his first harsh taste of Covey's treatment, and he later described it as a model for many other similar encounters. Covey asked Douglass to perform what was an impossible task for a young and inexperienced farm worker: to enter the forest with a cart pulled by partially trained oxen, in order to gather a load of wood. Douglass could not control the oxen and he spent much of his time chasing them or attempting to right the overturned cart. In the end, he destroyed part of a fence on the farm.

At the conclusion of this disastrous day, the young Douglass openly and honestly presented himself to Covey as a worker who had done his best under difficult circumstances. In one version of this tale, he even said "I was not without a faint hope of being commended for the stern resolution which I had displayed in accomplishing the difficult task."[29] But Covey did not accept the explanation Douglass offered. He ordered him back into the woods, cut three switches from a tree, and demanded that Douglass remove his clothes. In a final attempt to avoid a beating and humiliation, Douglass refused to undress himself, but Covey stripped him and brutally flogged him anyway. Frederick Douglass had been unmasked. He had been called a liar and had been whipped. It did not matter that he had told the truth, since he lacked the power to demand respect for his word. This was only the first of many similar encounters on Edward Covey's farm.

Douglass's final confrontation with Covey—the confrontation that is most accurately described as a duel—included many of the same elements as his first encounter. Douglass collapsed from heat and exhaustion while carrying wheat to a fanning machine on a hot August day. When Covey questioned him, Douglass presented himself as a man who had tried his best. Once again, Covey treated the presentation with contempt. He kicked Douglass and hit him in the head with a slat of hickory. Douglass then ran away to tell his master of the injustice, in the hope of wrapping himself in the protective covering of a more powerful man, "humbly entreating him to interpose his authority for my protection."[30] However, Thomas Auld also refused to accept Douglass's presentation of himself and sent him back to Covey. Desperate for some method of insulating himself from brutality, Douglass even agreed to carry a magical root supplied by a friend.

Nothing worked until he asserted his power in a duel. Ultimately, Douglass determined to resist—to risk his life by using physical force in order to stop Covey from beating him. It was this resistance that, according to Douglass, restored his "manhood." As he later described it, "It was a glorious resurrection, from the tomb of slavery to the heaven of freedom. My long-crushed spirit rose, cowardice departed, bold defiance took its place; and I now resolved that, however long I might remain a slave in form, the day had passed forever when I could be a slave in fact. I did not hesitate to let it be known of me, that the white man who expected to succeed in whipping, must also succeed in killing me."[31]

Douglass achieved his liberation by assuming the posture of a Southern man of honor—asserting his willingness to die in defending himself against an insult to his character and body. Covey might still regard him as a liar, but he could no longer unmask him through an attack on his body. We have no record of Covey's perception of this encounter, but Douglass clearly believed that he had protected his presentation of himself. When Edward Covey walked away from the encounter and failed to renew the attack, he had implicitly accepted Douglass's assertion of his liberty and equality.

Douglass's experience with Covey was unusual. Most slaves did not challenge their masters in the kind of face-to-face, open confrontation described by Douglass. The few who did often ended up beaten, sold, or killed. Douglass was lucky. He had challenged an "honorable" man who prized his reputation as a slave-breaker and who could not bear the humiliation of publicly announcing his difficulties with a slave by calling for outside assistance. But the odd circumstances that permitted Douglass's triumph in a duel—circumstances that restrained the master's power—stand in contrast to the more typical slave experience.

Masters generally saw slaves as people who lacked the power to keep themselves from being unmasked; this pattern underlay many aspects of master-slave relations. There were numerous ways in which masters unmasked their slaves. Certainly this was at least a part of the meaning contained in some of the coercive sex engaged in by white men in their attacks on black women. Southern law never recognized slave rape as a crime. Jefferson Davis may have been symbolically raped in cartoons; African American women experienced a more immediate experience of rape. The state imposed no legal sanction on masters who sought to violate their slaves. The power of the state would not be used to preserve the mask of respectability for African American females. The fear of local gossip, or a Christian ethic, or a watchful white mistress, or a knife hidden under a dress might sometimes prevent a rape, but rarely did these protections add up to the impenetrable layer of protection worn by a man like John Randolph when he announced to his guest "Sir, I am not at home." If a black woman said "Sir, I am not at home" to her unwelcome white guest, the visitor would most likely "give *her* the lie."[32] This was precisely what happened to a slave named Celia during the years when her master frequently visited her cabin at night.[33] It was a common experience for African American women.

Harriet Jacobs well understood the relation between honor and power when she tried to maintain the mask of respectability as she fought off the sexual advances of her master.[34] When she turned fifteen, her fifty-year-old owner, Dr. James Norcom, "began to whisper foul words" in her ear. "He told me I was his property," Jacobs later recalled, "that I must be subject to his will in all things." He followed her everywhere, trying to get her to submit to his advances—even as she walked outside after a day of work, or knelt by the side of her mother's grave. Sometimes he held a razor to her throat.[35]

It would be incorrect to suggest that Jacobs had no power as she confronted her master. In fact, she contended that Norcom never completed his rape.[36] At some moments, Jacobs successfully resisted by indicating a willingness to die rather than submit. Her master also had a concern for his reputation in the community. Sometimes Norcom's wife came to her aid, even though she clearly hated and resented her "rival." Moreover, Jacobs could sometimes use the threat of telling her well-respected free grandmother, Molly Horniblow, about Norcom's advances. Horniblow was a woman to be feared. Not only was she widely seen as a woman of extraordinary virtue and strength, but she had also "once chased a white gentleman with a loaded pistol, because he insulted one of her daughters."[37]

But despite these protections, Jacobs never lost her own sense of vulnerability to attack. In the end, her resistance left her with a feeling of humiliation rather than one of triumph. Unable to continue her connection to a free black man she hoped to marry, she struck at her master by having an affair with another white "gentleman," an "educated and eloquent gentleman" who expressed great kindness as well as sympathy for her condition. However, that relationship produced a feeling of degradation rather than liberation. The resulting pregnancy led to a shaming moment of rejection by her grandmother. When Molly Horniblow learned of the pregnancy, she condemned Jacobs as "a disgrace to [her] dead mother" and barred her from her house. Although her grandmother later realized that she had wrongly blamed the victim, Jacobs never forgot the humiliation of that initial rejection.[38]

Harriet Jacobs had resisted humiliation by her own master only to experience its equivalent from another master. At the time, she thought she had "chosen" her gentleman lover. Later, she realized that slavery and her own vulnerability had chosen him for her. "The remembrance" filled her "with sorrow and shame." "I wanted to keep myself pure," she later wrote, "and, under the most adverse circumstances, I tried hard to preserve my self-respect; but I was struggling alone in the powerful grasp of the demon Slavery; and the monster proved too strong for me. I felt as if I was forsaken by God and man; as if all my efforts must be frustrated; and I became reckless in my despair."[39] Her lack of the power to protect herself made it impossible for her to preserve a mask of respectability. Unlike John Randolph, when her unwelcome guest came to visit, Harriet Jacobs was "at home."

Similarly, many slaves experienced the act of being unmasked in public when they were placed on sale. Slaves repeatedly described the same patterns of humiliation during auctions. First, the trader or master made them lie—made them change their appearance as a way of snaring prospective buyers. Slave skin might be greased in order to create a healthy shine. Slave voices might be altered so that buyers would never hear the rebellious spirit that lurked beneath a newly greased skin. At a slave auction, in both a literal and a figurative sense, men of power created a new dress for their slaves.[40] The slave James Curry once described slaves on their way to sale: "They go bare-headed and bare-footed, with any rag they can themselves find wrapped around their bodies. But the driver has clothing prepared for them to put on, just before they reach the market, and they are forced to array themselves with studied nicety for their exposure at public sale."[41]

Slave sales often involved additional humiliation. Sometimes, slaves had to undress. Sometimes, prospective buyers poked into openings in the bodies of the slaves. As one ex-slave described it, "They 'xamine you just like they do a horse; they look at your teeth, and pull your eyelids back and look at your eyes, and feel you just like you was a horse."[42] Occasionally, slaves would resist. When one buyer put his hand in Martha Dickson's mouth "she bit his finger to the bone." But the bleeding man did not honor her for her spirited defense. He kicked her and killed her unborn child.[43]

The willingness of whites to unmask slaves continued even after death. Just as J. Marion Sims bought slaves in order to cut them open for experimental operations with new surgical instruments, many doctors used black cadavers for dissection. A black body lacked the layer of honor that could protect it from intruders.

Another form of humiliation commonly associated with slavery involved the assumption that the word of a gentleman needed to be honored, while the word of a slave could be treated with contempt. Southern law gave validation to this vision of slaves as liars when it forbade their testimony in court cases involving whites. A white man might be murdered or robbed in front of a hundred witnesses, but if these witnesses were slaves, their testimony could not be used to convict the criminal.[44] It was better to let a murderer go unpunished than to honor the words of slaves.

The importance of this legal rule for white society is highlighted by the way Southern courts interpreted certain difficult or ambiguous cases. For example, in 1828 a Kentucky court excluded the testimony of a white physician who described what he had been told by a slave patient. The court reasoned that if the doctor's words were no more than the undigested words of a slave, they could not be permitted legal recognition. But the judge went on to note that slave words need not always be excluded. They could enter the courtroom under special circumstances— circumstances that precluded anyone from mistaking their admission as an honor. The court would open its doors to slave words if they had been fully filtered through the mind of a white man. Here the judge cited a doctrine that permitted consideration of spontaneous oral statements surrounding an event as part of a total body of evidence. For example, if a slave uttered a cry of pain as a knife cut through his flesh, a white witness could mimic the cry in court as part of his description of the stabbing. As one South Carolina judge put the matter in his decision on a case that raised a similar issue: "The words of a negro are at least as significant as the cry of a brute animal, . . . and if any sound whatever, cotemporaneous with an act, . . . might serve to give meaning to the act, it would be admissible."[45] In other words, a white man in court could speak the "cry" of a slave only after it had become detached from its creator—only after it had changed from "the cry of a slave" into "the cry of a slave in the mind of a master."

The law did allow slave voices to enter the court as long as they simply parroted the words of white men. But that was only because they were not really slave voices. In 1854 a North Carolina court, for example, permitted a deaf-mute woman to draw up a deed of gift by communicating the necessary information through a slave who could understand her signs.[46] The slave could give voice to his mute white mistress, but could not give voice to himself.

Similarly, free blacks daily experienced the legal denigration of their words. Like their slave counterparts, they could not testify in court cases with white defendants.[47] The law also forced them to carry papers or to register with white authorities as proof of their condition as free men. It was a sign of their dishonored status that they could not assert their liberty through their own words. As one escaped slave described it, "I have known cases where free persons have been put to a great deal of trouble, & put in jail for a long time because they had lost their papers."[48] To lose one's papers was to lose the words of another man, words every free black was made to carry in his pocket and display on command.

The denigration of the words of African Americans in the legal system was part of a larger pattern. Although many masters developed relations with individual slaves they could trust, the vision of a slave as a liar or a trickster was more common. Masters frequently complained about theft on their plantations, about slaves feigning illness, about tools that mysteriously broke when the master turned away, and a host of other occurrences that seemed to demonstrate the deceit of slaves.[49] For example, when James Henry Hammond took control of his South Carolina plantation he faced a group of slaves who resisted his attempts to change their labor system from task to gang work. While seeming to obey his commands, they performed their work carelessly. In addition, slaves stole his hogs, appropriated his potato crop before it was harvested, dug a tunnel into his wine cellar and freely tasted of its contents, set fire to his buildings, and ran away. He came to trust a particularly skillful slave driver, but later discovered that the man was a "humbug" who permitted his fellow slaves to undermine the productivity of the plantation.[50] Hammond constantly struggled to determine which of his slaves sought to deceive him. But it was a task he, and most other masters, could never fully accomplish.

Masters repeatedly demonstrated the connection between their power and their ability to mask and unmask slaves—their ability to denounce the lie of the slave and impose their own version of the truth. James Curry once witnessed a whipping that seems to embody this attitude toward truth. The incident began when a forty-year-old fellow slave became involved in a complex scheme of theft. He had been approached by his brother-in-law's master, Lewis Morgan. Morgan had told him to buy stolen wheat from a slave on a neighboring plantation. Morgan said he would purchase it and arrange for its resale. Unfortunately for the slave, he was detected and brought before his master. Together they returned the wheat to its rightful owner, and both masters then proceeded to punish the thieving slaves. They took their slaves into the woods where "they were stripped and tied each to a fallen tree, extended upon it face downwards, with their feet, and hands tied under it." Then they were beaten "with willow sticks, from five to six feet in length." The beating was brutal, extending over a period of five hours with occasional relief supplied only to the masters in the form of a bottle of rum and a pail of water. But the brutality itself is less startling than the peculiar discussion that took place between master and slave during the beating. As James Curry described it, the master "would require the poor slave to confess the truth, and then to deny it, and then back again, and so on, beating him from truth to lie, and from a lie to the truth, over and over again."[51]

What a strange conversation! What was it about? Consider first what it was not about. The master was not at all interested in a thorough investigation. Here we do not see torture used as a mode of interrogation intended to produce true statements. The slave understood this perfectly. No part of his confession ever mentioned that the real instigator of the theft was Lewis Morgan, the brother-in-law of his master. The slave realized that this true information would only earn him a more brutal beating.[52] This conversation between master and slave was not about the causes of theft but about who controlled truth. By whipping the slave from truth to lie and from lie to truth, the master was telling both the slave and himself that truth was a matter of assertion and force—and the master had it in his control.

The same connection between truth and power can be seen in the attempts of some masters to select names for their slaves. Men of honor understood that to name a piece of the world was not only to give it meaning but also to assert power and control over it. It was to create the truth of the world. That is why men of honor were so sensitive to the disrespectful use of their own names. To attack a man's name was to attack a central part of the man himself.

Men of honor could never assume much control over the names of their slaves, but some made the attempt.[53] Some slaves resisted—but usually not through the direct and forceful confrontation characteristic of men of honor. Resistance took the form of an inner commitment to a name not spoken before the master, or to a name used only within the community of slaves. William Wells Brown felt what it was like to be a slave in a world where masters tried to control names. He resisted in a way typical of other slaves. His use of the name "William" had become offensive to his master because it was the name of a nephew newly arrived on the plantation. Brown was told one day that his name was engaged in an act of trespass. His master sought to unmask him—to strip his name away. His mother was ordered to select a new one for him. Brown later recalled that he thought this demand "one of the most cruel acts that could be committed upon my rights." At first, he resisted in a direct way. He simply told people that his real name was "William." But such open resistance was handled in predictable fashion. He was severely whipped several times. After that, he became known around the plantation as "Sandford."[54]

In the long run, Brown's master did not really win the battle of the names. Although Brown no longer openly called himself "William," he kept the name to himself. When he made his dash for freedom he took his old name with him. His liberty and his name seemed indissolubly linked. As he made his escape he even repeated the name secretly to himself, over and over again, as a means of preparation to enter a new free life. In the end, the name "William" outlived the master who tried to destroy it—appearing in the name of the author of one of the great fugitive-slave narratives. But the man who was William Wells Brown's master may never have appreciated the extent of his ultimate defeat. He had won the most crucial battle for a man of honor. When Brown resisted him on the plantation, he had him severely whipped. "William" then became "Sandford." A piece of the world had been renamed through assertion and force. An important new truth, publicly acknowledged, had been established in the world he dominated. Why should he care what "Sandford" chose to call himself in secret or in the safety of a refuge hundreds of miles away? Such a master shared the sensibilities of the slave mistress who whipped her slaves and then made them kiss the lash.[55] She did not really expect her slaves to love the lash—only to kiss it on command. To control the name and the kiss was not to control the soul. It was to control external rather than internal dimensions of personality and spirit. It was to control what mattered most to a master.

One slave, David Holmes, gave eloquent expression to many of the complexities involved in the issue of slave names in a world dominated by men of honor. After his escape from slavery he was interviewed by abolitionists in London in 1852. He explained to them that he did not know the name of his mother. She was known as "Holmes," but he did not believe that was her real name, "because slaves never have any name." "I'm called David, now," he explained. "I used to be called Tom, sometimes; but I'm not; I'm Jack. It didn't matter much what name I was called by. If master was looking at any one of us, and call us, Tom, or Jack, or anything else, whoever he looked at was forced to answer."[56] David (or Jack) Holmes seems to have understood the distinction between the names he was called and the name that was really his. But in front of his master, he had to respond to any name. It may not have been his real name, but it was the only name that mattered to his master.

The attempt by whites to control the names of blacks persisted even after slavery ended. Obviously, whites could no longer so easily instruct black parents in the naming of their children. But after emancipation, whites often called African Americans by any names they pleased and expected them to respond. A "humorous" story that circulated among twentieth-century blacks illustrates both this white practice and the kind of resistance that was possible for a man of dignity. It is a story that precisely repeats the antebellum pattern. A black man enters a store seeking to purchase a hat. A white clerk imposes a name on him, inquiring "Well, Bill, what will you have?" The black customer resents the imposition but shows his resentment only by leaving the store. He then proceeds to move from store to store, only to leave each one in turn as white clerks call him such names as "Son," or "Uncle," or "Mose." Finally, one clerk calls him "George"—which just happens to be his real name. He rewards the clerk by purchasing a hat. Here is an act of genuine subversion and resistance—but it is an act that none of the white clerks would ever appreciate. Blacks who laughed at the joke must have understood the irony and ambiguity of the situation, laughing all at once at the idiocy of the custom that produced the incident, at the white clerks who could not understand the behavior of their customer, and at the proud man who both resisted and failed to resist.[57]

The North Carolina slave Lunsford Lane experienced another version of this conversation about truth and power.[58] But it was his body rather than his name that was the object of assault. Men of honor took off his clothing and replaced it with a coat of tar and feathers. The story of how this came to pass is complex. Lane was an unusual slave. He seems to have had several powerful friends among the wealthy whites in his hometown, Raleigh. They even permitted him to buy himself—to purchase his own freedom. This was not easy to accomplish in antebellum North Carolina. In fact, the law did not allow him officially to become the agent of his own freedom. It compelled his dependence on white patrons. He had to trust their words and promises. One of them bought Lane and brought him to New York, where he was manumitted. Lane then returned to North Carolina as a free man, intending to earn money to pay for the liberty of the rest of his family. But he quickly ran into a formidable obstacle. North Carolina law forbade the permanent migration of free blacks from other states. He was forced to leave.

Lane then went north and told his story to many in the antislavery movement; he raised enough money to finish the emancipation of his family. However, by the time he returned to Raleigh on a visit to complete the transaction, news of his Northern activities and associations with antislavery and abolitionist leaders had preceded him. The white people of Raleigh had become incensed. They arrested him and accused him of delivering abolitionist lectures. It was then that he began a series of conversations that reveal a great deal about the relationship between truth and power among Southern gentlemen.

Lane was arrested before the regular magistrates and their attendants had arrived to open the courthouse for business. Instead, in an arena full of high emotion, the mayor and several justices of the peace heard his case in a large room in a local store. Angry citizens filled the store and the streets outside, generating an atmosphere that resembled both a regular legal proceeding and a preparation for a lynching. Yet despite the hostile atmosphere, Lane seems to have been treated with considerable respect. After reading the charge that he had delivered abolitionist lectures, the mayor asked him whether or not he was guilty—implying a concern for Lane's version of events. This testimony was permissible because the case did not involve a white. But Lane seems to have understood that he was not a man of honor whose words could be believed. With the uncanny sense that a simple assertion of either guilt or innocence would be seen as arrogance—as an attempt to impose a version of the truth on the world—Lane answered the charge with the more humble statement that he did not know whether or not he had delivered abolitionist lectures. He wanted the court to judge the truth of the charge. He would merely describe what he had done.

If Lane had really been alone in that courtroom—with no support from men of honor, from men of power whose words could be believed—he most certainly would have been dealt with harshly. He might never have left the town alive. But he was not alone. For one thing, he carried a letter from a powerful white man, a letter he had carefully solicited before daring to reenter the state. The letter was written by the master who owned his family and it promised that the governor of the state would protect him when he returned to Raleigh. Moreover, the courtroom contained several influential and wealthy whites who seem to have played the role of patron for Lane. When Lane finished his description of his activities, these "leading men" exchanged whispers with the mayor and determined the truth. Much to his relief, Lane discovered that he had not delivered abolitionist lectures. He was guilty of no crime and could safely complete his business.

Unfortunately, that decision was only the beginning of Lane's troubles. A mob consisting of less influential and less wealthy whites awaited him on the street. They disagreed with the decision of the "court." Lane's patrons, however, again came to his aid. They decided to escort him directly onto a train heading out of town and to complete for him the purchase of his family. Once again he had to depend on their word. But the mob intervened before he could leave the city. They followed him to the train, where they demanded a more "careful" investigation, including a search of his trunk. In order to head off a possible lynching, his white friends arranged for him to be rearrested and for his luggage to be examined for abolitionist literature. The search turned up nothing.

Still the mob was not satisfied, and again his influential friends had to come to his aid. They staged a late-night release from jail and a quick dash to sanctuary in one of their homes. But the mob, anticipating the ruse, lay in wait and grabbed him as soon as he left the jail. They marched him into the woods where they demanded that he tell them the truth about his abolitionist activities. Lane protested that he had already told the truth, and he repeated his courtroom story. But this group of whites, which no longer included his powerful patrons, seemed less sympathetic. As Lane later reported it, "They said that was not the truth." When Lane replied that he was "not in possession of any other truth on the subject," they stripped him naked and coated his body with tar and then with a layer of feathers. He had become the object of a public shaming.

Why did the mob feel compelled to cover Lane with a coat of humiliation? Obviously they felt that Lane had moved out of his subordinate place in the world. He had moved from slavery to freedom, had acquired wealth and powerful friends, and had been successfully able to manipulate the world. He had tried to put on clothes of his own choosing. The mob had stripped those clothes off his back and made him wear a new coat. If Lane wanted to attend their masquerade ball he had to wear the appropriate costume.

Lane was not the only object of the assault. The more complex purposes of the mob became evident in the words they spoke to him as they let him go. They told him that he was free to stay in Raleigh as long as he wished; he could complete his business and they would do him no further harm. Lane described these final words a bit differently in different places, but he was consistent about their general content. "Now we have done what we wished to do," he recalled them saying in one version of the incident. "Now go home, and be not afraid. You may do what business you please, and you shall not be hurt. We merely wished to let the aristocracy know that they could not have their own way."[59]

Like the master who whipped his slave from truth to lie and back again, the white mob was informing Lane about the relationship between truth and power. Consider the sequence of events. Lane spoke words in court that became true only after they had been supported by a letter from a white man promising the protection of the governor and by the intervention of a group of wealthy white patrons. But the mob refused to accept that version of the truth. When Lane fell into their hands they had before them a person who, although not a man of honor himself, had become connected to men of honor. The court and Lane's patrons had turned his words into truth. It was this assertion that disturbed the mob. In a sense, Lane had become the projection of a group of gentlemen. He was attached to men of honor. He was their nose. Unfortunately, he found himself in the hands of another group of "honorable" gentlemen, a group that sought to project a different version of the truth on the world; these gentlemen wanted to tweak the noses of the more wealthy men of the town. If a search of his trunk for abolitionist literature did not accomplish their goal, then tarring and feathering might do it. What better way to humiliate the honorable men who had created Lane's truth than by covering his body with a coat of contempt? "We merely wished to let the aristocracy know that they could not have their own way," they told him.

Although Lunsford Lane certainly preferred the coat of respectability supplied by his patrons to the coat of tar and feathers supplied by the poorer whites, the coats shared a meaning in the culture of honor. They both were coats of shame, masks not of his own fashioning—masks sustained by the power of other men. In this use of the language of honor, gentle paternalism and savage brutality conveyed a common meaning.

III

To understand the connection between masks and power in the language of honor is to gain other insights into the nature of master-slave relations. The master's devotion to honor may have operated as a check on the rise of an increasingly paternalistic slave system in the nineteenth century. The central feature of paternalism is often misunderstood as an affection that bound masters and slaves. But paternalism was less about love than about the depth and intimacy of the masters' intrusion into the lives of the people they owned. The tendency of the paternal impulse was to push masters to intervene everywhere. They sought to control food, housing, clothing, marriage, naming, medical care, religion, the organization and pace of work, law and order, visitation, and much more on the plantation.[60] However, although the masters' paternal ideals impelled them toward greater intervention, their devotion to honor limited the intrusion. Ironically, the language of honor may have restrained masters and helped create a space within which black culture could survive and develop. This worked in several ways.

Within the language of honor a black mask frequently lied, and it lacked the power to command respect. Masters often complained that they were unable to read the faces of their slaves. One Georgia planter lamented, "So deceitful is the Negro, that as far as my own experience extends I could never in a single instance decipher his character. . . . We planters could never get at the truth."[61] Mary Boykin Chesnut, a woman who understood and spoke the language of honor, gave eloquent expression to this problem when she pondered the question of whether slaves would remain loyal to their masters in the midst of the Civil War. Slaves, she believed, "will not rise and cut our throats in the rear. They are not really enemies of their masters—and yet I believe they are all spies for the other side. Inconsistent?" She scattered similar contradictory sentiments throughout her diary. On the one hand, she felt that the slaves of the South would be loyal to the Confederacy; on the other hand, she doubted they could be trusted.[62]

Repeatedly, she tried to read the faces of slaves in order to resolve her doubts. But Chesnut found those faces undecipherable. "I am always studying these creatures," she wrote in her diary. "They are to me inscrutable in their ways and past finding out." She saw "sphinxes" and "black masks" all around her. Once, shortly after slaves murdered her cousin Betsey Witherspoon, her elderly and ill mother-in-law emerged from her bedroom to warn guests at the dinner table not to eat the soup because it had a bitter taste—implying that it had been poisoned. While the dinner party continued uninterrupted, Mary Boykin Chesnut looked closely at the black faces around her in the hope of reading a reaction to the charge just leveled against them. But, she reported, "The men who waited at table looked on without change of face."[63]

Chesnut's search for meaning in faces was common for masters and mistresses who spoke the language of honor. It was a world where people read other people by their prominent surface features. And Chesnut's sense that black masks could not be read, that they obscured rather than revealed the truth, was also rooted in the language of honor. In the eyes of masters, a mask worn by a man of honor had a kind of stability. It was connected to the power of the person who wore it and was the central sign of his character. But a black mask—a mask that marked a person as outside the circle of honor—carried a more ambiguous meaning. It clearly was a mark of dishonor, but beyond that it had no easily discernible deeper content. Was it a face put on to please a powerful master? Was it a face that constantly changed with circumstances? In the language of honor, a black face could easily become a signifier disconnected from a signified.

People who spoke the language of honor rarely felt the urge to inquire deeply into the secrets hidden behind black faces. Generally, it was enough to note that such a face lacked honor. Except during times of slave rebellion, it did not matter what slaves said or thought in secret. Even the curious Chesnut did not probe far when she thought about slaves. Her search for meaning began and ended at the face. Neither she nor her contemporaries had an anthropological or even protoanthropological sensibility. Antebellum white Southerners often claimed that they "knew" their slaves. But their "knowing" largely consisted of accepting slaves at "face" value. And the face was always ambiguous. That is why twentieth-century historians who wrote about black culture by using sources generated by antebellum whites never found any black culture at all.

But sometimes it is useful not to be understood. A consequence of the inability of masters to "know" their slaves—a variation of the inability of powerful groups to "know" the people they dominate—was that it prevented masters from intruding even more deeply into slave life. Masters never probed deeply into the nature of African American religion, music, or family relations, and slaves achieved at least a limited degree of insulation from control.

Men of honor primarily demanded a mask of obedience from their slaves. They demanded obedience to explicit commands, the completion of assigned tasks, attendance at the sermons of white ministers, a look of contentment, a gesture of subservience, a change in a name—and all the other "superficial" features of obedience. They patrolled the roads, both literally and figuratively. Rebellious slaves rarely were sent to the penitentiary, the place designed to manipulate the "internal" transformation of criminals. Masters preferred whips to prisons because they believed, along with legal expert Thomas R. R. Cobb, that the slave could only be controlled externally, that he "can be reached only through his body."[64] Although it would be a considerable exaggeration to suggest that men of honor sought control only over the bodies of their slaves, it is appropriate to note that the body drew a disproportionate degree of attention. This method of control defined both the central brutality and the central limitation of the power of the slave regime. Damage to a slave's body could still leave deep inner scars—even if the external focus did permit a space within slave psychology and culture outside the reach of the master. As the historian Bertram Wyatt-Brown suggests, the demand for a mask of obedience could cause more than a superficial wound.[65] Moreover, we can see from a modern perspective that the simple dichotomy between an outer self and an inner self collapses at many points. But the mistress who told her slaves to kiss the lash might have done considerably more damage had she required her slaves to love it

Even the attempt to prevent slaves from learning to read should be understood as an external mechanism of control—analogous to the masters' patrolling the roads at night or whipping bodies. It was related to the language of honor. It was a control tactic designed to close off external sources of contamination, rather than to indoctrinate slaves through a program of reeducation. The example of Harriet Jacobs was an exception that illustrates the general practice. When James Norcom tried to force Jacobs into a sexual relationship he sought a deeper level of penetration than could be afforded by physical coercion. He demanded a "voluntary" compliance with his sexual demands. In the paternal spirit, he yearned for a seduction; he sought entry to her mind. As she later recalled, Norcom first "began to whisper foul words in my ear." Jacobs pretended not to understand, but Norcom persisted. When the watchful eyes of Norcom's wife made it difficult for him to whisper, he resorted to sign language, and "invented more than were ever thought of in a deaf and dumb asylum." Then Norcom discovered that Jacobs could read. At first, Jacobs reported, he seemed displeased. But he later came to a conclusion rare among Southern gentlemen: he could continue his seduction in the form of written notes. Jacobs here experienced literacy differently than most slaves, because Norcom's primary target was her will, not her body. For a man like Frederick Douglass, learning to read was a route to liberation. For Harriet Jacobs, at least in this context, learning to read opened another path for her master to enter. But what stands out about Jacobs's experience with literacy is its oddity. Masters did not produce a written literature of seduction for their slaves. The proslavery argument was not directed to a slave audience. Instead, most masters chose the more superficial tactic of enforced illiteracy.

The language of honor limited the focus of masters. Many masters who desired the love and respect of their slaves primarily focused on the care of their bodies. They presented food and clothing as gifts on ritual occasions. They provided good medical care. They arranged for the construction of decent housing. They tried to enforce a moderate pace for work. And they exercised mercy by learning to restrain their whipping. Such masters often interfered with other aspects of slave life, including marriage and religion. But their primary focus remained on the body.[66]

The language of honor, in placing a high value on bodies and surfaces, directed the energy and interest of masters as they tried to control their slaves. Generally, open and face-to-face verbal and physical confrontations could not be tolerated. Although masters were never pleased with other forms of disobedience, most came to accept them as an inevitable product of the dishonored condition of slaves—a product that was annoying but not severely threatening. Attitudes toward theft offer a good example. Every master would have loved to eliminate theft from his plantation, but few could accomplish this. Instead, most learned to live with it. The historian Drew Faust has described James Henry Hammond's accommodation by noting that once he decided he could not eradicate black theft, "he chose to define [it] . . . as a passive 'habit' rather than an assertive and powerful challenge to his control."[67] The proslavery theorist William Harper offered a parallel description when he noted, "Theft in a freeman is a crime; in a slave, it is a vice."[68] In other words, Hammond and Harper both concluded that theft was a symptom of the flawed character of slaves rather than an attack on masters. It was a symptom of dishonor. Such an analysis opened a space for the accommodation of theft on the plantation—a space not made available to open challenges to the master's authority. Similar spaces existed in the language of honor for the slaves' lying, poor work habits, and running away. They were understood as character traits of men with no honor rather than as modes of revolt. Many masters came to expect and to tolerate a certain level of such behavior as part of life with slaves. The language of honor created the space for such an accommodation. African Americans carved out a semiautonomous space on slave plantations; the language of honor may have deflected the masters' attention away from that space.

THREE

GIFTS, STRANGERS, DUELS, AND HUMANITARIANISM

SOUTHERN MEN of honor loved to give gifts. It is the central argument of this chapter that gifts were the most common means of
exchange for honorable men of the master class in the antebellum
South. Such men engaged in numerous market transactions, but these
were neither as frequent nor as significant in their lives as gift transactions. Gift exchanges flourished because they were so intimately connected to the values and behaviors associated with the language of honor
and slavery.

This contention may at first seem an exaggeration. Every student of the
antebellum South knows that masters were deeply involved in both a
local and an international market economy.[1] They grew cotton and other
crops for exchange in a world market. They borrowed money at interest
from each other or from banks or factors. They maneuvered to sell their
crops at the highest possible profit. They bought and sold slaves at prices
that reflected the slaves' potential productivity. They carefully recorded
their trades in plantation diaries. They bargained, calculated, and con-
tracted. By all these measures Southern masters seem to have lived
largely in the world of the market rather than the world of the gift. Although they may have given gifts to slaves at Christmas and extended
generous hospitality to their neighbors, these seem like minor activities
for men primarily engaged in crop production for market.

But gift exchange only appears peripheral in the lives of Southern men
of honor if "gift" and "exchange" are narrowly defined. Consider the concept of "gift." If one looks only for wrapped packages, or for particular
formal settings where gifts commonly appear, or for overt statements announcing that someone is giving a gift or being hospitable, then one will
miss most gift exchange in Southern culture. Perhaps the single most
important feature of gift exchange is that it is not identifiable through any
specific set of behavioral criteria. Consider a contemporary example.
Every morning as I walk to my office I engage in a classic market trans-

action. I buy the *Boston Globe* from a newsstand. I buy it because I want to read the *Globe* and the newsdealer sells it because she wants to earn money. But suppose the following events transform this interaction. Suppose I no longer want to read the *Globe*, and at the same time I discover that my newsdealer is sick and in need of money to pay medical bills. I therefore continue to buy the *Globe* because I do not want to diminish her income. Suppose she understands all this because a mutual friend tells her of my small act of generosity. Our behavior under these changed circumstances might appear to be what it has always been. I give her money and she gives me a newspaper and a "thank you." And yet our changed motives and knowledge would have fundamentally transformed the nature of our relationship and of our transactions. We would have moved from the world of the market to the world of the gift. The movement would not have been completely open and acknowledged. Both of us would probably be embarrassed if we overtly entered into an unambiguous gift relationship—if, for example, I simply dropped coins in her hand without receiving a newspaper in return. Therefore we would silently and mutually agree to allow our gift exchange to assume the outward form of a market exchange. But both of us would know that our transactions were transformed—that her "thank you" was a sign of gratitude for the receipt of a gift rather than for a completed market exchange. Southern men of honor engaged in numerous gift transactions of exactly this type.[2]

If gift exchanges cannot be identified by any particular set of behavioral criteria, then how is it possible to distinguish them from market exchanges? The differences are far more subtle than may at first seem apparent. One must examine the spirit and intent of the parties engaged in the exchange; one must examine the larger system of language and social relations that surrounds a particular instance of gift exchange. One of the key features of gift giving is that it must be undertaken in a spirit of generosity (or a simulated spirit of generosity)—without any overt calculation that it will produce some beneficial return to the giver. This is a paradoxical feature of gift exchange because, in fact, gifts almost always do produce great benefits for the giver—usually far greater than for the recipient. Givers almost always gather profits in the form of love, respect, power, prestige, status—or other return gifts.[3] My daily contribution to the newsdealer would have increased my own status far more than it would have increased her income. The extreme form of gift exchange known as the "potlatch" practiced by the nineteenth-century Kwakiutl tribe of the northern Pacific Coast region illustrates in exaggerated form the underlying dynamics of most gift exchanges. On special occasions, such as a marriage or the elevation of a new chief, Kwakiutl tribes and individuals engaged in orgies of generosity, struggling to give away or to destroy vast stores of their own wealth in a ritual that determined their social position.⁴ Those who gave or destroyed the most achieved the highest positions of status and power. Here is an activity that vividly demonstrates the central paradox of the gift· gift giving is "acquisitive generosity" that the giver must not openly recognize as acquisitive, since that would not be generous.

Just as it is easy to underestimate the pervasiveness of gift exchange in Southern culture by adhering to a too narrow definition of "gifts," it is easy to compound the mistake by following a too narrow definition of "exchange." Masters in the antebellum South engaged in large numbers of transactions in which no commodity or material good ever changed hands. Why should a study of gifts focus exclusively on the exchange of objects or money when people also engaged in countless other social exchanges such as pledging loyalty, insulting each other, and voting? The human exchanges that occurred on dueling grounds or at polling places were part of the same social world as the exchanges that occurred in slave or cotton markets. No one place of exchange can claim a privileged status because it shapes the others; they are all fields in which power, wealth, status, pleasure, and pain are distributed in a social world. We should study them all—not simply separately but also in relation to each other.

One fruitful way to begin to explore the connections among gifts, honor, and slavery is to look closely at a Southern duel. Such a focus may seem an oblique way to approach the subject. Why not study Southern hospitality or Christmas presents rather than duels, if the goal is to gain insights into gift exchange? The answer is simple. A study of the duel *is* a study of gifts. A description of an 1826 confrontation between John Randolph and Henry Clay should make the relationship clear.

I

At 4:30 in the afternoon of April 8, 1826, Henry Clay, secretary of state in the Adams administration, and John Randolph, a United States senator from Virginia, fired pistols at each other at a distance of ten paces. They fought near Washington, D.C., in a forest beside a bridge on the Virginia side of the Potomac. Randolph had insisted that they meet in Virginia. If shot, he wanted his blood to fall on the soil of his beloved native state. Only a handful of people witnessed the duel. Each man brought two seconds and a surgeon. In addition, two others looked down on the scene from the top of a small hill. One was Senator Thomas Hart Benton of Missouri, a friend of both Clay and Randolph. The duelists had agreed to honor him with permission to be a witness. The other was a slave variously known as "Johnny" or "John" or "John White," later described by

FIGURE 5. John Randolph.

Benton as Randolph's "faithful man" who "evinc[ed] the deepest anxiety for his beloved master."[5]

Tensions between Clay and Randolph considerably predated their encounter in 1826. As early as 1812, Clay had humiliated Randolph in the House of Representatives. Randolph, a strong opponent of the impending war with Great Britain, had tried to raise the issue preemptively, before President James Madison had delivered his war message. He had been speaking for more than an hour before his fellow congressman John C. Calhoun interrupted, complaining that the speech was out of order since there was no motion on the floor. Clay was Speaker of the House, and he ruled that before he could continue his diatribe, Randolph had to put forward a motion in writing. Randolph objected. But the House sustained Clay, and Randolph was silenced.[6]

According to the values of men of honor, this kind of encounter did not usually lead to a duel unless it included personal insults. Neither Clay nor Randolph had called the other a "poltroon," a "coward," a "liar," or something similar. Their conflict remained relatively abstract and impersonal. They confined their remarks to the issue of proper congressional procedure. Still, it would be wrong to see this kind of clash, and the thousands of others like it among antebellum Southern politicians, as divorced from the culture of honor. Randolph, like any man of honor, felt the sting of having been bested. He would lie in wait to make Clay and other political enemies submit at a later date. An abstract and impersonal encounter did not usually end in pistol shots, but any attack had to be resisted. Men of honor always held a grudge. Clay and Randolph repeatedly clashed in public during the years after 1812.[7]

The conflict that led to the 1826 duel had its most immediate causes in political disagreements. But unlike the 1812 encounter, it also involved personal insults. Clay had been under heavy attack by political opponents ever since he threw his support behind John Quincy Adams during the 1824 presidential election. Some of his political enemies suggested that Clay had sold his vote in exchange for political office. They believed their suspicions had been confirmed when Adams appointed Clay secretary of state. Clay was insulted by the insinuations. The "corrupt bargain" charge crossed the line from political disagreement to personal insult. When the accusation appeared in an anonymous article in a Philadelphia newspaper, Clay—believing he knew the source of the attack—issued a blanket challenge to fight a duel with any member of the House of Representatives who would acknowledge authorship. He was a bit surprised when George Kremer, a man not taken seriously by other members of Congress, stepped forward. Clay would not duel with a person of such low status; that sort of encounter would do little to repair his injured reputation. He backed off; he called for a congressional investigation of the charge and invited Kremer to present his evidence in public. Kremer never appeared to testify, and the charge of corruption remained unsubstantiated. But Clay felt that his status had been lowered by the insult and he stood ready to challenge any gentleman of note who even hinted at his corruption.[8]

In March 1826, John Randolph emerged as the man Clay would meet on the field of honor. The immediate precipitating event was a debate in the Senate over a mission, proposed by Adams and Clay, to send American delegates to a Panama conference in order to meet with representatives of the governments of Central and South America. Numerous issues related to this mission troubled the senatorial opponents of the Adams administration. Some suggested that attendance at the meeting would compromise official United States neutrality in the battle between the newly independent South American states and Spain. The Panama meeting would also likely authorize official relations with the black government of Haiti and involve the United States in discussions with countries that had some blacks in their governments and armies. This was highly offensive to representatives of the American slave states. Others feared that a United States association with the Latin American states would involve the nation in an "entangling alliance," and that cooperation with other states might compromise American sovereignty.[9]

The usual procedure of the Senate was to debate in closed session an issue like the Panama mission. But opponents of United States participation in the proposed meeting feared that if they could not engage in open debate, their voices would not be heard and the administration's position would win wide popular support. The Senate, therefore, passed a motion to debate in open session unless Adams objected that it would be prejudicial to existing negotiations. Adams sent back a response that some in the Senate—especially John Randolph—found insulting.[10]

The Adams reply infuriated Randolph. It prompted him to rise in the Senate and to deliver a vicious attack on the president, including several insulting remarks directed against the sensitive secretary of state, Clay. What made Randolph so angry? On the surface, the Adams note simply said it was up to the Senate to decide whether or not it would meet in open session. The substance of the reply might seem innocuous to a modern observer, but Randolph detected an insult buried in that substance. Adams had said that to meet in open session "involves a departure, hitherto, so far as I am informed, without an example, from that usage, and upon the *motives for which*, not being informed of them, I do not feel myself competent to decide" (emphasis added by Randolph). Randolph told the senators that this was a libel against all of them; it was an attack on their characters. Adams had implied that the senators had motives that did not appear on the surface of their motion. "The innuendo," he believed, "was that our motives were black and bad. . . . [W]ho made him the searcher of our hearts, and gave him the right, by an innuendo black as hell, to blacken our motives?" Part of this vitriolic speech included at least two insulting references to Clay, although neither mentioned him by name. One suggested that the Kentuckian Clay had fabricated the Latin American invitation to the Panama mission, or, as Randolph rather colorfully put it, that it was "a Kentucky cuckoo's egg, laid in a Spanish-American nest." The other reference was included in a statement to the effect that Randolph believed that in his opposition to the Adams message he was "defeated, horse, foot and dragoons—cut up, and clean broke down by the coalition of Blifil and Black George—by the combination, unheard of till then, of the puritan with the blackleg."[11] Blifil and Black George were characters in the novel *Tom Jones*. Everyone recognized that the Puritan was John Quincy Adams and the blackleg (a swindler and a professional gambler) was Henry Clay.

Clay was not present during Randolph's attack, but friends quickly reported the assault. They told him that Randolph had charged him with "forgery" and had called him a "blackleg." Clay was furious. Almost immediately, he dashed off a challenge note: "Your unprovoked attack of my character, in the Senate of the U. States, on yesterday, allows me no other alternative than that of demanding personal satisfaction." Clearly, Randolph had touched a raw nerve. Clay could have taken a more cautious and moderate course of action. After all, he had only heard a verbal report of the Randolph speech. He could have detailed in writing the purported insults and asked Randolph to verify their accuracy and explain their meaning. Such a course was a common practice in the world of honorable gentlemen. But given the earlier "corrupt bargain" charges and the aborted challenge to Kremer, Clay probably felt a powerful need to push this encounter quickly from the language of words to the language of bullets. He "demand[ed] personal satisfaction."

But the Clay-Randolph duel, like many other Southern disputes over honor, did not move easily from insult to battle. Much remained to be discussed, explained, and negotiated, especially after the seconds became involved. Clay had asked his friend General Thomas Sidney Jesup to deliver the challenge note to Randolph. But before handing over the letter, Jesup felt he needed to clarify one ambiguous point. All the parties to the dispute seemed to agree that Randolph, like any United States senator, had a privilege not to be held "personally accountable" for words he spoke in debate. Clay had heard (erroneously, as it turned out) that Randolph explicitly waived this privilege during his vituperative speech. But the reports must have been vague enough to have prompted Jesup to make his own inquiry on this point before he delivered the challenge note. Randolph replied that he agreed that the Constitution protected him from attack for words he spoke in the Senate, "but he would never shield himself under such a subterfuge as the pleading of his privilege as a senator from Virginia."[13]

Randolph then informed Jesup that another issue needed to be clarified. He pointed out that Clay already had "two pledges to redeem"—that is, that Clay needed to bring to closure two other affairs of honor before he could demand a meeting with Randolph. Clearly, Randolph intended to be nasty by bringing up these unredeemed "pledges": one was a reference to Clay's confrontation with George Kremer, the lowly representative; the other concerned a newspaper confrontation with John Quincy Adams himself.[14] Jesup immediately replied that Clay would not want to use these commitments as an excuse to postpone a duel with Randolph. Randolph answered in a way that paralleled his response to the issue of senatorial privilege. He carefully noted that it was *he* who would not hide behind these commitments. As Jesup described it, Randolph "said he had not the remotest intention of taking advantage of the pledges referred to; that he had mentioned them merely to remind that he was waiving his privilege, not only as a senator from Virginia, but as a private gentleman."[15] In other words, Randolph was interested in asserting that he had the right to refuse a duel with Clay, but that he would magnanimously refrain from exercising that right. His duel with Clay would be a gift and not an obligation.

Another striking feature of this Jesup-Randolph meeting is the great courtesy and mutual respect that both men displayed. Such behavior was typical of many dueling disputes, because the code of honor demanded that all participants—seconds as well as principals—had to regard each other as equals. In fact, one of the central purposes of the dueling ritual was to reaffirm the equality of the principals after it had been disrupted by an insult. Although events leading up to the duel might involve considerable maneuvering to lower the status of an opponent, the duel included elaborate displays of respect as all participants moved toward healing the rupture by a meeting of equals shooting pistols at each other. Hence, for example, Jesup graciously refused to carry Randolph's reply directly back to Clay because he believed that the senator "owed it to himself" to consult with his friends. As Jesup later described it, Randolph then "seized my hand" and said "You are right, sir. I thank you for the suggestion." Jesup noted that during the entire interview Randolph's "bearing was . . . that of a high-toned gentleman of the old school."[16]

Randolph then set out to speak with his friends and to find seconds. His first stop was at the room of Missouri Senator Thomas Hart Benton in Brown's Hotel. He wanted Benton as a second, but he did not extend the invitation once he ascertained that Benton was a blood relation of Mrs. Clay. Apparently, Randolph would have linked himself to Benton if the relationship had been by marriage, but a blood connection was a different matter. Blood created a bond with which Randolph would not interfere.[17] Benton would remain an observer and a mediator, but not a direct participant in the duel.

It was during this meeting with Benton that Randolph first stated his intention to allow himself to be shot at but not to return fire. Benton later said that Randolph had at least three reasons for this decision. First, he had no desire to hurt Clay in any way. Apparently, not only did Randolph genuinely respect Clay, but he understood that if he killed the secretary of state, a popular politician and a married man with relatively young children, he would become an object of scorn rather than of honor. Second, he believed that to shoot "would be to answer [for the words he had spoken in the Senate], and would be an implied acknowledgment of Mr. Clay's right to make him answer." In other words, the intention not to shoot, at least in part, an extension of Randolph's belief that Clay did not have the right to demand an answer on the field of honor for words spoken in senatorial debate. For Randolph to shoot at

Clay would have transformed the duel from his gift to his obligation. As Benton described it, "It was as much as to say: Mr. Clay may fire at me for what has offended him; I will not, by returning the fire, admit his right to do so." It was this same intention that prevented Randolph from explaining and thereby softening the meaning of his words when the seconds later tried to work out a compromise to abort the duel. Finally, Randolph was well aware that Virginia had laws that prohibited dueling. Like any man of honor, he would never have hidden behind these laws to decline a duel, but he would not go out of his way to "insult" the laws of his beloved state. He saw the act of not shooting at Clay as a good compromise. He would participate in the duel and yet show his respect for Virginia law by withholding his fire.[18]

This determination not to shoot kept coming up as an issue throughout the encounter. It presented a variety of problems for Randolph's friends as well as for Randolph himself. When he first informed his seconds that he would not "make [Clay's] wife a widow or his children orphans," they rushed to him for a midnight meeting. Randolph greeted them in the pose of a man of honor unconcerned with risking his life. He had just been reading *Paradise Lost*, and he kept them waiting as he expounded on one of his favorite passages. Finally, the seconds informed him of their objection to his decision not to shoot. One second, Georgia colonel Edward F. Tattnall, even threatened to withdraw from participation unless Randolph changed his mind. He did not want to watch his friend shot down. But Randolph would not budge, and he convinced Tattnall that a second's withdrawal at this time might be misunderstood by the public, and therefore he had to see the matter through to the end.[19]

For different reasons, Randolph's determination not to shoot was troubling to Thomas Hart Benton as well. He considered himself a friend of Clay as well as of Randolph. Perhaps because of his respect for Clay, his blood tie to Mrs. Clay, and his sympathy for the family, he had a strong desire to see Randolph carry through on his pledge to withhold his fire. Since several days passed between the initial challenge and the actual duel, Benton wondered whether Randolph would keep to his original intention. He visited him the morning of the duel in order to find out. Benton could not directly ask Randolph his question because that would imply a lack of trust. Instead, he described his previous night's visit to the Clay family—emphasizing the peaceful domestic scene he witnessed, including a child sleeping on his father's lap. Randolph understood perfectly and, although indicating some annoyance at Benton's lack of trust, reiterated his pledge not to shoot—to "do nothing to disturb the sleep of the child or the repose of the mother."[20]

However, Benton's lack of trust was not really misplaced. A duel was a complex and volatile interaction. New information, new insults, or new interpretations could easily disrupt a man's initial intentions. Two late developments moved Randolph to waver from his original determination not to fire. On the way to the dueling ground, Randolph's seconds informed him that Clay seemed to have a real desire to kill him. This impression came from their negotiations over the speed of the count. This was an important matter. The duel would begin when one second said "Fire." Clay and Randolph could shoot at each other while the second counted "one, two, three." All firing had to end at the word "stop." The seconds on both sides wanted a quick count. Part of their intention was to prevent anyone from taking careful aim and thereby to lessen the chances of injury or death. Another goal was to equalize two duelists of different skill by, as Benton later put it, "reducing the result as near as possible to chance."[21] But Clay apparently preferred a much slower count. Although he did finally agree to a quick count, Randolph's seconds interpreted Clay's initial position as evidence of a desire for blood. Actually, this probably was a misinterpretation. Clay was so unpracticed with pistols that he feared he would not get off any shot at all with a quick count. He did not particularly want to take careful aim, but he did want to shoot.

At any rate, when Randolph heard about the debate over the quick count he began to reconsider his plan not to shoot. At the dueling ground he hinted to Benton that he might shoot, and handed him a note (to be read at the completion of the duel) that explained his reasoning: "Information received from Col. Tatnall since I got into the carriage *may* induce me to change my mind, of not returning Mr. Clay's fire. I seek not his death. I would not have his blood upon my hands—it will not be upon my soul if shed in self-defense—for the world. He has determined, by the use of a long, preparatory caution by words, to get time to kill me. May I not, then, disable him? Yes, if I please."[22] It is clear that at the moment he penned these words he was not yet sure what he would do. But his reasoning reveals that he did not view the duel as a way to commit suicide. He was willing to risk his life, but not to face certain death. He wanted to pass near death and then to emerge back into life with his honor revivified. He wanted to become the master of death, not its victim. He had told Benton and his seconds about his original intention to spare Clay's life because he envisioned the awe in which he would be held as he walked from the dueling ground and back into the Senate. He took considerably less pleasure in the vision that he might simply be carried away and buried.

A second development on the dueling ground finally convinced Randolph to return Clay's fire. Randolph and Clay had assumed their positions on the field. One of the seconds began to rehearse the count as he would give it in a few minutes. Clay did not yet have his pistol; Randolph held his own pointed at the ground. Just then, Randolph's gun fired. It was an accident, although that was not obvious to everyone at first. This was a delicate and dangerous moment. Randolph was furious that his intentions might be misunderstood. People might think that he sought to kill an unarmed Clay in order to save his own life. Immediately, for all to hear, he turned to Colonel Tattnall and said, "I protested against that hair trigger." Apparently, in his attempt to save Randolph's life, Tattnall had secretly set the pistol on a hair trigger, and Randolph's heavy glove had touched it off. Benton later reported that, immediately, Clay's seconds delicately raised some questions about the accident, but the very fact of their inquiry "was of a nature to be inexpressibly painful to a gentleman's feelings." Finally, according to Benton, Clay himself intervened "with the generous remark that the fire was clearly an accident; and it was so unanimously declared." This must have disturbed Randolph even more. He had originally intended to give Clay a gift, but the accidental firing permitted Clay to give him one instead.[23]

It is a bit of a puzzle why the accidental discharge of his gun determined Randolph to return Clay's fire. No evidence on this subject is available; one can only speculate. Perhaps he felt so humiliated by the accident that he simply lost his temper. Or Randolph could have calculated that Clay's knowledge of the hair trigger might make him more determined to draw blood. Randolph did not welcome certain death, and thus he may have become even more interested in wounding his adversary. It is also possible that Randolph calculated that the accidental firing before the duel followed by a refusal to fire during the duel might afterward be unfairly judged by the public. Perhaps his failure to shoot in the duel might be understood as an admission that he already had taken his first shot. Perhaps people would laugh at a man who seemed to misunderstand dueling custom—shooting and not shooting at the wrong moments. It is impossible to know what flashed through Randolph's mind as he shot at Clay. What is known is that the accident triggered a powerful reaction.

At any rate, both men missed in their first exchange of shots. Randolph's bullet hit a stump behind Clay and Clay's bullet hit the dirt behind Randolph. Benton then moved in to mediate. Clay dismissed him "with that wave of the hand with which he was accustomed to put away a trifle," telling him *This is child's play!* Randolph too wanted to shoot again. However, by this time he had collected himself and returned to his original intention. Now he regretted his first shot and wanted to reframe the meaning of the duel. His first shot seemed to show that he wanted to kill Clay and that he had contempt for the laws of Virginia. He would do it properly the second time. When Clay's next bullet also failed to injure Randolph, Randolph fired his pistol into the air. *"I do not fire at you, Mr. Clay,"* he announced. The two men then walked toward each other and shook hands. Randolph, noting a bullet hole in his clothing, remarked *"You owe me a coat, Mr. Clay."* Clay immediately replied, *"I am glad the debt is no greater."* Benton later reported that, within a few days, "the parties exchanged cards, and social relations were formally and courteously restored."[24] The duel had healed their wounds.

II

The duel between Clay and Randolph illustrates many of the complex connections among gifts, honor, and slavery in the antebellum South. Perhaps the best way to begin to understand these connections is to recognize the central role played by images of domination and subordination—of mastery and slavery—throughout the dueling encounter.[25] The Clay-Randolph duel was a conversation between two men in which each tried to remain a master and to avoid becoming a slave. In the end, both men accomplished their goals by risking their lives and by exchanging a series of gifts in a confrontation that demonstrated their equality.

The Clay-Randolph encounter, like virtually all Southern duels, began with an imbalance in the relationship between two gentlemen. One man insulted and shamed another in public—one man declared he was dominant and the other was subordinate. An imbalance in the relationship between two Southern gentlemen was highly volatile because it immediately evoked images of mastery and slavery. Virtually all insults involved the imputation of "slavelike" behavior—of being a coward, thief, liar, or something similar. Moreover, just as it was not possible to be a partial slave, it was not possible to be slightly insulted. All insults were equal in the sense that they implied that someone had been reduced to a slavish condition. Honor and dishonor, like mastery and slavery, were total conditions. A man was usually in one state or the other and only spent a brief moment in transition.

Randolph's speech in the Senate was the precipitating event that prompted Clay to issue his challenge, but that speech should not be understood in isolation from the events that led up to it. Both Clay and Randolph entered the conflict concerned about their status as honorable gentlemen. Clay had suffered from the "corrupt bargain" charges and his silly encounter with George Kremer. Randolph, always a man with a thin skin, had taken great offense at Adams's attempt to question the motives of the senators. Although Adams did not personally refer to him, Randolph felt as if he had been called a liar—as if Adams had said his appearance covered some deep, dark secret.

FIGURE 6. "The Late Henry Clay and His Faithful Companion."

Randolph and Clay saw themselves locked in a battle over mastery and subordination. In his Senate speech, Randolph had referred to Clay as a forger and a swindler. This direct, personal insult created an inequality between the two men. Clay felt that he had to respond to the insult. As he later described it, "Submission, on my part, to the unmerited injury, I can only say, would have rendered existence intolerable."[26] Slaves, not honorable gentlemen, were the people who "submitted." Instead of "submission," Clay exhibited the behavior of a master and wrote a challenge note in which he "demand[ed]" personal satisfaction.[27] However, Randolph refused to allow Clay to "demand" anything of him. Randolph understood that he and Clay were playing a deadly game. As they engaged in a ritual designed to reestablish their equality, they each had to watch carefully to avoid falling into a slavish condition. Randolph pointed out that he could speak in the Senate without being held personally accountable for his words and that Clay was first obligated to settle other affairs of honor. Clay could not "demand" a duel, but Randolph would offer it to him freely—as a gift.

The duel exposed Randolph as a man obsessed with giving. Not only did he shower Clay with gifts, but during the course of the encounter he also gave gifts to his seconds, to Thomas Hart Benton—even to his bank. As part of his preparation for the duel, Randolph planned, in the event of his death, to give a commemorative gold coin to each of his seconds as well as to Benton. With this in mind, he sent "his faithful man, Johnny" to obtain the coins at a United States branch bank. Johnny returned empty-handed. The bankers had told him they had no gold coins in stock. This infuriated Randolph; he suspected that they had lied to "his man." "Their name is legion!" he screamed, "and they are liars from the beginning." Randolph called for his horse, and with Johnny riding his customary forty paces behind, he arrived in a rage and demanded to withdraw all his money immediately in the form of silver coins. Finally, a cashier intervened and miraculously turned up a few gold coins. Still, Randolph punished the bank by closing out his account, although he ultimately accepted a banknote in payment rather than several wheelbarrows of silver coins. But even then his problems with the bank continued. Shortly after the termination of the duel a runner from the bank arrived and announced that Randolph had been overpaid. Randolph denied this "demand" for repayment in a manner parallel to the way he denied Clay's "demand" for a duel. "I believe *it is your rule*," he told the runner, *"not to correct mistakes, except at the time, and at your counter."* However, after the runner had left, Clay turned to his friends and announced that he would return the money on Monday since *"people must be honest, if banks are not."* In other words, Randolph would not pay upon "demand," but would offer the money to the bank as a gift.[28]

Randolph ultimately distributed the gold coins. He had gone to the dueling ground with nine coins and a note in his pocket. The note was to be opened upon his death; it directed that three coins each should be given as gifts to Benton and his seconds. The coins were to be made into seals in his memory. Randolph did not die, but he insisted on bestowing the gifts anyway. Shortly after leaving the dueling ground he gathered his friends around him and announced "Gentlemen, Clay's bad shooting shan't rob you of your seals. I am going to London, and will have them made for you." Randolph kept his word, even tracking down and copying the design of a family seal that Thomas Hart Benton never even knew existed.[29]

Why did Randolph embark on this orgy of gift giving in the midst of his dueling encounter? He seems to have understood that the giving of a gift was a distinguishing mark of men of honor and of masters. The institution of slavery was deeply implicated in the meaning of gift giving in antebellum Southern society. Between master and slave, gifts could only flow in one direction.[30] A slave could own nothing and therefore could give no gifts. One of the central characteristics of the condition of enslavement, as seen through the eyes of masters, involved the inability to give gifts. Similarly, since a slave could make no contractual or other demands on a master, everything he or she received came as a gift. According to the logic of the slave regime, masters did not give gifts to slaves only at Christmas. All transactions involved the giving of gifts; food, clothing, and shelter were supplied as gifts by the master.[31] The same was true of nonmaterial transactions. Every "howdy" or other kind word that a master bestowed on a slave assumed the form of a gift. Clearly, market and other motives frequently played a role in a master's decision to supply the necessities of life to slaves. Masters would make no money if slaves died of malnutrition or exposure. The neighbors might gossip about a master who dressed his slaves in tattered rags. The slaves would not work if they were not properly supplied. But these kinds of selfish motives are often present in gift exchanges, and they need not fundamentally change the nature of the transaction in the mind of the giver. For example, I am aware that my neighbors would gossip if I failed to give my daughters gifts on their birthdays. I also know that the internal peace of my household would be destroyed if holidays did not come with presents. Gift givers frequently benefit from the act of giving. But a gift remains a gift as long as its benefits to the giver are not calculated in the kind of overt and explicit terms that dominate the transaction.

Several features of master-slave interaction suggest that masters regarded that involvement as a one-way gift-giving relationship. Perhaps most central was the master's refusal to allow slaves to make demands. Just as John Randolph refused to allow Henry Clay to demand a duel, masters refused to allow slaves to demand the basic necessities. They might give them the necessities—but only in the form of gifts. They might even sometimes suggest that slaves were entitled to these necessities.[32] But it was an entitlement to a gift, just as modern parents believe that children are entitled to birthday presents. It was an entitlement that could never properly be demanded or bargained for by the slave. Masters regarded slave demands—whether stated or acted upon—as acts of rebellion.

The language of the gift was frequently the language of mastery. "Gave" may have been the single most common verb used by planters to describe their relations with slaves. Thomas Chaplin of South Carolina wrote many diary entries in a form echoed by planters throughout the South: "Gave the Negroes a part of the morning to get their corn"; "Gave ... [potatoes] out to the Negroes for allowance"; "Gave out the cloth."[33] The same language appears in the diary of Bennett Barrow, a brutal Louisiana planter: "Gave the negroes shoes," he wrote, "gave the negroes Cappor 'Blankets,'" "gave the negroes a dinner," "gave the women a dress."[34] Masters gave; slaves received.

Since all this giving resulted from no explicit demands or bargaining, most masters could think of themselves as men of great generosity. Few masters ever kept their slaves at the level of bare survival. Most thought that they gave their slaves much more than was minimally required for life. The brutality associated with slavery seemed to pale next to the far more frequent instances of generosity. That is why so many masters could lament the lack of gratitude on the part of disloyal slaves. It is why a master like Thomas Chaplin, rereading his antebellum plantation diary from a postemancipation vantage point, could append a note stating that "the Negroes did not care as much about us as we did for them."[35] It is why so many masters experienced a sense of ingratitude and betrayal when their slaves deserted them in the midst of the Civil War.[36]

The gift relation was just as deeply implicated in emancipation as it was in slavery. Prior to the abolition of slavery, masters could liberate individual slaves only by awarding them freedom as a gift.[37] Slaves could never purchase themselves in market transactions because they could give nothing to their masters. Masters might permit slaves to purchase themselves, but that was only a roundabout way of giving slaves a valuable gift. But an emancipation that assumed the form of a gift from the master could only be partial. Because one of the distinguishing characteristics of a master was the ability to give gifts, and one of the distinguishing characteristics of a slave was the inability to give gifts, an emancipation that assumed the form of a gift paradoxically reconfirmed the master-slave relationship. Such an emancipation might destroy the legal institution of slavery without attacking the heart of the dependency relationship—at least as it appeared in the minds of masters. Slavery involved more than law. Just as slave marriage could exist in a world where slave marriage was illegal, slavelike dependency could exist in a world where slavery was illegal. This helps explain why the Skipwith family, emancipated by the Virginian John Hartwell Cocke in 1833, wrote letters to him for twenty-five years that began with the salutation "dear Master."[38] It also explains why images of Abraham Lincoln and Northern soldiers as great emancipators—as bringers of the gift of freedom to the down-trodden—actually worked both to liberate and to degrade newly freed slaves. The same insight clarifies the important issue at stake when, in the middle of the twentieth century, the historian W. E. B. DuBois rejected the notion that emancipation was a gift and argued that American slaves liberated themselves.[39]

The deep connections between gift giving and emancipation illuminate the behavior of the many prominent late-eighteenth- and early-nineteenth-century planters who provided for the freedom of their slaves in their wills. John Randolph freed his "faithful man John" along with his other slaves in just this way.[40] But if this generous act is read in the context of what is now known about gift exchange in the master-slave relationship, the ambiguous meaning of freedom when dispensed by the grant of a master in a will becomes clear. John had been at the dueling ground, and at the bank, and in countless other contexts in which his master distributed gifts great and small. He must have understood the connection between gifts and mastery. If Randolph had not freed him in his will, John would have passed into the hands of another owner—once again, no doubt, to bear witness to countless future acts of generosity from a new master. Instead, Randolph prevented that transfer and in effect reached out from the grave in an attempt to remain John's master (or superior) forever. John Randolph had given John the gift of liberty, just as he had given Henry Clay the gift of life, and the magnitude of the gift was, at least in part, intended to dwarf all future gifts. This may sound a bit harsh as a description of the noble act of a generous man. But it really is no more than an elaboration of the paradox of generosity in a slave society, and of the tragic structure that inevitably tainted the best deeds of the most well intentioned masters.

Sometimes—perhaps often—the giving of a gift by a master to a slave (or later, by a white landowner to a black freedman) completely lacked any underlying spirit of generosity. Sometimes it involved the mere form of a gift exchange, with nothing of its substance. But the mere form of a gift exchange seems to have been vitally important to masters and their postemancipation landowning descendants even when it had no content. The spirit of paternalism died long before the style of paternalism.

This is brilliantly illustrated in "Frankie Mae," a short story written by Jean Wheeler Smith and set in the mid-twentieth-century Mississippi delta.[41] It is a tale of a gift relationship at its moment of collapse. Old Man Brown and his family live and work on the cotton plantation of Mr. White Junior, first as sharecroppers and then as workers paid a daily wage. Following a long tradition of economic relations between blacks and whites in the South, the arrangement more closely resembles a gift than a market connection. White Junior extends credit to Brown and his family over the course of the year, lending them money or supplies or medical services while keeping a record of their crop share or accumulated wages. But for Brown this experience of credit is no different from the experience of receiving a gift. It is never a clear exchange for work completed; it is never the result of a specific negotiation; it is never the result of a demand. Only once each year does Brown come before White Junior for a final settling of accounts. But both the timing (at Christmas) and the setting (with White Junior seated at a table with a ledger, a stack of money, and a pistol) offer good clues that the final accounting is not a market moment. Typically, White Junior glances at his ledger to discover that he has been too generous with his gifts of credit during the year. Brown owes him money. But no matter, the spirit of Christmas is in the air and White Junior counts out a few dollars: "Here's you some Christmas money. . . . Pay me when you settle up next year."[42] Next year is always the same. Brown never gets any more than "Christmas money."

Frankie Mae, Brown's bright and lively daughter, innocently intrudes into this world of Christmas money. Completely unaware of the dangerous ground on which she treads, she attempts to transform the gift relation—or at least the empty shell of the gift relation—into a market relation. Encouraged by her family, and impelled by a powerful desire to better herself through education, Frankie Mae learns to read and write. By the age of thirteen she is able to keep her own record of the transactions between White Junior and her father. This time, she believes, Christmas will be different. This time, or so her records seem to say, White Junior will not give them a gift at Christmas. Instead, he will owe them money. This time, they can demand payment. For once, it will be a "Brown" rather than a "White" Christmas. She even convinces her more realistic father that her new knowledge will transform the world.

But the world does not lend itself to such easy transformation. At the moment of accounting, with White Junior solemnly seated behind his ledger sheets, his money, and his pistol, with Frankie Mae seated hopefully before him and her father nervously standing behind her, we learn that this Christmas will be no different. White Junior tells them that they have earned nothing, that once more they will return home with no more than a gift. But Frankie Mae is young and she learns the lesson slowly. "I been keeping a book for my daddy," she proudly announces. "And I got some different figures. Let me show you."[43] Perhaps she did not fully understand the revolution in her words. Perhaps she did not understand the way an accounting ledger could threaten a world. But White Junior did. His face grew red, and his hand moved toward the pistol on the table.

This confrontation, however, did not end in blood. White Junior would not allow the form of the gift to die so readily. First, he conveyed his threat through words, noting a missing $350 charge from a doctor's visit to Willie B., one of Brown's other children. But Frankie Mae would not give up. She knew that Willie B. only had a broken arm and that the doctor had stayed twenty minutes; "that couldn't a cost no $350." She did not understand the insurrection embedded in her innocent use of the language of the market. But White Junior and all the black workers in the room understood it quite clearly. White-knuckled, clutching his pistol, White Junior felt compelled to expose the naked power that lay behind this and all other acts of generosity in white-black relations during and in the wake of slavery. He "spat thick, brown tobacco juice onto the floor," spattering it onto Frankie Mae and her father. "Nigger," he said, "I know you ain't disputing my word. Don't nobody live on my place and call me a liar. That bill was $350. You understand me?" Frankie Mae still did not understand and she turned to her father: "Tell him no, Daddy." But Brown did not "tell him no." He came close, fingering the hidden gun in his pocket. He came close until he envisioned his own death or penitentiary sentence and the eleven mouths his wife would be left alone to feed, and he answered "Yessir ... I understand." And Frankie Mae finally understood as well. White men of honor gave gifts. They did not bargain or trade. They did not accede to contractual demands. They did not allow their pronouncements to be questioned, or as White Junior rather bluntly put it, "Long as you live, bitch, I'm gonna be right and you gonna be wrong. Now get your black ass outa here."[44] Perhaps in the Mississippi delta of the mid–twentieth century the words assumed a cruder form than they would have among the Virginia gentry of the early nineteenth century, but they conveyed a meaning John Randolph would have understood.

But a world where a gun barrel openly and brutally compels the acceptance of "generosity" is a world where gift exchange is near collapse. Frankie Mae herself did not live to witness the collapse. That Christmas gift—accompanied by the spit of White Junior's tobacco juice—killed her. Her body lived on for a number of years, but without the lively spirit that had animated her as a child. Ironically, in the end Brown tried to keep her body alive by requesting another gift from the man whose earlier gift had killed her spirit. When Fannie Mae was giving birth to her fifth child, Brown needed money to take her to the hospital—but White Junior could not be bothered. He was hosting a garden party and said he would help tomorrow. White Junior killed Frankie Mae twice: once by giving her a gift and once by denying her a gift. Only then did Brown say "no." Only then did he join the workers' strike on the White Junior plantation. Only then did he leave the world of the gift.

III

If the sole meaning of gift exchange had been to enhance the position of the giver at the expense of the recipient, then every gift given to a Southern man of honor would have been understood as an insult. At a deep level, every gift given to a Southern man of honor *was* a potential insult. Every gift came wrapped in meanings associated with the gift of a master to a slave. That is why John Randolph was disturbed when Henry Clay generously refused to allow further inquiry into the meaning of his improperly discharged pistol. It is why Randolph expressed contempt for his bank by rewarding it with the gift of a return of its overpayment. It is why the exchange of courtesy common in the Clay-Randolph duel and in many other duels should, at least in part, properly be understood as another form of the exchange of insults.

But gifts involved more than degradation when they were part of a *system* of gift exchange among men of honor. Gifts flowed in only one direction in the master-slave relationship. Men of honor, on the other hand, both gave and received gifts. To be immersed in a system of reciprocal gift giving was to be part of a community of free men. In fact, gift exchange was one of the defining features of that community.[45]

This double quality of the gift as potentially degrading and divisive on the one hand and potentially defining of a community of free men on the other is demonstrated in a description of a "hospitality" exchange in 1857 Virginia. The story is part of a collection of humorous tales written and illustrated by the Virginian David Hunter Strother, under the pseudonym "Porte Crayon." Like many works of travel literature, the accounts here are based on real experiences. Similar descriptions can be found in the diaries and letters of many other Southern gentlemen.[46] The story begins when the traveler Porte Crayon enters a tavern and encounters a group of "teamsters and drovers." Immediately, he is greeted by a bully named Tim Longbow, described as a "strapping, insolent-looking fellow, six feet three in his boots, and somewhat in liquor." The scene is accompanied by an illustration in which Longbow brandishes a whip, evoking images of both teamster and master. Longbow also brandishes aggressive words, referring to Porte Crayon as a man with a "beard as black as a Mexican Greaser's" and then offering him a drink. Here we can see the unambiguous coupling of an insult and a gift. Longbow seeks to degrade the stranger, Crayon, by making him enter into a one-way gift relationship. He hopes to force Crayon to swallow two insults together: the comment that he is a "Mexican Greaser" and the drink offered in hospitality.

FIGURE 7. "Tim Longbow."

But Crayon will not play the role of degraded gift recipient. He tells
Longbow to "hold his peace" and refuses the drink. Longbow knows that
his mastery has been challenged by the refusal of his gift, and he insists
that Crayon follow the custom of the country and either "drink or fight."
Happily, they avoid bloodshed at the last moment when the innkeeper
intervenes just as Longbow advances to the attack and Crayon draws his
knife. The innkeeper mediates a compromise to which they all now refer
as a "point of honor": Crayon agrees to drink—but only a glass of water.
In other words, Crayon accepts a gift in order to avoid an insult to Long-

FIGURE 8. "The Triumph."

bow, but it is a gift of no value and hence one that does little to demonstrate the mastery and generosity of the giver.

The boisterous Longbow, however, like John Randolph, is a man obsessed with the need to assert himself by bestowing gifts. Repeatedly he draws Crayon into a kind of battle of generosity reminiscent of the potlatch of the Kwakiutls. First he offers the assembled company in the tavern the gift of a clever tall tale; he tells of an extraordinary swimming

journey. Then he turns to Porte Crayon and asks him to join the community by presenting the gift of a story of his own. Crayon responds with the
offering of a fantastic story of life at the North Pole. It was common for
Southern men, whenever they gathered in groups, to exchange these
types of stories as gifts. Men on hunting trips frequently bound themselves together as a community by exchanging exaggerated tales of their
heroic exploits in field and stream.

Everyone in the room seemed to understand this gift exchange through
stories as a kind of competition of generosity. Each man tried to offer the
company the most impressive gift. In the end, Tim Longbow conceded
that he had been beaten, but it was a beating that did not reduce him to
slavery because it was part of a system of gift exchange. He acknowledged
that he had been bested but he did not have to grovel. In fact, Longbow
gave Crayon another gift—his hat—as a way of admitting the defeat without degrading himself. He crowned the champion in good "democratic"
fashion, reminiscent of the way Southern voters crowned their political
leaders. It was a crown that he would expect back if he bested Crayon in
a later confrontation. But, at least on this occasion, Tim Longbow did
not stand a chance. Crayon went on to offer the company an impressive
series of card tricks and then to outplay Longbow in a fiddling competition. In the end, it was clear to everyone that Crayon had given them the
gifts of greatest value. The entire company honored him by carrying him
on their shoulders around the room— or, to put it another way, the entire
company recognized Crayon's triumph and awarded him the gift of
honor.[47]

What was the difference between the confrontation of Longbow and
Crayon in a nineteenth-century Virginia tavern and the confrontation of
Frankie Mae and White Junior on a twentieth-century Mississippi planta-
tion? In many ways they were quite similar. Both were stories about gifts.
In both tales the gifts came with a taint of degradation attached to them.
In Mississippi the gift of money came with the spit of tobacco juice; in
Virginia the offer of a drink came with the remark about a "beard as black
as a Mexican Greaser's." Both stories had moments when a man's word
was challenged as part of an attempt to reject a gift. Both showed gift
givers defending their words along with their gifts: White Junior telling
Frankie Mae "Nigger, I know you ain't disputing my word" and Longbow
ominously asking one skeptic, "Are you a-misdoubting of a gentleman's
word?"

The central difference between the two stories lies in the arena of reciprocity. In the Virginia tavern all the white men gave gifts (even if all the
gifts were not exactly equal). Longbow gave drinks, told stories, played
the fiddle, and gave away his hat; Crayon told stories, performed card

tricks, and played the fiddle; the rest of the company carried Crayon around the room. But on the Mississippi plantation only White Junior gave the gifts. The stories illustrate a significant difference between reciprocal and one-way gift relations. In the Virginia tavern a community was created; on the Mississippi plantation a community was destroyed.

These distinctions between one-way and reciprocal gift relations help clarify why the Clay-Randolph duel worked to reestablish peaceful relations. The duel was an opportunity for the exchange of gifts. The gift exchange allowed each man to demonstrate his status as a master and a man of honor. Although each gift might have come with a hint of degradation, the reciprocity of the exchanges pushed the degradation deeply into the background. First, consider a few of the smaller gift exchanges that surrounded the duel. Randolph gave his seconds commemorative medals and a festive dinner; Randolph's seconds gave him the valuable gift of agreeing to become involved in the duel, putting their lives at risk for him. Every man extended the gift of courteous language to every other man. Clay gave the gift of a challenge to Randolph, a gift he had earlier refused to give to the lowly George Kremer. Randolph agreed to give the duel to Clay, although Clay had no right to demand it. Clay gave Randolph the courtesy of preventing further inquiry into his accidental shot.

But the most important gift exchange of the Clay-Randolph duel, and of all other Southern duels, was the exchange of shots. It may be difficult for us to take seriously the idea of a bullet as a gift, yet that only serves to demonstrate how far removed we are from the world of men of honor. It is easy for a modern observer to misunderstand the central point of the duel. Although some men dueled in order to kill a hated adversary, the vast majority dueled in order to demonstrate that they possessed the central virtue of men of honor: they did not fear death.[48] The central purpose of a duel was not to kill, but to be threatened with death. Hence, the exchange of shots on a dueling ground should be thought of as a double gift exchange. Each man shot a bullet and gave his adversary a chance to demonstrate that he did not fear death; honor was more important than life. And each man allowed his adversary to shoot at him, and therefore paid him the compliment of acknowledging his social equality. Men, after all, only dueled with their social equals. Perhaps no other human activity has ever allowed men to demonstrate such a spirit of generosity. The exchange of shots on the dueling ground differs from the exchange of presents at Christmas only because of its excess. Like the potlatch, or like human sacrifice to the gods, the duel should be seen as an extreme form of gift exchange.

This way of looking at the Clay-Randolph duel brings to light the problematic nature of Randolph's "generous" decision to spare Clay's life. Randolph's shot in the air contained more than a hint of the kind of

FIGURE 9. "Sunday Amusements at New Orleans—
Duel at the Half-Way House."

gifts that masters gave to slaves. Masters thought that they protected the lives of slaves while they risked their own. If the only bullet exchange between Randolph and Clay had involved Randolph's shot in the air, it is likely that Clay would have demanded a real duel and a real exchange of shots. The reason Clay accepted the shot in the air was that he already had received a shot near his hips. By the time of the "magnanimous" shot, Randolph and Clay had become embedded in a system of gift exchange. That is why they could end the duel with a set of joking comments about credit and debt. Randolph could announce "You owe me a coat, Mr. Clay," and Clay could respond "I am glad the debt is no greater," without either man feeling degraded by the relation.

The importance of reciprocal gift exchange for Southern men of honor also clarifies several aspects of their political lives. Many Southern statesmen envisioned election to office and service in the government as part of the culture's larger system of gift exchange.[49] The South Carolina governor and senator James Henry Hammond repeatedly gave expression to the deep connections among honor, gifts, and politics. He stated them most bluntly in the privacy of his diary during his notorious confrontation with his fellow political leader Wade Hampton II. Hammond and

Hampton never liked each other, despite their marriage to sisters. In 1843, their differences escalated into an open break that led to a bitter, lifelong mutual hatred. Hampton learned that his four teenage daughters had been involved in a secret sexual relationship with Hammond. This violation might easily have led to a duel or some other kind of violent assault. But—perhaps because Hammond was governor, or because both parties had a desire to prevent an open public discussion of the violation, or because the two men wanted to avoid inflicting further misery on their wives—their dispute never erupted into violence. Instead, Hampton sought vengeance against Hammond by spreading rumors about his honor and by trying to prevent him from winning election to public office.

Hampton's tactic succeeded for a considerable period of time. For many years, Hammond lived in partial disgrace at his Silver Bluff plantation. But in exile, Hammond harbored a dream of redemption. Some day he would emerge once again with his reputation and his honor restored, and a gift exchange would be the mechanism of his redemption. Some day, he hoped, the people of South Carolina would present him with the gift of election. "Ever since my rupture with Hampton," he confided to his diary, "and the consequent damage to my reputation, I have entertained the hope that the State would some day raise me from the dust and cleanse me from every stain. To do this effectually it must have been the *Act of the State*, performed without any prompting from me. I have endeavoured on every proper occasion to prove myself worthy of thus being redeemed. But I have felt that any self-seeking, much less truckling on my part would destroy the healing virtue of this act and I have there[fore] scrupulously avoided it."[50] Rarely had a Southern political leader so clearly articulated the relationships among honor, gifts, and political office. Hammond understood that his honor could be restored only if his election came as a gift of the people. Involvement in "self-seeking" or "truckling" activities would have transformed his election from a gift into a market transaction.

In 1857, Hammond's dream became reality. The South Carolina legislature elected him to the United States Senate. Not surprisingly, he was particularly pleased that he had expressly withdrawn his name as a candidate and yet had still been elected. As he described it in his diary: "This is a signal triumph over all my enemies and, speaking as a mere mortal, a full compensation and more for all I have endured. It wipes off every calumny and puts my name among the foremost of So[uth] Ca[rolina] without a stain. Indeed, since John Rutledge was appointed Dictator in the Revolution no man of SoCa has ever been *forced* against his *expressed refusal* into so high an office."[51] Election to office was sweet because it assumed the form of a gift.

Hammond's attitude toward political office was common among men of honor in the antebellum South. Many shared his view that to seek election openly would mean transforming the transaction from a gift into a market relation. Although many of these men craved office as a sign that they had been honored by the people, they felt compelled to hide their desires. Throughout the antebellum period political leaders from all over the South wrote diary entries and letters to friends telling the same story over and over: they saw themselves elected to office "innocent of solicitation," they "did not seek the position of a candidate," they "did not seek favour or office," they never "asked or sought the support of any," nor did they exhibit "a personal solicitude about the office."[52] Similarly, it was a common feature of Southern political life that men of honor loved to retire from office and then be recalled from retirement by constituents who surprised them with election. Such men looked down on political leaders who seemed to calculate and to manipulate. James Henry Hammond nicely summarized the attitude of men of honor toward political men who marketed themselves when he complained that Pierce Mason Butler was "a shrewd man, overshrewd. He thinks 'too precisely on the event.'"[53] Such a spirit of calculation was quite different from the spirit of the gift.

Why did Southern men of honor not feel degraded by receiving election as a gift? At one level, it is difficult to distinguish the gift of money to Frankie Mae on a Mississippi plantation from the gift of office to James Henry Hammond on a South Carolina plantation. Frankie Mae told White Junior that she did not want his gift of Christmas money; he forced her to take it. James Henry Hammond announced that he did not want the gift of election, and yet he took it after he was "*forced* against his *expressed refusal.*" Yet Hammond felt honored by his gift and Frankie Mae felt degraded by hers. The central difference involves the reciprocal exchange present in Hammond's transaction and its absence in Frankie Mae's transaction. Hammond and other Southern men of honor thought of public service as a way to give gifts to the community. They thought of themselves as sacrificing wealth and time and subjecting themselves to great inconvenience for the public good. Hence, they thought of their election and their service in office as a gift exchange. They received the gift of office; they gave the gift of service. Frankie Mae, on the other hand, only received the gift of money and a bit of tobacco juice.

It is not easy to measure the degree to which gift exchange dominated the practice of politics in the antebellum South. The problem is rooted in the difficulty of distinguishing market from gift transactions. Consider, for example, the practice of "treating" constituents to drinks or to a sumptuous banquet just before an election; or the lavish hospitality that Thomas Jefferson bestowed on guests who went to Monticello; or the extravagant house that James Henry Hammond built in Columbia and the opulent parties he held there.[54] Little in these behaviors clearly determines whether they are market or gift transactions. Did these men trade their drinks and hospitality for votes, power, and prestige? Almost certainly not, but the only way to demonstrate that is to look at the spirit of their exchanges—not just at the absence of overt calculation, but also at the larger meanings of their actions in a slave society that followed a system of honor. In other words, the importance of the gift in Southern politics is related to the importance of the gift on dueling grounds, in taverns, and in the relations of masters and slaves.

Significant parts of the network of credit and debt that surrounded Southern masters were connected to the larger system of gift exchange in slave society. It is important not to exaggerate the linkage; most loans from professional factors or from banks are best understood as market transactions. Sometimes, business relations between masters and factors blossomed into friendships that included gift exchanges at holidays, but such transactions did not dominate the relationships.[55] Factors wanted to profit from marketing planters' crops, and planters wanted to have their crops marketed at the highest possible prices. If factors and planters sometimes exchanged gifts, it was only as an adjunct to their primary market relationships.

But the elaborate network of loans among planters, and the common practice of cosigning notes or standing surety for the debts of family and friends, are best understood either as full-fledged gift exchanges or as exchanges that straddled the indefinite border between the market and the gift. Consider the practice of cosigning notes as security for loans. Typically, this type of transaction had its origins in a market relationship in which a planter sought a loan from a bank or a factor. If the lender doubted the planter's ability to repay, the planter was asked to secure the signatures of friends or relatives who agreed to assume responsibility in the event of a default. This request often pushed the planter into the world of gift relations. A man who was asked to cosign a loan could expect no specific gain from the transaction, only the assumption of risk. Hence, men gave their signatures as gifts, endorsing the character of the man who made the request without calculating the possible gains achieved by the transaction. Men who requested signatures did not feel degraded by the transaction because they were usually embedded in a system of gift exchanges of signatures, sometimes giving their signatures and sometimes getting the signatures of others.

Like many other prosperous Southern men of honor, James Henry Hammond frequently cosigned the notes of other gentlemen. Some of these transactions nicely illustrate the ways in which men of honor saw their signatures on notes as gifts that evoked all the relations associated with honor. For example, in 1840 Hammond became involved in the network of indebtedness incurred by his fellow South Carolinian James Hamilton. Hamilton was the type of man whose request for a signature or a loan was virtually impossible to deny. He was a prominent gentleman of honor who had served as a state legislator, as a congressman, and as the governor of South Carolina. By the late 1830s he had become enmeshed in an elaborate speculative scheme involving land and loans in Texas. Hammond, like many other prominent South Carolinians, had been drawn into Hamilton's speculative network through several requests to cosign loans. Hammond agreed, but only because he saw his signature as part of a larger system of gift exchange. As he described it in one 1841 diary entry, "I endorsed his [Hamilton's] paper for $12,500 last Feb. year knowing that he could not or barely could pay his debts. I thought him a noble fellow. He had done me many little kindnesses, and I felt like risking something for him."[56]

At one point during his tangled financial relationship with Hamilton, Hammond seemed to think of their relationship as involving market rather than gift considerations, but other men of honor quickly reminded him of the impropriety of shrewd calculation in such a context. His lapse occurred under the pressure of having to pay for a note on which Hamilton had defaulted. Hammond had joined with three other prominent South Carolina gentlemen in endorsing a loan for Hamilton, each assuming five thousand dollars' worth of responsibility for a twenty thousand-dollar note.[57] Unbeknownst to the cosigners until ten months too late, the note had become due. Hamilton had been unable to pay, and they had all become liable. Faced with the loss of a significant amount of money, Hammond began to think about the transaction as a market exchange. He calculated that he and the other cosigners could avoid payment by arguing that the bank had failed in its obligation to notify them as soon as the note became due. Had they been promptly informed, he and the other cosigners could have avoided monetary loss by attaching Hamilton's property. Hamilton's financial collapse now made that impossible. But Hammond's suggestion to the other cosigners that they should make an argument in order to avoid payment evoked a powerful negative response. These men of honor thought of their signatures as gifts. As Hammond described it in his diary, "they do not think it honorable [to maneuver to avoid payment] . . . and are making quite a flourish of their indifference to the loss etc." Once admonished by his fellow men of honor, Hammond became quite defensive and a bit embarrassed by his own more calculating view of the matter. He felt disturbed "that any man thinks me a whit below the most elevated ideas of honor."[58]

Usually, however, Hammond had a less ambivalent view of the meaning of his signature. He clearly understood that his refusal to endorse the note of a fellow planter had implications that extended beyond the world of the market and into the world of gifts and honor. One rejected planter, he believed, "will be very hurt and very angry and do me all the injury he can."[59] It probably came as no surprise to him that when Wade Hampton accused him of molesting his daughters, one of the first acts that symbolized their break was the return of an endorsed note.[60] Hammond's signature had been part of the network of gift connections that united him with Hampton in the community of honorable gentlemen. The return of the signature was a way of announcing that the community had been dissolved. Although market concerns were never entirely absent from Hammond's decisions to offer his signature or an outright loan to a family member or a friend, these concerns were always intertwined with meanings surrounding gift exchange and honor. At one point in his diary Hammond summarized his financial dealings in the following terms: "I have made many hazardous loans and have been led purely from sympathy to do this and to endorse for friends by whom I have lost $20,000. I have also been swindled a thousand times in trades, have allowed agents to injure me materially rather than mortify them, and made, to gratify another, a ridiculous purchase of Texas Scrip, which cost me some $8,000."[61]

Bennet H. Barrow of Louisiana was involved in a similar network of loans and endorsements with family and friends. Sometimes he even borrowed money in order to give loans to members of his family. He also liberally endorsed the notes of gentlemen who requested that gift. Like Hammond, he lost significant amounts of money by this practice, and like Hammond, he could rarely bring himself to withhold his signature.[62] The liberality displayed by Barrow and Hammond, and the immediate financial losses they sustained, were quite common among wealthy Southern planters. One historian has estimated that as many as 20 percent of these loans were never paid back.[63] Men like Barrow and Hammond knew perfectly well that their loans and endorsements were poor investments, but they could not stop the flow of gifts that defined them as honorable gentlemen in the community of masters.

IV

Southern men of honor did not give gifts to everyone. They were most generous to kin. They also gave to neighbors and friends, as well as to slaves and other dependents. Sometimes, especially for men of wealth and power, the realm of the gift extended over a broader domain, encompassing friends of friends, members of the same or a higher social class, political allies, residents of the state, and even travelers in the neighborhood.[64] But Southern generosity always had limits. The world of the gift had an inside and an outside. Men of honor gave no gifts to strangers.[65] A stranger was someone to ignore, to laugh at—or to engage in trade.

Frederick Law Olmsted felt what it was like to be a stranger while traveling in the Southern backcountry during the 1850s. In Mississippi, one local informant told him that he would not be able to find a lodging ahead on the road because all the planters had told their overseers, "Take a stranger in, and I'll clear you out!"[66] The rich planters of the area were hospitable only "among their own sort." They gave great parties, "but they were all swell-heads ... they'd never ask anybody but a regular swell-head to see them."[67] Olmsted's experience confirmed the warnings. He recounted a tale of travel in Virginia in which he made a harrowing search for a lodging while ill. "We don't take in strangers," he was told by one planter; "[We are] not accustomed to take in strangers," said a second; "We don't take in travelers," explained a third; "Yer ken go on to de store," yet another informed him. Finally, at the store, he was given a bed, but he had to pay for it with cash.[68] Olmsted reported that only twice during a journey of four thousand miles through the South was he given a night's lodging or a meal without having to pay for it.[69]

Olmsted concluded from these experiences that Southern hospitality was a myth. He was genuinely puzzled by the claim that slave society bred generosity in masters. All he experienced in his continual search for lodgings were closed doors or requests for money. But Olmsted misunderstood the institution of Southern hospitality. It was not a myth; it simply had a border, and he was usually on the wrong side of it. Like all Southern gifts, hospitality did not extend to the world at large. It excluded strangers. Southern men of honor were hospitable to some people and not to others. The "regular swell-heads" of Mississippi did give parties—but they had a limited guest list.

It is difficult to know exactly why Olmsted so frequently found himself outside the border of hospitality. In part, it must have been because he was a Northerner traveling at a moment of heightened sectional tension. The dispute over slavery and the fear of slave insurrections incited by "outside agitators" diminished the realm of Southern hospitality. Or perhaps it was a class issue—a situation in which his clothing and manner did not readily identify him as a man of sufficient respectability to warrant special attention. It could also be that he sometimes traveled on routes that were so heavily used that a more open hospitality would have posed too great a financial strain on the planters. The reasons cannot be known with any certainty. The definition of a stranger was not rigid and fixed. It varied with time, place, and circumstance.[70]

But men of honor always established a border that limited the realm of the gift. It was important, for example, for men who dueled. Since the whole point of the duel was to heal a breach within the community of gentlemen through an extreme form of gift (or bullet) exchange, it made no sense to duel with a stranger. John Lyde Wilson's dueling code—a description of common Southern dueling practices as well as a guide to proper dueling, published in 1838—included some revealing remarks on the problem of strangers. He warned seconds, "If a stranger wish you to bear a note for him, be well satisfied before you do so, that he is on an equality with you; and in presenting the note, state to the party the relationship you stand towards him, and what you know and believe about him." Similarly, Wilson suggests that a man challenged by a stranger has "a right to a reasonable time to ascertain his standing in society, unless he be fully vouched for, by his friend."[71] These pieces of advice were really the same: a gentleman should avoid involvement in a duel with a stranger. Wilson directed both seconds and principals to find out about the character and background of a stranger before beginning the gift exchange of the duel. In other words, they were advised to exclude the stranger until he was no longer a stranger.

In a parallel way, the law and practice of "poor relief" in the antebellum South also excluded strangers. Public opinion and the law held masters responsible for the care of old and sick slaves. Family members had to contribute to the support of their less fortunate relations. Beyond the family and the plantation, the poor only had a claim to assistance from their "place of settlement"—generally the place where residence had been established for at least one year. A justice of the peace could order a transient indigent back to his or her place of settlement. By and large, the honorable men of the antebellum South did not assume responsibility for the poverty of strangers.[72] Such a practice was not confined to Southern states, but only in those states was it embedded in the powerful network of ideas and practices surrounding gift exchange and slavery.

The line that separated the world of gift exchangers from the world of strangers was important to the South Carolina planter Thomas Chaplin. Chaplin was always in financial trouble, and he depended heavily on loans, cosignatures, and other gifts from his kin and neighbors. Although he generally received more gifts than he gave, he struggled to give enough to avoid complete humiliation and degradation. That is why he was so happy to bring sumptuous dinners to the local agricultural society—delighted to supply five times what his neighbors could eat. But his insatiable need for gifts occasionally pushed against the limits of what people could or would give him. At one point, he wrote in his diary that he had to return three slaves he had hired because "no one will stand my security, & I am too proud to ask any & everybody." After the Civil War—after he and his kin and neighbors lost much of their accumulated wealth—Chaplin reread the description of his inability to find a man to "stand . . . security." He appended a revealing lamentation: "Where are they now, that were so particular & saving then—no better off today than I & some dead & gone, & their leavings belong to *strangers*. They saved, saved, for strangers."[73] Here, for Chaplin, was one of the great humiliations of the Civil War—the wealth of the community of gift exchangers had been shifted into the pockets of strangers.

Not surprisingly, strangers in the South could easily become objects of humor or of practical jokes. When Porte Crayon entered as a stranger into a Virginia saloon, the local ruffian immediately singled him out for a humorous assault. The South Carolinian William John Grayson recounted several similar stories about the way hunting clubs sometimes treated strangers. One tale involved a Scotsman, Mr. Robert Brown, who was newly arrived in Charleston. Grayson noted that "the young stranger was invited to club as all strangers were." As part of his initiation into the community he was asked to get drunk along with the members. Brown imbibed only what he considered appropriate and then refused to drink any more. The club members repeatedly insisted that he drink, but he remained stubborn. They then proposed a race, with Brown given a five-yard head start and the entire club in pursuit. If the club caught him he had to drink with them; otherwise he was free to go. Brown won the race, but as he ran back to his home he must have questioned any reports he had ever heard about Southern hospitality.[74]

Grayson told another story of a "foreigner" invited to a club meeting. The members knew of his fear of slave insurrections, so they gave a fake alarm: "Everyone pretended to be frightened, the stranger took to the woods; guns were fired and yells and other noises kept up during the night. The next morning, the victim was found in a tree half-dead with fear and shivering with cold"—destined for enshrinement in this book as another illustration of the fate of the stranger in the world of gift exchangers.[75]

Identification of the barrier that excluded the stranger can help us understand how some Southern men could think of themselves as honorable and generous even as they engaged in the calculations associated with market transactions. Trade with a stranger was the moral equivalent of making fun of a stranger who entered a saloon or a hunting club. A generous man of honor did not think he had lost his generosity because of the way he treated strangers. The men who made Frederick Law Olmsted pay for the bed in which he slept lost no honor if they allowed their neighbors and their kin to sleep in the same bed free of charge during other nights of the year.

The border that defined the stranger also played an important role in the sectional controversy. Southern men of honor often reverted to the image of the stranger as a way of indicating their alienation from the North. The Negro Seamen's Acts, designed to exclude blacks who were "strangers" from Southern seaports, drew a clear border around the realm of Southern hospitality. When Massachusetts sent Samuel Hoar to South Carolina in order to test the constitutionality of these laws in the courts, he received the greeting that a stranger would. The South Carolina state legislature charged that Hoar had come to the state "as the emissary of a foreign government, *hostile to their domestic institutions*, and with the *sole* purpose of subverting their internal peace." They authorized his expulsion.[76] Carolinians defined Hoar as a foreigner who had invaded their "domestic" and "internal" world. Abolitionists, suspected abolitionists, vagrants, and other strangers received similar welcomes in many parts of the South throughout the antebellum period. The insurrection panics that periodically swept the South frequently focused on the danger to slavery posed by strangers from the North. Many Southerners came to view secession as one of the best ways to keep out the strangers—the outside agitators—who posed such a grave threat to slave society.[77]

The border that excluded the stranger was permeable. Men could move through it, sometimes quite easily. The sectional crisis made movement across the barrier more difficult for some people, but such movement was possible. Sometimes, a willingness to fight was helpful. As one Southern man said of his relations with a friend, "When we had nothing else to do we quarrelled; it is a sure sign of a good friend when he loves you enough to quarrel with you. Strangers don't care a picayune, and won't quarrel about you any way."[78] Porte Crayon began his move out of the realm of the stranger by drawing his knife in a Virginia tavern. Verbal and written references from other men of honor also helped. According to John Lyde Wilson's code, a stranger could enter the gift exchange of a duel once he produced proof of his status as a gentleman, and the word of another gentleman was an important part of that proof. Similarly, Frederick Law Olmsted discovered that he was hospitably treated "by gentlemen to whom he was formally presented by letter."[79] Thomas Chaplin reported that a man appeared one day at his plantation "with a paper signed by a captain of a vessel, stating that he was deserving of charity, having been robbed by pirates in coming to this [country] from Switzerland with his family of everything he had in the world."[80] Chaplin helped this stranger because a gentleman—"a captain of a vessel"— corroborated the man's sad story. Some men crossed the border by drinking. Robert Brown, the man chased by an entire South Carolina hunting club, could have left the realm of the stranger had he agreed to get drunk with his pursuers. One British traveler on a steamboat in the South discovered that a few drinks created a warm atmosphere; "as soon as it was known that I was on a hunting expedition, a dozen invitations had been extended to me by the planters, pressed with the usual warmth common to Southern hospitality, before I had been three hours on board the boat."[81] On the other hand, evidence of ungentlemanly conduct could just as easily transform a member of the gift community into a stranger—a man not to be dueled with, or to be given charitable donations, or to be offered hospitality.

While the line that divided gift exchangers from strangers was permeable, it was a border nonetheless—a vitally important demarcation in the culture. It limited the vision of a man of honor, keeping his focus local rather than universal. Or, to state the matter in a slightly different way, the barrier that defined the stranger also deadened humanitarianism. It was not that Southern men of honor felt no sympathy for the suffering of strangers; they simply felt no responsibility. As the historian Thomas L. Haskell has argued, the type of men likely to develop a sense of responsibility for the suffering of strangers lived primarily in a market world, in a world of contract, in a world where men could visualize and see realized the remote consequences of their calculations and actions.[82] But the obligations of a man of honor in a gift-exchange culture ended at the border that separated him from strangers.

The proslavery argument offers one of the most striking examples of the limited responsibility men of honor felt for strangers. As part of their defense of slavery, many Southern writers wrote about the horrible working and living conditions experienced by the free workers of England and the Northern states. George Fitzhugh described how "the free laborer rarely has a house and home of his own; he is insecure of employment, sickness may overtake him at any time and deprive him of the means of support; old age is certain to overtake him, if he lives, and generally without the means of subsistence; his family is probably increasing in numbers, and is helpless and burdensome to him."[83] In his epic poetic defense of slavery, William J. Grayson envisioned the free laborers of England in the following terms:

> In squalid hut—a kennel for the poor,
> Or noisome cellar, stretched upon the floor,
> His clothing rags, of filthy straw his bed,
> With offal from the gutter daily fed.[84]

Edmund Ruffin believed that the free laborers of England "have not the family comforts, or the care for the preservation of their health and lives, enjoyed by every negro slave in Virginia and Mississippi."[85] George Frederick Holmes argued that "there is scarcely one revolution of a wheel in a Northern or European cotton-mill, which does not, in its immediate or remote effects, entail more misery on the poor and the suffering than all the incidents of servile misery gathered in [*Uncle Tom's Cabin*]."[86] James Henry Hammond, in one of his letters to the English abolitionist

Thomas Clarkson, repeatedly condemned the condition of the free working classes, and concluded that "in Great Britain the poor and laboring classes of your own race . . . are more miserable and degraded, morally and physically, than our slaves."[87]

But despite all their descriptions of the misery experienced by the free workers of Great Britain and the North, no proslavery theorist ever suggested that Southern masters should do anything about it. James Henry Hammond might describe the horrible life of a ten-year-old child working in an English coal mine, but he never felt the need to work for the liberation of that child. Like all proslavery writers in the culture of the gift, Hammond had a local vision of responsibility. Southern masters, it was felt, should be responsible for the care of their slaves, other dependents, kin, and "neighbors." Northern and British capitalists should be responsible for the care of their workers.[88] In the world of honor and gift exchange, misery was a local problem.[89]

The same point can be stated a bit differently. Southern gift exchanges shattered time and cut apart space. Recall the distinction between a gift and a market transaction. Gifts are given in a spirit of generosity, without explicit calculation. The way to transform a gift into a market exchange is to link it to other events in time and space. If I begin to think of the birthday present I give as related to birthday presents I have received or will receive, or as part of a network of birthday presents, I will have moved from the world of the gift into the world of the market. A gift is a gift precisely because of its isolation in time and space. Hence, those immersed in the culture of gift exchange become skilled in addressing local rather than universal concerns. Their good deeds assume the form of charity to people closely linked to them in space and time, rather than the form of humanitarian aid for remote strangers.

FOUR

DEATH

JOHN BROWN arrived in Harper's Ferry, Virginia, with hundreds of rifles and revolvers—as well as with pikes to be used by slaves to impale their masters. Not only did many abolitionists support him, but he seemed to command wide sympathy throughout the North. Brown's captured papers included maps indicating that his scheme of insurrection was vast in scope.

Many white Southerners reacted to news of the invasion with a potent mixture of hatred and panic. Susan Hillers Darden of Mississippi wrote in her diary that the Brown conspirators "ought to be hung; burning would be nothing but right."[1] Jeb Stuart informed one of Brown's wounded followers, "You son of a bitch. You had better keep silent. Your treatment is to be that of midnight thieves and murderers, not of men taken in honourable warfare."[2] All over the South "unsound" strangers found themselves under arrest as suspected "emissaries" of Brown's "army."[3] Many hitherto moderate Southerners became converted to the cause of secession as the only remaining protection against future enemy invasions.

And yet some Southern men of honor—men who passionately despised abolitionists—had a few words of praise mixed in with their denunciations of John Brown. Because the language of hatred and fear so dominated the Southern reaction to the Harper's Ferry raid, the words of praise have never become the object of serious historical analysis. But in some ways those words constitute the most interesting aspect of the response to John Brown. Why should Southern masters have said anything good about a man whom they despised?

The part of John Brown's character that some men of honor could not help admiring was his apparent bravery—his willingness to confront death without fear. It is the central argument of this chapter that the attitudes about death and honor revealed in these positive reactions toward Brown appeared in many other contexts throughout antebellum

Southern culture. Together, they constituted a system of variations on the belief that lay at the heart of the worldview of masters: free and honorable gentlemen, unlike the slaves they governed, were not afraid to die. For honorable men of the Old South, mastery over the fear of death seemed a precondition for life as free men. Hence, when seen through their eyes, John Brown may have failed to liberate any slaves, but he succeeded in confirming his own liberation. There was a deep irony to this liberation, for it required Brown's death and it signified his absorption into the worldview of the men he sought to destroy. No Southern gentlemen ever explicitly suggested that John Brown would make a good master—but they came close.

It matters little where one begins a search through the mind of the master class. An extraordinary number of roads lead back to the subject of death and its connection to honor and mastery. Death obsessed men of honor because it established the great divide in their social order. Death, honor, and mastery were the central subjects under discussion not only when Southern men of honor watched John Brown hang, but also when they lay on their deathbeds, when they confronted rebellious slaves, and when they defended slavery in the abstract.[4]

I

Edmund Ruffin should have hated John Brown. The Virginia agricultural reformer and proslavery theorist had been an active Southern nationalist for more than a decade before Brown's 1859 invasion.[5] For many years Ruffin had preached to less radical Southerners about the dangers of Northern abolitionism, but he had not been able to convince them of the urgent need for protection by secession. The Harper's Ferry invasion suddenly transformed Ruffin into a prophet. He had warned of just the kind of horror brought to Virginia by John Brown.

Edmund Ruffin's 1859 diary entries contain numerous contemptuous references to John Brown. He variously referred to Brown as a man who had been a leader of "brigands, murderers & robbers," as a "fanatic," and as a "villain of unmitigated turpitude."[6] Ruffin also understood the potent symbolism of the pikes Brown had intended for slaves to use against their masters. He distributed a sample pike to every governor of the fifteen slave states, with instructions for prominent display in their statehouses as "impressive evidence of the fanatical hatred borne by the dominant northern party to the institutions & the people of the Southern States, and of the unscrupulous & atrocious means resorted to for the attainment of the objects sought by that party."[7] No historian could suggest that Edmund Ruffin was a friend of John Brown.

And yet what stands out in Ruffin's diary entries on Brown are the words of praise embedded within the general condemnation. After first hearing the full story of the raid and the man behind it, Ruffin remarked that he was "a very brave & able man" and that "it is impossible . . . not to respect his thorough devotion to his bad cause, & the undaunted courage through which he has sustained it, through all losses and hazards."[8]

Ruffin was even more impressed with the way Brown faced execution. He believed that a man revealed his true character in the face of death. A man who loved his life so much that he dared not risk it, a man who trembled when confronted with a bullet, a knife, or a hangman's noose—such a man could be dismissed with contempt; such a man could never become a formidable adversary. Hence, Ruffin went to extraordinary lengths to be present at the execution. He wanted to see Brown ascend the scaffold, to watch the rope as it tightened around his neck, and to behold the last twitchings of his dying body. Ruffin wanted to "read" Brown at the moment of his death.

It was not easy for Ruffin to gain access to the scene of the execution. The authorities feared a possible last-minute abolitionist rescue attempt, and civilian spectators had been excluded. Brown was to be put to death in an open field surrounded and heavily guarded by a large military contingent. Rather than miss the event, the sixty-five-year-old Ruffin drew on his influence with the commanding officer at the execution and arranged to become a military cadet for the day.[9]

Ruffin was exhilarated by the opportunity. The day began for him at two o'clock in the morning, when he joined the "grand rounds" inspection of security arrangements. At four he rested a bit on a sofa, but arose again at dawn in order to march in parade with the other cadets.[10] By nine o'clock he had arrived on the execution field; he waited in formation for an additional two hours. Ruffin was delighted to discover that his military company was positioned closest to the gallows. He had a clear view from a distance of fifty yards. Shortly after eleven, John Brown arrived in an open wagon, seated on his coffin, his arms tied behind his back at the elbows. From this point on, like a reader confronted by an important text, Ruffin watched Brown's every gesture with careful attention.[11]

As the wagon passed the gallows, Ruffin thought that Brown seemed fearless as he "looked . . . intently" at his place of death. Brown needed some assistance leaving the wagon because his arms had been tied, but Ruffin noted that he marched up to the scaffold "with readiness & seeming alacrity." Ruffin could not hear what Brown said while standing on the gallows, but later learned that "he said very little, & nothing that was not required, & in relation to the work in hand." Overall, Ruffin concluded that Brown's "movements & manner gave no evidence of his being either terrified or concerned, & he went through what was required of him apparently with as little agitation as if he had been the willing assistant, instead of the victim."[12]

Ruffin watched closely as the executioners adjusted the halter around Brown's neck, tied his ankles together, and placed a hood of white linen over his head. Then there was a delay as Brown's military escort continued to file into place. The respite lasted a full five minutes, during which Ruffin speculated that Brown must have felt that any moment could have been his last. Ruffin was impressed by what he saw of a man under extraordinary stress, standing at the edge of his life. "Brown stood erect," he later wrote, "& as motionless as if he had been a statue. Not the smallest movement, or shifting of position was visible . . . & no shrinking or failing of the body to the mind."[13]

Ruffin thought that Brown, even in the act of dying, maintained his dignity. When the sheriff gave the signal and the platform dropped, Ruffin looked carefully for signs of panic in the form of movement; he could find nothing but small, apparently involuntary muscle spasms. He detected no movement at all for about a minute, and then he saw a slight jerk of the hands. Brown's body swayed gently in the breeze for five minutes before Ruffin again noticed motion in the form of small, convulsive leg spasms. After a half hour, physicians examined the body. After forty-five minutes, they cut Brown down and placed him in his coffin.[14]

Ruffin never thought of Brown as a true man of honor. He hated and felt contempt for him both before and after Brown's death. He strongly objected to the sight of several military companies that accompanied Brown's body away from the field: "It seemed like offering evidences of respect & honorable attention to the atrocious criminal."[15] Ruffin also noted his lack of deep respect for the mere "physical or animal courage" displayed by Brown. Yet any reader of Ruffin's diary description of the Brown execution can easily detect the powerful admiration buried within the contempt—admiration for the abolitionist's "complete fearlessness of & insensibility to danger & death."[16]

The governor of Virginia, Henry A. Wise, expressed even greater appreciation for John Brown. Like Edmund Ruffin, Wise was no friend to abolitionism. He was a slaveholder and an advocate of the values of Southern honor expressed in the duel.[17] Although Wise was not an early supporter of secession, he was a staunch supporter of slavery who firmly believed that the South could preserve its peculiar institution while remaining within the Union. Yet when he returned to Richmond after interrogating Brown at Harper's Ferry, he delivered a speech that both condemned Brown and was full of praise for him. "He is a bundle of the best nerves I ever saw cut and thrust and bleeding and in bonds," he told a group of Virginia militiamen. "He is a man of clear head, of courage, fortitude, and simple ingenuousness. He is cool, collected, and indomitable; and it is but just to him to say that he was humane to his prisoners, ... and he inspired me with great trust in his integrity as a man of truth. He is a fanatic, vain and garrulous; but firm, truthful, and intelligent. His men, too, who survive, except the free negroes with him, are like him. [18]

In the same speech, Wise paraphrased words of praise for Brown from Colonel Lewis Washington, a Virginian who had been a hostage and was present at the moment of Brown's capture. Washington believed that Brown "was the coolest and firmest man he ever saw in defying danger and death. With one son dead by his side, and another shot through, he felt the pulse of his dying son with one hand and held his rifle with the other and commanded his men with the utmost composure, encouraging them to be firm and to sell their lives as dearly as they could."[19] Even a man whose life had been placed in danger by Brown could not help admiring him.

Some white Southerners felt that Governor Wise had gone a bit too far in praise of Brown. Edmund Ruffin feared that the governor's speech might be used as propaganda by Northern abolitionists.[20] But throughout his life Wise remained unwavering in his admiration for Brown. During Reconstruction, Wise applied to General Alfred H. Terry, who was in command of the occupation, for repossession of a building on his land that had become a school for African Americans taught by a woman who was reportedly John Brown's daughter. When a friend commented on the irony, the mention of Brown's name only triggered a powerful statement of praise from Wise. "John Brown!" he cried out. "John Brown was a great man, sir. John Brown was a great man."[21]

Edmund Ruffin, Colonel Lewis Washington, and Governor Henry A. Wise were only briefly "acquainted" with John Brown. Ruffin's primary relationship with Brown had been conducted at a distance of fifty yards. Washington had spent a day with Brown, and Wise had been with him for only a few hours. Yet these Southern gentlemen admired the abolitionist. John Brown had displayed the virtue most important for men who accepted the values of the culture of honor. John Brown had faced death without fear. At a deep level, they may have sensed that their hated enemy was also their comrade. A free white man had led an attack on slavery that reconfirmed the central values of honorable masters.

II

Many Southern men of honor aspired to die the death of John Brown. They did not seek to become abolitionist martyrs, nor did they crave the indignity of hanging, but they admired a style of death that demonstrated mastery and control rather than fear and submission. The most honorable death for a Southern gentleman came on the battlefield.[22] This was certainly not uniquely true of the South, but such a death had special meaning in a slave society. Death in battle seemed to involve a masterful gesture of resistance to submission. Soldiers confronted death erect, unafraid, standing up to the enemy opposition. When Colonel Francis Stebbins Bartow of Georgia chose to face death in battle and volunteered for service in the Civil War, he wrote to Governor Joseph E. Brown "I go to illustrate Georgia"—suggesting that he carried his honor and the honor of his state into the war with him. And when he was mortally shot on the battlefield at Manassas he proudly proclaimed a defiant resistance: "They have killed me boys, but I never gave up." His dead body was treated with great respect. Colonel Bartow lay in state in the Savannah City Hall, surrounded day and night by an honor guard, while solemn visitors came to pay their respects. His family and friends placed him in a lead-lined coffin (to limit offensive odors), draped it with a Confederate flag, and surrounded it with "chaplets of laurel appropriately intertwined, the offerings of the ladies of Charleston and of Savannah." His funeral cortege included all available local officers of the army, navy, and militia. The mayor, the city council, and nearly all the citizens attended. They tolled church bells, brought flags to half-staff, and fired artillery in his honor. One witness to the events concluded that "Colonel Bartow's name will live in the history of these Confederate States, and his noble daring on the field of Manassas be remembered by all, and especially by those whose state he illustrated in such a signal way by his undaunted courage and chivalrous valor."[23] Southerners reenacted similar scenes for many other honorable men killed in battle.

But only a tiny fraction of Southern men of honor died of wounds sustained in battle. The vast majority died of sickness in their beds. For the most part, nineteenth-century Southern men of honor followed the conventions of dying common to other American men of the time. The proper death included several key features. The dying person should be surrounded by close friends and relatives. He had to be fully aware of his impending demise and face it "calmly," with "clear eyes" and "Christian fortitude." However, Southern men of honor subtly departed from one convention of their age. They had a bit of trouble with the idea that a proper Christian death should be a "submissive" death.[24] They did not openly disagree with the idea that death involved a submission to God's will, but their behavior on their deathbeds indicates that they could not fully accept death as an act of obedience. They thought of their dying as a part of their living. A man of honor could not die with the kind of Christian submission that smacked of passivity and servility. It was one thing to die calmly and without a struggle; that was the way John Brown had faced death on the scaffold. It was the way Colonel Francis Stebbins Bartow died at Manassas. But, in the minds of Southern gentlemen, Brown and Bartow had been resigned and accepting in the face of death, not submissive. Colonel Bartow announced that though they had killed him, he had not given up. Edmund Ruffin admired the way John Brown had "marched up to the scaffold" and "stood erect." That was precisely the way old and sick Southern men of honor hoped to die, even as they overtly professed obedience to the will of God—always in control, never in a subservient position, marching and erect.

Edmund Ruffin's death serves as a good illustration of the kind of dying many believed appropriate for an old and sick Southern man of honor. Not many followed Ruffin's specific example, but they shared the values reflected in his reasoning about death. At one level, Ruffin's death was quite unconventional. Just as the Civil War ended, he put a musket in his mouth and blew off the top his head, "scattering his brains and snowy hair against the ceiling of [his] room."[25] Yet in another sense, it was a typical honorable death for an old man; it demonstrated mastery and control rather than dependence and submission.

Several factors influenced Ruffin's choice of suicide, but they all involved a desire to avoid being placed in a submissive or dependent posture.[26] He envisioned suicide as a free choice of death over loss of liberty. On a political level, Ruffin preferred death by his own hand because he did not want to live under "Yankee rule" and "enslavement" after the South's defeat in the Civil War. He devoted the last paragraphs of his diary (penned as the final segment of an extended defense of his suicide) to a denunciation of the "Yankee race." A separate memorandum about his burial ended on a high-pitched note of defiance: "And now, with my latest writing & utterance, & with what will be near to my latest breath, I here repeat, & would willingly proclaim, my unmitigated hatred to Yankee rule—to all political, social & business connection with Yankees, & to the perfidious, malignant, & vile Yankee race."[27] He had even found biblical precedent for the choice of suicide rather than continued life after military defeat: Jews had killed themselves rather than submit to rule by their conquerors.[28]

Ruffin's defense of his suicide included a parallel personal dimension. He could not face life as a dependent old man. The war had cost him his accumulated wealth, and he would have had to live his last years on charity from his son. As he noted with dismay in the final pages of his diary, "I am now merely a cumberer of the earth, & a useless consumer of its fruits, earned by the exertions of others." Moreover, his health was seriously declining; he suffered from significant hearing loss, blindness at night, hand tremors, occasional dizziness, and periods of incontinence.[29] He dreaded a prolonged death that would involve dependence.

Ruffin had become familiar with death during the years before he took his own life. In addition to watching John Brown be hanged, he had seen death on the battlefield, in the 1840 suicide of his close friend Thomas Cocke, and in the loss of an astonishing thirteen members of his family after 1844—including his wife and five daughters. By the time Ruffin made his decision in favor of suicide at the end of the Civil War, it was clear that he would not die in battle or be hanged. His choice was between suicide and the possibility of a lingering period of ill health. Ruffin had written vivid descriptions from his personal observation of both types of death. Two of his descriptions stand out as unusually detailed: one of his daughter Jane's slow death, and the other of his friend Thomas Cocke's suicide. Given his values as a man of honor, it is easy to see why he preferred suicide. He would not die like his daughter Jane, whom he described as "remarkable for her uniform gentleness & docility," "with the most perfect obedience to her parents," a woman who died with "calm resignation & submission to the will of God," who "submitted quietly and calmly," even compliantly ingesting the prescribed opium she detested because of her "gentle & dutiful disposition."[30] Instead, he chose the death of his friend Thomas Cocke, a man who had a "stronger mind" and a "nobler heart" than any other human; a man whose weakness in illness was a "mortification to his pride"; one who firmly resolved, "I cannot bear it—& I *will not* bear it"; a man whose suicide stood out among all others "in long deliberation and preparation of the plan, & in the regulated & cool determination with which it was executed"; a man who was "seated upright" when he placed a gun in his mouth, who blew off his head but whose "body did not seem to have been moved in the slightest degree, either by the tremendous concussion, or by any struggle of the body in the act of death."[31]

On June 17, 1865, Edmund Ruffin ended his life.[32] Like Thomas Cocke, he had carefully planned his death, probably for at least two months. He waited until his son was near, but not near enough to stop him. He then wrote the lengthy justification of the act in his diary, and penned the memorandum describing in detail his wishes regarding his burial and funeral. He wanted to be buried simply, in the clothes he was wearing, along with an "over-wrapping" of an "old sheet or blanket." He preferred no coffin of any kind so that his remains would return quickly to the soil, and so that he might "be buried as usually were our brave soldiers who were slain in battle." Ruffin clearly saw his death as analogous to the honorable death of a warrior. He ended with a final curse for the "vile Yankee race" and placed a silver gun in his mouth. As his son described it, "He was in a sitting position in a chair, braced against the arms of the back and no doubt put the mussle of the gun in his mouth. The butt of the gun rested on a trunk before him and he pulled the trigger with a forked stick." Edmund Ruffin, Jr. reported that after the gun exploded, his father's "body remained in its position."[33] In an extraordinary parallel to the deaths of Thomas Cocke and John Brown, Ruffin remained erect and unmoving in the act of dying.

Most Southern men of honor rejected suicide as an appropriate mode of death. Religious constraints turned them away from the path followed by Ruffin. Most died of natural causes in their beds. Yet even in their beds, men of honor sought to echo deaths like those of Edmund Ruffin, Thomas Cocke, John Brown, and soldiers who died in battle. Consider the death of the great South Carolina political leader John C. Calhoun. During the final days of his life, Calhoun kept dragging himself to the Senate, repeatedly refusing to stay quietly in bed. When a friend asked how and when he would like to meet death, he reportedly replied, "I have but little concern about either; I desire to die in the discharge of my duty."[34] Too weak to deliver his own last speech in March 1850, he sat upright, pale and weak in his seat, while Senator James Mason of Virginia read it for him.[35] The next day, Varina Davis saw him enter the Senate chamber supported by two colleagues, weak and burning with fever. Yet, she reported, "his eagle glance swept the Senate in the old lordly way," even though by the end of the session he was virtually carried out of the chamber back to his bed.[36] To the repeated astonishment of his colleagues, Calhoun kept returning to his seat each day for the next week. Later, his senatorial colleague Andrew Pickens Butler employed imagery that echoed Varina Davis when he described Calhoun's presence during these final days as "the exhibition of a wounded eagle." It is little wonder that Governor Whitemarsh B. Seabrook turned to military language when he eulogized Calhoun in his message to the South Carolina legislature. "Our faithful sentinel," he explained, "died at his post."[37]

Like Seabrook, witnesses to Calhoun's final moments also developed images that suggested command and control rather than submission. Senator Andrew Pickens Butler informed his colleagues in his eulogy that at the moment of his death, Calhoun "evinced recognition and intelligence of what was passing," and that "one of the last directions he gave, was to a dutiful son, who had been attending him, to put away some manuscripts, which had been written a short time before, under his dictation."[38] The "directions" Calhoun gave and his "dictation" to a "dutiful son" were virtually the only details of the death offered by Butler in this public speech. Here was a master, in full command at his death. Congressman Abraham Venable conjured up a similar image when he told his colleagues that during Calhoun's last days, "I witnessed with astonishment the influence of his mighty mind over his weak physical structure." Venable saw Calhoun, during the final moments on his deathbed, as "calm, collected, and conscious of his situation, but without any symptom of alarm, his face beaming with intelligence, without one indication of suffering or pain." Calhoun did not sink slowly away. He was cut down, almost like a soldier in battle. "The lustre of that bright eye remained unchanged," Venable later recalled, "until the silver cord was broken."[39]

John Randolph of Virginia also died in a style that emphasized his mastery and control. Joseph Parrish of Philadelphia, a Quaker physician—a man who did not share the values of the culture of honor—wrote the central eyewitness account of Randolph's death. Yet even through the filter of Parrish's narrative it is possible to detect the standard outlines of an honorable gentleman's style of death. Randolph spent a fair portion of his last moments correcting the doctor's pronunciation. The night before his death he had Dr. Parrish read aloud from a newspaper, and then took him to task for mispronouncing certain words. When Parrish began to defend his choice of pronunciation, Randolph "sharply replied 'There can be no doubt of it'"—and was satisfied only after the doctor had conceded the point. Later, when Randolph experienced a sense of "remorse" about past misdeeds, he coupled it with a command to Dr. Parrish to write the word down so he could see it.

On the very day of his death, Dr. Parrish tried to comfort Randolph's apparently distraught slave, John, by suggesting a possible recovery. Randolph emphatically contradicted the doctor. Finally, during the hours just before his death, Randolph issued a series of commands that would assure his slaves' manumission and provide for their financial support after he had died. Virginia law permitted Randolph to manumit slaves in a will, but in order to provide for their financial support he had to make the declaration on his deathbed in the hearing of a white witness who had to remain with him, uninterrupted, until his death. With no explanation at all, Randolph made the declaration to the bewildered Dr. Parrish, and then directed his slave John to lock the door. Only after considerable explanation and persuasion did he agree to allow Dr. Parrish to attend another sick patient and to permit the substitution of other white witnesses. John Randolph died the way he had lived—issuing commands until the moment when he became incoherent.[40]

Edward Spann Hammond's description of the 1864 death of his father, James Henry Hammond, evokes the same sense of a powerful man seeking to remain in command during illness and death. The elder Hammond's life had been devoted to retaining control over everyone and everything in his domain. This desire for control had even extended to his body, especially to a virtual obsession with the regularity of his bowel movements. His modern biographer, Drew Gilpin Faust, has noted that James Henry Hammond's father had early given him advice that guided him throughout his life: "Keep your Bowels open." Since early child-hood, whenever they had failed to open with regularity, he took control. Hammond frequently resorted to enemas and powerful laxatives—medications heavily laced with mercury. Faust speculates that Ham-mond's attempt to control his body may ironically have led to mercury poisoning and debilitation.[41] Edmund Ruffin had blown off his head; James Henry Hammond had destroyed a different part of his anatomy. Although Hammond's intention had not been suicide, it was similar to Ruffin's in that it involved an attempt at control.

Edward Spann Hammond described his father as weak and sometimes confused as he lay on his deathbed, but never submissive. The day before his death, James Henry Hammond carefully examined his tongue in a mirror, declared his condition to be "very bad," and began his final prep-arations to die. He instructed his son that his place of burial should be near a pair of large hickory trees with "a fine view of Augusta and the Sand Hills." He directed that his father's grave be moved and that his own sons be buried near him. Then, with a note of defiance against Yankee rule and any future attempt to desecrate his grave, Hammond addressed his son in a way Edward Spann Hammond later described thus: "with a thrilling earnestness, looking at me and pointing his finger." "But mind," he ad-monished his son, "if we are subjugated, run a plow over my grave." It was extremely important to him that his dead body should not become an object of contempt, for he "repeated again most impressively the last injunction."[42]

On the last day of his life, James Henry Hammond would not keep still. He commanded his son to play the fiddle for him and "the negro chil-dren" to sing to him. He gave detailed advice on how to excavate a bitu-men bed. Appropriately, Hammond's final moment of life involved a struggle to rise, and (according to his son) his face in death had "features calm and placid, lips closed naturally, eyes wide opened, brilliantly but not unnaturally luminous, and a look of profound thought and brightest intelligence, as if something most curious and interesting was just un-raveled."[43]

The pattern seems clear when one contrasts the descriptions of the deaths of these Southern men of honor with those of Southerners outside the tradition.[44] The Reverend Charles Colcock Jones, a Presbyterian min-ister, described the death of his slave Jack in 1850 in a way that identified him as a slave:

> But oh, how happy was his deathbed! Not a murmur; a smile for every-body; and his mind clear and stayed on the Saviour to the last! His exercises were very remarkable. No doubt; no distress. He expressed himself ready to depart. Told his mistress "he was in God's sight but a filthy rag," but "his

hope was in Jesus"; that "his Saviour was shedding unnumbered mercies all around him." He told me "it was a blessed thing to have a good master and mistress"; that "he could not begin to speak of God's mercies to him."[45]

This description has some elements that are consistent with the death of a man of honor—dying without a murmur, with a clear mind, and with a readiness to depart. Other elements, however, make it obvious that Jack was no Edmund Ruffin, John C. Calhoun, John Randolph, or James Henry Hammond. Such men could never have died with a smile for everybody, nor would they have likened themselves to filthy rags.[46] Most importantly, this description of a slave's death lacks the references to resistance and command common in accounts of the deaths of honorable men.

Similarly, Ella Gertrude Clanton Thomas, the mistress of a plantation, lovingly described the death of her mother in the postwar era in a way that clearly identified her as a woman. Thomas prayed that her mother would not succumb to a "sudden death," but that was precisely the death preferred by men of honor. They wanted to be cut down at a high moment, like men in battle or in duels, in their prime. Moreover, Thomas's mother had all the submissive qualities associated with a virtuous woman. She was asked as she lay on her deathbed if she trusted in Jesus; "'Yes I do' was her simple childlike reply," according to her daughter. Thomas reported that her mother "lived a life consecrated to the duties she was called upon to perform, that of a faithful wife and a devoted conscientious mother."[47] She died in the quiet and unassuming style considered appropriate to that life.

III

Slave rebellions provided a peculiar challenge for men of honor. These men, after all, believed that one of the distinguishing features of slaves was their inability to confront death without fear or submission. Men of honor believed that every slave had chosen a life of humiliation over an honorable death. It was precisely this preference for life that marked them as slaves. But what about rebel slaves? A modern observer might judge the "success" of a revolt by such criteria as the number of masters killed, the number of slaves who achieved their "freedom," the panic the revolt created within the master class, or the length of time it lasted. Certainly, antebellum men of honor were interested in all these aspects of slave rebellions. But they were centrally concerned with the way rebel slaves confronted death. A slave who faced death with the bravery that Edmund Ruffin saw in John Brown had to be considered a free man. Such a rebel would be seen as having cast aside one of the central marks of his enslavement. Like John Brown, he would be perceived as a villain who deserved to be hanged. Yet whatever his formal legal status, he would be hanged as a man who had transcended his position as a slave. In the eyes of men of honor a rebel slave might achieve the greatest success by dying erect and without fear.

It is painfully ironic that in the web of meanings woven by the language of honor, virtually all forms of slave resistance—including slave rebellions—served to strengthen rather than to weaken the myths of men of honor. The most common forms of slave resistance did not involve open and overt rebellion. The Louisiana planter Bennet H. Barrow, for example, kept a running record of examples of slave misconduct on his plantation for the years 1840 and 1841. They provide good documentation of the kind of slave resistance encountered by masters on most plantations. Barrow's slaves pretended to be sick, undertook slow or careless work, lied, ran away, engaged in petty thievery, stayed up too late, left their houses without permission, were "impudent," and arrived late to work.[48] All of these forms of resistance disturbed Barrow, and they lowered the productivity of his plantation. But they also reconfirmed Barrow's belief that he deserved to be the master and the people he owned deserved to be the slaves on his plantation. The resistance encountered by Bennet Barrow from his slaves was quite different from the resistance observed by Edmund Ruffin when he watched John Brown. It did not involve a confrontation with death. Hence, Barrow never wrote about the "fearlessness" of his slaves, of their "insensibility to danger and death," of their "bravery," or of how they stood "erect" when they faced him. Barrow's slaves were "inattentive," "neglectful," "careless," "impudent," "lazy," "liars," and "rascals." In other words, they had the personalities of slaves. The typical forms of their resistance confirmed their status when seen through the eyes of a man of honor like Barrow.

But what about rebel slaves who actually did engage in open rebellion? What about men like Nat Turner and those who followed him? Virtually no white Southern gentleman ever remarked favorably on their bravery and willingness to face death.[49] When Nat Turner and his followers had their actions translated into the language of honor, even as they confronted death, they remained slaves.

The basic outlines of the insurrection are well known. The Nat Turner rebellion took place in Southampton County, Virginia, in 1831. Turner was a highly religious slave leader with a deep hatred of the men who held him in bondage. Turner believed that he had experienced a series of heavenly visions that mandated that he should lead slaves in an insurrection against their white masters. During late August 1831, convinced that an atmospheric phenomenon that seemed to create a spot on the sun was a sign from heaven to begin his rebellion, he gathered a handful of other slaves and they began to move from plantation to plantation, killing all white men, women, and children, and picking up more slave recruits as they went along. He may have had seventy followers at the height of the insurrection. At least fifty-seven whites died before the state militia put down the rebellion. Although most of the rebels were immediately captured or killed (with many executed after swift trials), Turner himself managed to elude his pursuers for more than two months, hiding in the woods while avoiding a furious manhunt. In the end he too was captured, tried, and executed.[50]

As soon as news of the insurrection began to spread throughout the South, it became subject to interpretation. Southern men of honor could read about the event in a flood of newspaper accounts, in statements by Governor Floyd of Virginia, and, ultimately, in the widely circulated *Confessions of Nat Turner*. When filtered through the language of honor, much of what contemporaries heard about the insurrection from published sources reconfirmed their belief that the slave rebels remained slaves, and were not men willing to risk their lives in a bid for freedom.

Immediately after the outbreak of the insurrection, newspapers described Turner as a trickster who manipulated and fooled all the slaves around him. This image left the impression that the slaves involved in the rebellion had been deceived by Turner and had not voluntarily chosen to confront death in a quest for liberty. The *Richmond Enquirer* of August 30 described Turner as "artful, impudent and vindictive." Later, it noted that Turner had "used every means in his power, to acquire an ascendency over the minds of the slaves. A dreamer of dreams and a would-be Prophet, he used all the arts familiar to such pretenders, to deceive, delude, and overawe their minds."[51] The *Richmond Compiler* of September 3 printed a letter from a resident of Jerusalem (the town near the heart of the insurrection) that maintained that Turner was "a bold fellow of the deepest cunning, who for years has been endeavouring to acquire an influence over the minds of these deluded wretches."[52] John Hampden Pleasants, editor of the popular *Richmond Constitutional Whig*, described Turner on September 3 as "the first contriver" of the revolt, as a "shrewd fellow," and as a man who "by various artifices had acquired great influence over the minds of the wretched beings whom he has led into destruction. It is supposed that he induced them to believe that there were only 80,000 whites in the country, who, being exterminated, the blacks might take possession."[53] The *Constitutional Whig* of September 26 published a letter from a resident of Jerusalem that noted that through fake acts of divination, Turner had "acquired an immense influence, over such persons as he took into his confidence."[54]

Nat Turner's own *Confessions* included a similar image of the leader as shrewd manipulator. The *Confessions* has always been a difficult document to interpret because it purports to contain Turner's words as dictated in his jail cell to a white lawyer, Thomas R. Gray. It is virtually impossible to know how much of this document accurately represents Turner's voice, and how much contains Gray's distortions. But it sometimes closely echoes language that appeared in earlier newspaper reports, reports written long before Turner had been captured; this might be an indication that the *Confessions* includes, at least in part, Thomas Gray's interpretation of Nat Turner.[55] The *Confessions*, like the earlier newspaper accounts, evokes the image of the rebel leader as manipulator: Turner admits "knowing the influence I had obtained over the minds of my fellow servants." When he describes the initiation of the revolt, he says "I now began to prepare them for my purpose."[56]

Another aspect of the image of Turner as trickster and manipulator involves repeated references to his use of the atmospheric effects on the sun to convince other slaves that God would protect them. Thus, the *Richmond Compiler* of September 3, 1831, noted that Turner was "superstitious himself" and that "his object has been to operate upon the superstitious hopes and fears of others; and the late singular phenomenon of the Sun, enabled him to fill their minds with the most anxious forbodings, regarding it as an omen from Heaven, that their cause would result prosperously."[57] In several accounts of the episode, whites seemed to have made the sun, rather than any human agency, largely responsible for the entire rebellion. The *Constitutional Whig* of September 3 concluded, "We are inclined to think that the solar phenomenon exercised considerable influence in promoting the insurrection; calculated as it was to impress the imaginations of the ignorant." A later article noted that it was no surprise, given the wild imagination of Nat Turner, "that the singular appearance of the sun in August, should have tempted him to execute his purpose. . . . Nat encouraged his company on their route, by telling them, that as the black spot had passed over the sun, so would the blacks pass over the earth."[58] One can see a similar image in proslavery writer Thomas R. Dew's later account of the episode. "Nat," he wrote, "a demented fanatic, was under the impression that heaven had enjoined him to liberate the blacks, and had made its manifestations in loud noises in the air, an eclipse, and by the greenness of the sun. It was these signs which determined *him*, and ignorance and superstition, together with implicit confidence in Nat, determined a few others, and thus the bloody work began."[59]

Turner's *Confessions* described a far more elaborate heavenly dimension behind his decision to lead the rebellion. Turner reported that he had felt chosen by God for a special purpose early in his life, that his ability to read and to write came to him as a miraculous gift, that the Holy Spirit had spoken directly to him on several occasions, and that he had seen special signs such as blood on the corn and hieroglyphic characters on leaves in the woods. These signals from God convinced him that he had been chosen to lead a slave rebellion. Almost certainly, this discussion of the religious aspect of the revolt came more from Turner than it did from Gray's interpretation of Turner. The earlier newspaper accounts had not elaborated the sacred dimensions of the revolt in such detail. Moreover, Turner's description here fits a common pattern in which African American rebellion was deeply connected to religious inspiration.[60] But when read by Southern men of honor, Turner's statement that he was inspired by God rather than by superstition would not have seemed to make a meaningful distinction. Both sources of inspiration involved the idea that Turner was a deluded fanatic who thought he acted in response to an imagined command from some higher authority.

Some whites, in their search for causes of the rebellion other than the desire of slaves to risk their lives in a bid for freedom, turned away from the sun and superstition toward the idea of other forms of "outside agitation." There were many ways to deny the agency of Nat Turner and the other slaves killed in the rebellion. One North Carolina newspaper maintained that the revolt had been stimulated by the publication of David Walker's and William Lloyd Garrison's incendiary writings.[61] John Floyd, the governor of Virginia during the insurrection, wrote to the governor of South Carolina, "I am fully persuaded, the spirit of insubordination which has, and still manifests itself in Virginia, had its origin among, and eminated from, the Yankee population, upon their *first* arrival amongst us, but most especially the Yankee pedlers and traders."[62] In his message to the legislature about the insurrection he offered a powerful image of black preachers as conduits of incendiary information from other states.[63] Likewise, William Gilmore Simms, a South Carolina novelist and proslavery writer, blamed the rebellion on abolitionists.[64]

Southerners used the idea that slave rebellion was the product of outside agitation far beyond the specific context of the Nat Turner rebellion. Such agitation was commonly blamed for almost all instances of slave rebellion. South Carolinians pinpointed the cause of the 1822 Denmark Vesey conspiracy in the turmoil of Santo Domingo and the Northern attack on slavery during the Missouri crisis.[65] The theme was echoed by many proslavery thinkers. William Harper wrote that attempts at insurrection had always been excited by "the agitation of the abolitionists and declaimers on slavery."[66] James Henry Hammond believed that slaves would never think of revolt "unless instigated to it by others."[67] For white gentlemen of the Old South it was Yankee pedlers or abolitionists or tricksters who lay at the root of every rebellion—not slaves voluntarily risking their lives for liberation.

Some accounts of the Nat Turner insurrection even suggested that many slaves joined the rebellion because of their desire to *avoid* the risk of death. One writer noted that most of the insurrectionists "had to be guarded" during the rebellion "by some two or three of the principals, furnished with guns; with orders to shoot the first man, who endeavored to escape." According to this vision, Turner had his own problem with runaway slaves and discovered that only the threat of death could keep them under control. Another report noted that one rebel gave himself up to his master because he feared "starving in the swamps or being shot."[68]

A related idea, widely circulated at the time of the rebellion, was that it took only a small number of white men to subdue slaves in a direct and open confrontation. Since slaves would not stand up in the face of death, their rebellion could easily be suppressed by a few gentlemen. In the midst of the initial panic, large numbers of militiamen had been called to serve, but later it became clear to some that they were not needed. One officer on the scene reported a skirmish in which four whites confronted twenty blacks and "the whites repulsed them, killed 3 or 4, and took several prisoners." General Broadnax reported that "a force of 20 resolute men . . . could easily have put them down." Thomas R. Gray, in the introduction to Nat Turner's *Confessions*, noted that "it is not the least remarkable feature in this horrid transaction, that a band actuated by such hellish purposes, should have resisted so feebly, when met by the whites in arms. . . . More than twenty of them attacked Dr. Blunt's house on Tuesday morning, a little before daybreak, defended by two men and three boys. They fled precipitately at the first fire; and their future plans of mischief, were entirely disconcerted and broken up."[69]

The idea that rebel slaves feared death extended even to Nat Turner himself. Accounts of his final apprehension universally lingered over his failure to resist his captor or to risk his life. Long before his actual arrest, reports claimed that he had been captured and that, although heavily armed, he "made no resistance."[70] Hence, when Turner finally was seized, the descriptions cited behavior that had long been anticipated. All accounts marveled that the notorious rebel was captured by one man, that he put up no resistance, and that he engaged in an act of subservience at the final moment of confrontation. One widely circulated description noted that Turner had been discovered in a cave by local resident Benjamin Phipps. Phipps "immediately pointed to kill him with his gun, but he [Turner] exclaimed 'don't shoot and I will give up,' he then threw his sword from the Cave." Another report maintained that Turner "displayed no sort of enterprise in the attempt to escape, nor any degree of courage in resisting the person who captured him." Another further embellished the image of subservience by describing how Turner "submissively laid himself on the ground and was thus securely tied—not making the least resistance." Moreover, it noted that Turner had wanted to give himself up long before but "could never summon sufficient resolution." Virtually every account of the capture mentions the symbolic moment when Nat Turner chose to throw down his sword rather than fight to the death.[71]

Gray reverted to the same imagery in his introductory remarks to Turner's *Confessions.* "This 'great Bandit,'" he maintained, "was taken by a single individual ... without attempting to make the slightest resistance." Most importantly for any honorable Southern gentleman who might read this account, Gray added the detail that Turner "begged that his life might be spared." Turner himself reported in the *Confessions* (or at least Gray said he reported) that Phipps cocked his gun and aimed it; "I requested him not to shoot and I would give up, upon which he demanded my sword. I delivered it to him, and he brought me to prison."[72]

All these descriptions of Nat Turner and his followers as cowards do not mean that Southern gentlemen failed to be concerned about the menace posed by the rebels. Cowards, after all, can be dangerous. They can kill people by stealth. They can kill if their lives are not in immediate danger. No theme received greater attention in the accounts given by whites than the ferocity and brutality of the rebels. It was possible to recognize the threat posed by a submissive, treacherous, bloodthirsty rebel slave, but it was not possible to respect him. For Southern gentlemen, Nat Turner was a dangerous man as well as a man with no honor; he was a man who killed unarmed women and children, but when confronted by a threat to his own life he was a slave who "laid himself submissively on the ground."

It would be wrong to suggest that there was no significant overlap between the way Southern gentlemen thought of Nat Turner and the way they thought of John Brown. Both men were vilified as insane fanatics. The major differences lay in the virtual absence of the language of submission, and in the occasional respectful remarks about bravery, in descriptions of Brown. Nothing illustrates this contrast more dramatically than the differential treatment given their bodies. Before the execution, Governor Wise had received a request for Brown's dead body from a professor of anatomy at the University of Virginia. "We desire," wrote Dr. A. E. Peticolas, "if Brown and his coadjutors are executed, to add their heads to the collection in our museum. If the transference of the whole bodies will not exceed five dollars each we should also be glad to have *them.*"[73] The request for Brown's head had a powerful meaning in the language of honor. Dissection of a dead body was an extreme form of degradation and expression of contempt. But Dr. Peticolas misread the prevailing sentiment about John Brown. Wise refused the request, and the dead body of John Brown was returned to his wife for a "triumphal" trip to the North.

Even after Wise's decision, John Brown still almost lost his head. Doctors who examined his dead body at the jail refused to certify his death because his head seemed so remarkably intact. His face was not discolored, his eyes did not protrude, and he was covered with no discharge from either the nose or the mouth. Even at the moment of death, it seemed, brave men retained their noble features. One doctor proposed the removal of Brown's head and another suggested a massive dose of strychnine. They feared that a not-quite-dead John Brown might be aroused from his coffin by "galavinic batteries" once he was returned to the North. But the doctors apparently hesitated to mutilate Brown even in death. They broke for lunch, and certified his death upon their return.[74]

In contrast, decapitation and bodily mutilation were central features of the Nat Turner revolt. Long before Benjamin Phipps captured Nat Turner, one newspaper incorrectly reported that Turner's head had been cut off and placed on display atop a pike on a public road.[75] It was a report that reflected the prevailing sentiment. From the moment the revolt began to collapse, whites engaged in a veritable orgy of decapitation. One group of whites apparently cut off the head of the slave rebel Henry Porter. It was reported to be in the possession of a militia surgeon, who carried it around the county.[76] One cavalry company from Murfrecsboro, North Carolina, decapitated fifteen slaves and placed their heads on poles for display. Another rebel head was posted at the intersection of the Barrow Road and Jerusalem Highway—a crossing thenceforth known as "Blackhead Sign Post."[77]

Nat Turner, like John Brown, suffered death by hanging, but his body was not treated with the kind of respect accorded that of John Brown. One account maintained that "General Nat sold his body for dissection, and spent the money on ginger cakes." Although it is probable that Turner was dissected after his death, the idea that he would sell his body for ginger cakes seems a likely invention of a white witness. It is inconceivable that the Virginia authorities would ask Nat Turner's permission to have his body dissected—or that anyone would pay a slave for the use of his body after death when they would not pay him for its use when he was alive. More believable are the comments by William Sidney Drewry, who interviewed still-living witnesses to the revolt and wrote in 1900 that "Nat Turner's body was delivered to the doctors, who skinned it and made grease of the flesh. His skeleton was for many years in the possession of Dr. Massenberg, but has since been misplaced." Drewry then remarked in a footnote about the specific content of the interviews he conducted while in Southampton County, "There are many citizens still living who have seen Nat's skull. It was very peculiarly shaped, resembling the head of a sheep, and at least three-quarters of an inch thick. Mr. R. S. Barham's father owned a money purse made of his hide."[78] It matters little whether such stories were true or merely imagined. Either way, they illustrate the same attitude toward Nat Turner's corpse.

John Brown's body lies moldering in a grave. Nat Turner's body has likely been beheaded, scattered, and misplaced, and perhaps turned into a purse. Even in death—at least in the language of honor—Brown retained his freedom and Turner retained his slavery.

Could it have been otherwise? In other words, did men in the culture of honor approach the free man John Brown and the slave Nat Turner with categories and assumptions that mandated their interpretation, no matter how the rebels behaved? What if Nat Turner had resisted at the moment of his capture? What if John Brown had begged for mercy when a noose was put around his neck? Although it would be wrong to preclude the possibility that some changed "facts" could have generated changed interpretations (especially in the case of John Brown), it is more important to recognize the difficulty of such a transformation. For one thing, "facts" do not exist independently of their interpretation. Did Nat Turner "submissively" lie on the ground at the moment of his capture? Perhaps Benjamin Phipps saw it that way—or perhaps it was so understood by someone who spoke to Benjamin Phipps. But what did Nat Turner think he was doing? Turner tells us in the *Confessions* that "he knew it was impossible for him to escape as the woods were full of men; he therefore thought it was better to surrender, and trust to fortune for his escape."[79] In other words, Turner's submission might have been part of his resistance. Sometimes an act of submission is not an act of submission. Gestures tremble with ambiguity even as they are placed in interpretive frameworks.

But more significantly, both Nat Turner and John Brown (or rather, their interpreters) generated plenty of "facts" that could have been used to develop radically different visions of their behavior. These accumulated "facts" became part of secondary themes within the central theme. The Virginia artist and writer David Hunter Strother visited John Brown in his jail cell; he thought that Brown "denoted the most ungovernable fear" when he heard noises outside that implied that Brown might be lynched. But he also found Brown "cool and unapologetic" during his trial, and, like many others, he saw no signs of fear during the execution.[80] Similarly, some doctors *did* want to cut off John Brown's head, although ultimately they did not do so. Reactions to the Nat Turner rebels included similar inconsistencies buried in the general pattern. One newspaper report contained a reference to a wounded slave, "a man aged about 21, called Marmaduke, who might have been a hero, judging from the magnanimity with which he bears his sufferings."[81] The slave Will Artis chose suicide rather than capture. This could easily have been understood as a choice of death over loss of liberty—if anyone had bothered to elaborate it. At least one newspaper reported that Turner did not tremble at the moment of his execution, although it quickly followed with the observation that he sold his body for dissection in exchange for ginger cakes.[82] There was much material in the *Confessions* that did not imply that Nat Turner was a coward.

These observations suggest the need for a renewed appreciation of the way the language of honor shaped the white male understanding of the world. The belief that slaves and others with no honor preferred their lives to their liberty made it likely that men of honor would come to understand Nat Turner as a coward or a madman. To have seen him otherwise would have been to "emancipate" him. Similarly, this view left open the possibility that John Brown *could* be understood as fearless. John Brown's behavior played a significant role in shaping the perceptions of men like Edmund Ruffin and Henry Wise, but these perceptions were formed and limited by the framework of the language of honor. In the end, the assumptions embedded in the language of honor made it likely that Nat Turner, and not John Brown, would lose his head. The language of honor created and destroyed Brown and Turner in its own image.

IV

The idea of slavery as an alternative to death reached deeply into the abstract thought of men of honor. It is quite evident in the single most influential proslavery work produced in the immediate wake of Nat Turner's rebellion—Thomas Roderick Dew's *Review of the Debate in the Virginia Legislature of 1831–1832*. The Turner revolt had generated a serious debate over the possibility of emancipation, and Professor Dew of the College of William and Mary wrote a summary analysis of the issues.[83] His essay became a widely circulated classic in the antebellum Southern defense of slavery. It was republished in 1852 as part of the compendium *The Pro-slavery Argument as Maintained by the Most Distinguished Writers of the Southern States*.[84]

Historians have long recognized the importance of Dew's 1832 essay in the history of proslavery thought. It has often been seen as the turning point in the development of the South's defense of slavery as a positive good rather than as a necessary evil. The historian Larry Tise has argued persuasively that the central significance of Dew's essay is that it attacked the idea that blacks could be freed and colonized outside the United States. This coincided with William Lloyd Garrison's abolitionist assault on colonization; together these unlikely allies discredited a once popular movement.[85] However, there is another way to read Dew's essay: not so much for the larger conclusions of its central formal arguments or for the ultimate effect of its ideas on policy as for its underlying discussion of the connection between slavery and death. It seems as if no matter what paths Dew wandered down in his complex defense of slavery, he came back to the subject of death. Just as the language of honor provided the lens through which Southern gentlemen viewed Nat Turner, it also structured many of the arguments they used to defend slavery.

Dew began with a discussion of the origins of slavery. This was an attempt to show that slavery was a universal, natural institution. He considered four major causes of slavery under the headings "Laws of War," "State of Property and Feebleness of Government," "Bargain and Sale," and "Crime." All four of these causes brought him back to the idea of slavery as an alternative to death. He reserved his longest discussion for the laws of war as the "most fruitful source of slavery."[86] His central argument here was that in early hunting societies, death was the usual result of capture in war. To illustrate the argument, he conjured a frightening image of early American "savage" warfare in which "the prisoners are tied naked to a stake. . . . All who are present—men women and children—rush upon them like furies. Every species of torture is applied, that the rancor of revenge can invent: some burn their limbs with red hot iron, some mangle their bodies with knives, others tear their flesh from their bones, pluck out their nails by the roots, and rend and twist their sinews."[87] The horrors of "savage" warfare, in Dew's account, only became tamed with the rise of slavery. Slavery was the civilized substitute for death in war because the victor's interest induced him to enslave rather than to kill his captives.[88]

Dew's discussion of the other causes of slavery also rested on the image of enslavement as a substitute for death. A feeble government and a severe imbalance in the distribution of property sometimes led the poorer part of the population to seek the "protection" offered by slavery.[89] Dew also argued that the most common reason for sale into slavery was the threat of death by famine.[90] Finally, he argued that enslavement was a proper punishment for some crimes, including some crimes that would usually be capital offenses. In African murder cases, according to Dew, the nearest relation of the victim could kill or enslave the murderer.[91]

The idea of slavery as an alternative to death also appeared in Dew's discussion of the advantages the world had gained from the institution.

Here, he repeated the argument that slavery ended murderous, "savage" warfare.[92] He also noted that the Indians could have been saved from slaughter if they had been enslaved. Slavery, Dew believed, was the only remaining alternative to their ultimate extinction.[93] Similarly, Dew maintained that children died in great numbers in "savage" society, and that slavery saved their lives and improved the lives of their mothers.[94]

Dew also considered the specific origins of American slavery in the slave trade, and once again he reverted to the subject of death. He recognized the brutality of the trade and condemned the high death rate of slaves during the middle passage. Yet he also argued that with the rise of the slave trade, "great care was taken in the preservation of the lives of prisoners, in consequence of the great demand for them occasioned by the slave traffic."[95] Dew was no defender of the slave trade, but he found it important to note the way it sometimes saved lives.

The most famous portion of Dew's essay involved a discussion of the impossibility of colonization. In this section he wandered from the subject of death. He described the economic devastation that would descend upon Virginia if it emancipated and deported its slave population. Dew also argued that it was economically impossible even to halt the increase of the Virginia slave population, and that it was a fantasy to believe that the slaves' places as workers would ever be assumed by free laborers. But the subject of death reemerged when he turned to the question of what would happen to the black population if it was returned to Africa. Freedom would bring death. Among other things, the African climate and its diseases would kill the liberated slaves; they could not provide food for themselves; they would have no houses; and they would be slaughtered by neighboring tribes.[96] Although not every portion of Dew's argument turned on the idea of slavery as a substitute for death, a significant segment of the essay directly or indirectly depended on the concept. The connection between slavery and the avoidance of death was the single most common theme developed in this classic proslavery work.

Dew was not alone. The idea of slavery as an alternative to death was an important concept for many antebellum proslavery thinkers, although few devoted as much space to the subject as did Dew. Some gave it more explicit and prominent expression than others, but in any case it appeared with remarkable frequency. It was such a basic and deep idea that it burst forth in the works of proslavery thinkers who rooted their logic in different assumptions or who otherwise profoundly disagreed with one another.

Many proslavery writers shared Dew's ideas on the origins of slavery.[97] William Harper, for example, in his *Memoir on Slavery*, used the concept of slavery as a substitute for death in a refutation of the idea of liberty as an inalienable right. He expressed amazement that a man could be condemned for selling himself into slavery: "Who will say that the man pressed by famine and the prospect of death, would be criminal for such an act? Self-preservation as is truly said, is the first law of nature. High and peculiar characters, by elaborate cultivation, may be taught to prefer death to Slavery, but it would be folly to prescribe this as a duty to the mass of mankind." Undoubtedly, Harper considered himself among the "high and peculiar characters" who would choose death over slavery.[98] But no black could be expected to make the "high and peculiar" choice.

William J. Grayson, the author of an epic poem in defense of slavery, drew on the link between slavery and the avoidance of death, referring at one point to people who became slaves as "the captive band in recent battle spared."[99] Edmund Ruffin also related slavery to the avoidance of death in his essay "The Political Economy of Slavery." In a discussion of war as a source of slavery, he argued that

> where civilization and refinement were so low . . . the prisoners of war would be put to death. . . . But where any advances had been made in regular industry, and especially where the right of private property in land had been established, the expediency of making domestic slaves and laborers of prisoners of war would soon be acknowledged and acted upon. Thus one of the earliest effects of the institution of slavery would be to lessen the horrors of war by saving lives that would otherwise be sacrificed.[100]

The idea of enslavement as a substitute for death sometimes appeared in the religious defense of slavery. Dew himself had referred to biblical accounts of the Israelites replacing a harsh death penalty with the comparatively mild punishment of slavery for prisoners captured in war.[101] The Reverend Thornton Stringfellow similarly argued that the "servants" referred to in the New Testament "were such as were preserved from death by the conqueror, and taken into slavery."[102] The same idea appeared in other portions of the religious defense. For example, it was an important part of white Southerners' understanding of the biblical story of Ham. Elaborations of this tale were often part of the Christian proslavery answer to the "scientific" racist argument that blacks were a different species permanently inferior to whites, and hence enslaveable. The story of Ham was a powerful myth, useful for the simultaneous refutation of scientific racists, the acceptance of the biblical account of a single human creation, and the justification of slavery.

The story of Ham as it appeared in the Bible was a relatively simple tale. As one historian of the subject summarized it:

> Noah had three sons, Ham, Shem, and Japheth, from whom the earth was peopled. One day Noah drank too much wine and fell asleep naked inside

his tent. Ham, the father of Canaan, saw his father's nakedness and went outside to tell his brothers. Shem and Japheth, looking the other way, covered Noah. Upon waking, Noah "knew what his younger son had done unto him" and said, "Cursed be Canaan; A servant of servants shall he be unto his brethren." Then he added, "Blessed be the Lord God of Shem, And Canaan shall be his servant. God shall enlarge Japheth, And he shall dwell in the tents of Shem; And Canaan shall be his servant."[103]

The Ham story (after elaboration) offered one resolution to a tension in white Southern Christian thought: how blacks could be fellow human beings and yet deserve to be slaves. The myth could serve this purpose as a result of the common belief that Ham was black, Japheth was white, and Shem was Indian. The sons of Noah were seen as the prototypes of the races of America. Noah had cursed blacks into slavery and prophesied the movement of whites into the tents of the Indians.

My concern here is not with a full analysis of the meaning and use of this myth in Southern society; I merely want to note the way in which death crept into the Southern elaboration of the Ham story. The curse on Ham's children had been slavery, yet many Southern thinkers felt compelled to add that this punishment was a substitute for death. For example, Iveson L. Brookes of South Carolina argued that Ham deserved "decapitation" for his crime, but that a merciful God chose to punish him "by flattening his head, kinking his hair, and blackening his skin"—thereby making him black and subject to slavery.[104] The same idea appears in the proslavery pamphlet *African Servitude: When, Why, and by Whom Instituted: By Whom, and How Long, Shall It Be Maintained?*: "Our first parents broke the first command on the first table, by disobeying the true God, and obeying that usurper, the devil, the god of the world—the legal consequence of which was death of body and soul. Ham, the son of Noah, broke the first command on the second table, by scorning and deriding his father, the legal consequences of which seem to be the death of his body, or the forfeiture of it for the benefit of others."[105] In other words, Ham merited death or its equivalent, enslavement. Slavery substituted for death.

Samuel Cartwright suggested a parallel link between slavery and the avoidance of death in his reading of the curse placed on Cain. He believed that the mark of Cain—the mark that prevented him from being slain—was black skin. And this was the mark that also made him enslaveable. "The wild Arabs," Cartwright wrote, "and hostile American Indians invariably catch the black wanderer and make a slave of him instead of killing him, as they do the white man."[106]

Most significantly, the portion of the proslavery argument that emphasized the kind, paternal relations between master and slave was an elaborate discussion of the idea of slavery as an alternative to death. An important part of the view of slavery as paternal was the notion that death lurked everywhere outside the institution. In this way of seeing the world, for example, Africans, once freed of the international slave trade, faced death. Cartwright reported a missionary's description of a "capricious mulatto chief" in "Central Africa" who sent his officers to a "poor fellow" who had committed a minor offense. They arrived with an empty bag and this message: *"The king says you must send me your head."* Cartwright blamed this brutality on the end of the international slave trade and the consequent decline in the value of an African life. "Empty bags," he wrote, "are now filled with heads instead of cowries." The "Soudan" had become depopulated.[107] Just as Thomas R. Dew had argued that colonized African Americans would quickly be exterminated if they were returned to Africa, Cartwright maintained that the withdrawal of a connection to American slavery would completely destroy the rest of the African population.

Similarly, many proslavery writers argued that if freed and permitted to remain in the South, the African American population would be exterminated. William Harper believed that the two races could not live together as equals in peace, and that "aggression would beget retaliation, until open war—and that a war of extermination were established. From the still remaining superiority of the white race, it is probable that they would be the victors, and if they did not exterminate, they must again reduce the others to slavery."[108] Jefferson Davis believed that emancipation would bring extermination because the black population would not be able to provide itself with the necessities of life. In the midst of the Civil War, he thought he saw the first signs of decline. His 1863 message to the Confederate Congress told of Northern armies that occupied Southern territory and recruited able-bodied male slaves into their ranks, leaving the aged as well as women and children to care for themselves. "Without clothing or shelter," he told the gathered legislators,

> often without food, incapable without supervision of taking the most ordinary precautions against disease, these helpless dependents, accustomed to have their wants supplied by the foresight of their masters, are being rapidly exterminated wherever brought in contact with the invaders. . . . There is little hazard in predicting that in all localities where the enemy have gained a temporary foothold the negroes, who under our care increased six-fold in number since their importation into the colonies by Great Britain, will have been reduced by mortality during the war to no more than half their previous number.[109]

Josiah Nott, like many other white Southerners faced with emancipation after the Civil War, fully expected to see the African American population disappear—"like the Indian and other inferior races." The image guided his perception. In 1866, Nott reported that "the Negroes are dying in idleness around this city [Mobile, Alabama] from disease and starvation."[110]

The idea that death was inevitable without the protection of slavery extended into the general critique of free labor. Many proslavery writers argued that the exploitation of all workers in a free society led them down the road to death. William Harper prominently cited a report on prostitution in England that maintained that prostitutes "die like sheep with the rot.... Those that die are, like factory children that die, instantly succeeded by new competitors for misery and death."[111] James Henry Hammond quoted at length the British parliamentary reports that chronicled the brutality and death visited on the exploited laboring poor of England.[112] George Fitzhugh read the same parliamentary reports and offered an even more thorough critique of the world of free labor—a world of competition "that places all mankind in antagonistic positions, and puts all society at war. What can such a war result in," Fitzhugh wondered, "but the oppression and ultimate extermination of the weak?" Some proslavery writers described the "savage" world before American slavery as the world of the cannibal; George Fitzhugh evoked the same imagery to describe the cannibal world of a free-labor society. "You are a Cannibal!" he admonished each of his capitalist readers, "and if a successful one, pride yourself on the number of your victims quite as much as any Fiji chieftain, who breakfasts, dines and sups on human flesh."[113]

In the imagery of paternal proslavery writers, while death stalked the rest of the world, life flourished safely within the protecting walls of enslavement. With the occasional exception of a man like Nat Turner—a man polluted by outside agitators—slaves survived. Most commonly, proslavery writers cited the protection afforded slaves because they were the valuable property of masters. A slave's life was not cheap in the antebellum South. William Gilmore Simms believed that "the interests of the owner are sufficient protection for the slave." Therefore, "it is his policy to prolong his life, to preserve his health, to promote his strength, and to give him contentment. These objects imply adequate food and clothing, indulgent nurture, moderate tasks, and, as much, if not more leisure, than is usually allotted to the laboring classes in any country."[114] E. N. Elliott, president of the Planters' College of Mississippi, argued that under slavery the master had an obligation "to the slave of protection, and a comfortable subsistence."[115] The editor of a New Orleans newspaper contrasted the threat of death faced by free workers with the protections afforded to slaves: "A white laborer," he wrote, "with the unrestricted command of all his physical energies, may be exposed to starvation, because nobody is inclined to use or pay for them; whereas the black laborer, whose thewes and sinews are the property of his master, is certain at all times of food, shelter, and clothing, and generally of kind treatment."[116] Similar statements appear in the writings of every paternal proslavery thinker. Over and over they voiced the same refrain: in a world where death by violence or neglect threatened everyone, masters protected the lives of their slaves.[117] The retreat into slavery was a retreat from the threat of death into the promise of life.

FIVE

BASEBALL, HUNTING, AND GAMBLING

SOUTHERN MEN OF HONOR did not play baseball during the antebellum period. They enjoyed a variety of other sports and diversions, including hunting, racing horses, and betting on various card, dice, and other games. But they showed little interest in baseball. Despite the wishful thinking of some early publicists, antebellum baseball was not the "National Game." Only after the Civil War, only after slavery had ended and men of honor had lost their central place in Southern culture, did baseball begin to take root in the South. To understand why Southern gentlemen preferred the hunt and other games to baseball is to understand much about the complex connections among games, slavery, and honor among masters of the Old South. Southern men revealed themselves in the games that gave them pleasure.

I

Baseball mythology has hitherto combined with Civil War mythology to make it difficult to analyze the sectional origins of the game. In order to study the history of antebellum baseball, it is necessary to appreciate the power of the myths that have come to surround it. Even before the war, early nationalist sports writers, eager to discover a single sport loved by all Americans, ignored the Northern regional roots of baseball. In 1857, the pioneer sports publicist William T. Porter referred to "the National Ball Play of our country" in the pages of his journal *Spirit of the Times.*[1] After the Civil War, the image of baseball as the national sport attained a nearly sacred status in the culture. It was an important symbol that demonstrated that the United States had always been a single nation. Charles A. Peverelly, in his popular survey of American sports, described baseball as "The National Game . . . peculiarly suited to the American temperament and disposition."[2] America had just been split by a bloody civil war, but Peverelly's portrait of the universal appeal of baseball created an image of unity. In phrases that echoed the words of contemporary sporting journals, Peverelly contended that the game offered "excitement and *vim*" with "no delay" for two and a half hours. Americans, he believed, needed constant stimulation in order to sustain their interest because "they are too mercurial and impulsive a race not to get drowsy and dissatisfied with anything which permits their natural ardor to droop even for a brief space of time." Moreover, baseball was not costly in terms of equipment or time. Unlike foreign, "aristocratic" games, anybody in America could play. "The great mass," Peverelly contended, "who are in a subordinate capacity, can participate in this health-giving and noble pastime."[3]

The image of baseball as the national game achieved powerful reaffirmation in the late nineteenth and early twentieth centuries under the guidance of the promoter and sporting-goods entrepreneur Albert G. Spalding and the president of the National League, Abraham G. Mills. Their central contribution was to achieve official sanction for the idea that "America's National Game" was invented by Abner Doubleday and had not evolved from the English ball game of "rounders." The campaign began in 1889. Spalding had just returned triumphantly to New York after leading an American baseball team on a world exhibition tour. He had played in Honolulu, Australia, England, and even in the shadow of the great pyramids. Mills was one of the speakers at a dinner at the Delmonico Restaurant to welcome the players home to America. In a stirring address, he told the audience (which included such notables as Mark Twain and Theodore Roosevelt) exactly what they wanted to hear: that "patriotism and research" had proven the American origins of the game of baseball. Anti-English shouts of "No rounders!" erupted from the excited crowd.[4]

Official recognition of the American origins of baseball came in 1907. Responding to a 1903 article in support of the "rounders thesis," Spalding called for the creation of a special commission to settle the matter once and for all. In the face of considerable contradictory evidence and virtually no supporting documentation, the commission (headed by Mills) endorsed the Abner Doubleday story—a story that quickly became myth and has since proved remarkably resistant to destruction. In an inspired moment of spontaneous generation, according to the apocryphal tale, Doubleday transformed the old game of "town ball" into baseball. He stepped onto a field in Cooperstown, New York, in 1839 and explained his creation to teams from Otsego Academy and Green's Select School. Baseball was born of a virgin in a virgin land.[5]

The overt focus of the Doubleday myth was to free baseball from its association with England, but it also freed baseball from any special association with New York or New England. To label baseball the "American Game" was to wipe away regional variation; it disguised the Northern origins of the game and its slow growth in the South. In the Doubleday myth the story of baseball became "American," excluding both external and internal "foreigners." It was far more than coincidence that Abner Doubleday, the mythic inventor of baseball, was also the mythic Northern Civil War officer who "sighted the first gun in defense of Fort Sumter" when it came under Confederate attack.[6] In the world of myth, both of his achievements helped obliterate the Old South. He threw out the first as well as one of the last balls in the Civil War.

Spalding himself gave the fullest elaboration of the myth and its implications in his 1911 history, *America's National Game*. The book began with two drawings. One was a portrait of Uncle Sam, sleeves rolled up and baseball bat in hand as if about to step up to the "batter's slab" (as it was then called), with the caption "America's National Game." The second was more complex in structure but identical in theme. In the background was a map of the United States and a flag decoration. In the foreground stood an umpire surrounded by four oval portraits of men playing baseball. The caption explained it all: "East and West, North and South 'Play Ball.'"[7] Both drawings portrayed an America united in its devotion to a single game.

The text extended this theme. Spalding claimed that baseball was the national game with "all the attributes of American origin, American character and unbounded public favor." Then, in a frenzied piece of alliterative writing that echoed what Peverelly and others had said decades earlier, he described the way baseball exemplified the American national character: "As no other form of sport it is the exponent of American Courage, Confidence, Combativeness; American Dash, Discipline, Determination; American Energy, Eagerness, Enthusiasm; American Pluck, Persistency, Performance; American Spirit, Sagacity, Success; American Vim, Vigor, Virility." In an illuminating illustration of these themes Spalding offered a short comparison between the American game of baseball and the English game of cricket. Cricket, he argued, was "too slow; [i]t takes two and sometimes three days to complete a first-class Cricket match; but two hours of Base Ball is quite sufficient to exhaust both players and spectators." Moreover, unlike cricket, baseball was a democratic game in which "the son of a President of the United States would as soon play ball with Patsy Flannigan as with Lawrence Lionel Livingstone." Finally, in marked contrast to the quiet and genteel demeanor of cricket players and fans, baseball was "War," with players sliding in the dirt and fans screaming in frenzy.[8]

But Spalding had it wrong. Baseball had its origins in the English game of rounders, and it evolved in America as a sectional sport of the

AMERICA'S NATIONAL GAME

FIGURE 10. "America's National Game."

EAST AND WEST, NORTH AND SOUTH
"PLAY BALL"

FIGURE 11. "East and West, North and South 'Play Ball.'"

Northeast. There is considerable evidence that New York and New England provided the soil in which American baseball grew. The earliest sports books setting forth the rules of the game were published in Boston and Providence during the 1830s. "Massachusetts [or New England] town ball" and "New York ball" were the names used to designate the two most popular early versions of the game as it developed from rounders.[9] New York was also the home of the first organized baseball clubs for grown men.[10] The entry of adults into the game marked an important change in the history of American ball games. Children throughout the nation had long played various games with balls. They came with names such as base, one old cat, stool ball, rounders, feeder, and bat and ball. But New York seems to have been the place where grown men first began to play with balls and developed the modern rules of the game. The political boss Thurlow Weed told of a baseball club in Rochester, New York, that included fifty prominent citizens and held regular matches in 1825.[11] The first organized team about which we have much information was the Knickerbocker Base Ball Club of New York City. It played informally in Manhattan as early as 1842. In 1845, under the leadership of Alexander Joy Cartwright, the team wrote a constitution, printed a set of rules, and rented a playing field in Hoboken, New Jersey. Shortly thereafter, the sport exploded in popularity throughout the New York region. One historian estimates that by 1858 there were approximately fifty adult baseball clubs in Manhattan and Brooklyn, along with a minimum of sixty "junior" clubs. Ignoring the regional nature of their sport, these teams and others from the area formed themselves into the "National Association of Base Ball Players."[12]

From the New York area and from New England, organized baseball spread west. By the late 1850s baseball clubs existed in many cities of western New York as well as in Cleveland, Philadelphia, Chicago, Detroit, Minnesota territory, and San Francisco.[13] However, for many years New York remained the center of baseball.[14] During the Civil War, more than half of all the baseball clubs listed in the "Base Ball Directory" were from Brooklyn and New York. Although the percentage of clubs from the New York area diminished significantly shortly after the Civil War, most of the growth was in the Midwest.[15]

It is possible to compile a substantial list of notable Northern men who took a strong interest in antebellum baseball. No comparable list exists for the South. During the 1840s Walt Whitman developed a love for the game that lasted his entire life. In 1846 he wrote an editorial for the *Brooklyn Daily Eagle* that declared that "the game of ball is glorious." He included "a good game of baseball" in his long catalogue of distinctively American activities in his epic poem "Song of Myself."[16] "Boss" Tweed of New York was an enthusiastic baseball fan and promoter. He enticed ballplayers to New York by putting them on the city payroll.[17] Abraham Lincoln, too, apparently enjoyed the game of baseball.[18]

It would be incorrect to suggest that no Southerners played baseball or other ball games before the Civil War. Southern children certainly played ball games throughout the eighteenth and nineteenth centuries. In 1859 a few groups of young men even organized several adult baseball clubs in New Orleans.[19] But overall, it seems clear that during the antebellum period the sport became a significant game for grown men in New York and New England while it was largely ignored by Southern masters and men of honor.

The evidence of Southern baseball during the Civil War is slight. Albert G. Spalding, for example, made grand claims about Confederate baseball without any supporting evidence. In his history of the game, he wrote about a series of matches played between Northern and Southern soldiers during quiet moments in the Virginia campaign. But his evidence was based solely on unsubstantiated rumors. "I have not," he wrote, "found any soldier of either army to corroborate these rumors or to deny them."[20] Bell Irvin Wiley, in his classic study of the common soldier of the Confederacy, noted that some Southern soldiers played baseball while in camp, but one of the two examples he cited included the observation of an officer that his men played baseball "just like school boys." The other made several references to the "boys" playing the game. Neither example indicates that the game had yet risen to the status of an activity appropriate for a *man* of honor.[21]

One of the most famous Civil War baseball stories concerned a game between Northern prisoners and Southern guards in Salisbury, North Carolina. A lithograph of the game has raised its status to mythic proportions. But the evidence that exists about this game indicates that it was the Northern prisoners who taught the Southern guards to play a sport with which the guards were not familiar.[22] Perhaps the classic tale of the relationship between Southern men of honor and baseball during the Civil War should not assume the form of the intersectional game at Salisbury. The central part of the tale is better told by George Haven Putnam of New York. Many years later, he recalled a Civil War game played by Northern soldiers outside their fortifications in the Deep South. While the ballplayers focused on fielding and hitting, Confederate skirmishers attacked them, shot the right fielder, captured the center fielder, and stole the baseball. Northern and Southern men shared the field during this encounter, but they were involved in different games.[23]

Baseball did not grow rapidly among Southern men of honor because it seemed to embody a set of values at odds with their culture. Baseball did not fit. This is not to suggest that baseball had a fixed nature that forever halted the triumph of the game. The meaning of a game can be reinterpreted; societies undergo transformations. But Southern men of honor initially had a negative reaction to the game. One source of tension is illustrated in the baseball reminiscences of Ken Leitner, once a slave in South Carolina. He was witness to a rare event in antebellum history: a master attempting to play baseball. During an interview in the 1930s he remembered the day long ago when for the first time "Marse Bill Kitchen

. . . went to de bat, and de very fust lick, him knock de ball way over center field." Everyone then screamed at the master, "Run Kitchen! Run Kitchen! Run Kitchen!" But Kitchen stood still and shook his head: "Why should I run? I got two more licks at dat ball!" The fielders retrieved the ball and tagged him out. With that, according to Leitner, "Marse Bill throw de ball down and say: 'D——n sich a game!' "[24]

Ken Leitner's description of events witnessed more than seventy years earlier does not offer much detail for analysis. The incident, however, is suggestive in several ways. Given his age and the date of his interview, it is safe to assume that the baseball game he described occurred no earlier than the late 1850s.[25] It is also clear that the South Carolina gentleman "Marse Kitchen" had never before been exposed to the game—at the very moment when New York bubbled with more than one hundred *organized* baseball teams. Leitner's description allows us to witness the moment of first contact—the moment when a master first met a baseball. It is a revealing moment. "Marse Kitchen" seems to have had little trouble hitting the ball. He smacked it on "de very fust lick." Perhaps he had already hit balls with a bat as a child. But he could not understand the running. He would not play baseball.

Why did Kitchen "damn" the game rather than run? Masters and men of honor did not run from anything.[26] "Marse Kitchen" probably knew all about the kind of men who would "run." They were slaves or dishonorable cowards or contemptible office seekers. Every Southern newspaper was full of advertisements for slaves who had "run away."[27] Masters were the men who tracked and captured these runaways. Moreover, dishonorable deserters "ran away" from the fire of the enemy, fleeing rifle "balls" in a way that paralleled the motions of players fleeing balls as they ran the bases. In contrast, men of honor "stood their ground." Men of honor did not "run away" from dueling encounters. They faced their opponents in an open, forthright, and steady manner. Men of honor did not "run for office."[28] They "stood," once they had been called by their constituents. When Kitchen played baseball he had little trouble standing at the "slab." But he could only "damn" the game that demanded that he run from a ball.

The act of running in baseball implied a change of position that seemed inappropriate to a man of honor. When a baseball player stands at the plate he stands as a subject ready to hit a ball as an object. But once he hits the ball, the roles are reversed as a result of no cause other than a rule of the game. The ball in the hands of an opponent becomes the subject and the batter becomes its object. In fact, this type of reversal is at the heart of baseball and is one of the reasons it was early touted as a "democratic" game. There was no fixed or privileged position in the game. This was especially true in antebellum baseball, in which even the pitcher did not have a special status. The job of the pitcher was to throw the ball so that it could be hit, rather than to strike out batters. Players took turns hitting the ball, catching the ball, and running the bases.

But this type of role reversal, which involved an arbitrary switch from subject to object, could not have made sense to a man of honor. It was not that men of honor believed in the impossibility of role reversal. Men did lose honor; men with the qualities of masters sometimes demonstrated the qualities of slaves. But when these reversals did occur they were always *caused*—by loss in some confrontation, or by the manifestation of a flawed character trait. Baseball, on the other hand, had arbitrary reversals built into the rhythm of the game. Kitchen could take "licks" with his bat but he could see no reason to run from the ball. Masters did not whip and expect to be whipped in turn. They could take a "lick" at a slave, but would not tolerate the reverse. A caning was one of the worst forms of humiliation for a man of honor. A man hit with a cane was transformed from an active, independent subject into an object. Similarly, it was the slaves who ran while the masters chased. Attempts at a reversal were called slave rebellions, and they were brutally suppressed.

The Northern city rather than the Southern plantation was the home of American baseball. In the city, baseball achieved its greatest popularity, especially among white-collar and blue-collar workers. The game seemed to satisfy middle-class urban men.[29] Early baseball clubs were not "professional" teams in the modern sense; the players did not make a living from the game. Baseball clubs were fraternal orders of young men engaged in a social activity. They consisted of workers, craftsmen, or owners of small businesses who worked in the city and played baseball during their leisure hours. The original Knickerbocker baseball team was just such a group. The team's leader, Alexander Cartwright, was a bank teller and volunteer fireman. The antebellum roster of the team included merchants, clerks, brokers, insurance men, a "Segar Dealer," a hatter, a cooperage owner, a stationer, a United States marshal, and a handful of people who called themselves "professionals" or "gentlemen."[30] Other early clubs had a decidedly more working-class membership. One historian estimates that between 75 and 80 percent of the members of baseball clubs between 1855 and 1870 "could be found in occupations running from journeymen and clerks to master craftsmen and small shopkeepers."[31] Sometimes workers in a particular shop would organize themselves into a baseball team. Team names might reflect the work of the players: "the compositors and pressmen of the *New York Daily Times*," or "the American Banknote Company." Some teams consisted of journeymen and master craftsmen shipbuilders; butchers had teams; government clerks formed "nines," as did many volunteer fire companies.[32]

Several historians have noted the way in which baseball fit the lives of this urban population.[33] For one thing, the length of the game seemed consistent with the demands of work in cities. Games usually began at three or four o'clock in the afternoon and lasted no more than four hours. It was possible for players to work all day and still complete a game by sundown. Urban Americans had neither the patience nor the time to engage in any sport at greater length. Spalding highlighted this as an important difference between the "democratic" American game of baseball and the more "aristocratic" English game of cricket—a game that often lasted all day and sometimes even two or three days.[34] Baseball also seemed to offer a form of exercise that reinforced middle-class urban values. Unlike many other sports of the time, baseball (in its middle-class, urban form) did not involve gambling, public drinking, or bloodshed.[35] Baseball allowed men who worked indoors all day to engage in "healthful" outdoor activities, free from the "corruptions" common to other sports of the era. Even women of "delicate sensibilities" could attend these "morally pure" contests.[36] Finally, baseball seemed to emulate and thereby to reinforce the patterns of urban work. Baseball teams engaged in carefully organized group production. Players worked together to produce "aces," or runs. Their efficiency could be calculated and measured in a rational and scientific way.[37] Here was a game that players, spectators, administrators, and reporters began immediately to describe in statistical terms. Moreover, the language of baseball was the language of work. Team players were supposed to practice. Early baseball reporters assumed that the discipline and hard work of the players invariably produced success.[38]

II

For many of the reasons that baseball pleased urban middle-class men, it failed to excite masters and men of honor. Southern men much preferred the sport of the hunt. Northern men in cities also sometimes hunted, but it was not so central to their culture. Just as baseball gave expression to Northern middle-class male values, the hunt gave expression to the core values of Southern men of honor.[39] One significant element of the hunt for Southern men of honor involved the issue of time. It took two to four hours to play a baseball game; hunters often planned excursions that lasted several days. One writer in the *Southern Literary Messenger* suggested that the most pleasant way to hunt deer was to camp by a stream for a week to ten days.[40] Although it was certainly possible to hunt for a single day, even a "short" foray into the field frequently consumed many hours. One Georgia hunter complained that his hunting day had been cut short; he could only pursue game between nine o'clock and four o'clock because his "boy" was too cold.[41] Northern men seemed attracted by the speed of baseball; Southern men relished the exorbitant length of the hunt. The same attitude toward time seems evident in the Southern willingness to listen to and admire long political speeches. Great Southern oratory took hours and hours—sometimes even days. Although the tradition of the long speech had once also flourished in the North, it was fading during the antebellum period.[42]

The hunt also fit into the world of Southern men of honor in the way it gave expression to ideas about death. The contrast with baseball is striking. Baseball denies death in several important ways. It is not just that no bodies are carried off the field at the end of the game. It is also that the game repeatedly refuses to put people into final resting places. The player at bat who is "put out" always returns later. When a side is retired it always comes up to bat again. An error in the field might be followed by a good catch. One of the greatest insights into the game of baseball is Yogi Berra's observation that "it ain't over till it's over." But the phrase does not even go far enough. Actually, "it ain't over even when it's over." As those of us who are fond of the Boston Red Sox can attest, there is always the next game or the next season. The same was true for nineteenth-century baseball clubs.

Hunting contains a different message about death. Hunters keep repeating their destruction of game, but the hunted always end up dead. The message of the hunt is that the hunter dispenses death. The hunted dies. In a sense, to paraphrase the baseball slogan, in the hunt "it is over even before it starts." Death is certain. The only question is how it will occur. In baseball, the game goes on; in the hunt, the "game" dies.

Sometimes in hunts, men of honor seemed to enjoy *approaching* a reversal. Sometimes injury or death threatened the hunter. Many Southern journals, newspapers, and novels contained stories of dangerous hunts. Sometimes, the hunter briefly became the hunted. Sometimes, the rifle of the hunter misfired as the bear approached. But the point of this type of encounter was not actually to engage in a reversal; it was only to come close. The point of telling these hunting stories was to demonstrate that the reversal had not occurred. Every good hunting story ended with a dead animal rather than a dead hunter. Approaching a reversal only highlighted that it had not occurred.

A central belief of Southern men of honor was that mastery of people was rooted in mastery of death. Men of honor thought of themselves as men who did not fear death; they could kill or be killed, but would not tremble. They could be shot at in battle and yet not run from the bullets. They could stand fearlessly in a duel while bullets passed or entered them. In the eyes of men of honor, slaves and other subordinates held their inferior positions precisely because they feared death. A man who was willing to die could never be forced to kneel.

The hunt gave expression to the idea that men of honor controlled the passage into death. It may seem self-evident that hunting was about killing animals. But it is extraordinary how often this idea was buried by participants and observers. Death was always surrounded by other considerations. Hunters loved to write about the skills they developed in the hunt. They loved to talk about the beauty of nature in field and stream. But if skill development and the appreciation of nature were the central features of the hunt, they did not have to be connected to the killing of animals. If improved hunting skills were the goal, one did not need to load a gun and actually shoot it. One could throw paint at an animal. If the appreciation of nature were the goal, one could simply take a walk in the woods. These aspects of hunting were subordinate to the central purpose of the enterprise: the killing of animals in a way that demonstrated mastery over death.[43] William Elliott's description of hunting devilfish in South Carolina nicely sums up the form of all hunts: "the lances were ready, and soon consumated the work of death; after which we all joined in merry procession toward the shore."[44] Here was the core of the enterprise for Southern men of honor: the consummation of the work of death followed by the procession.

It was mastery over death that was celebrated when a young hunter's face was daubed with the blood of his first kill. It was common practice for experienced hunters to dip their hands into the blood of the dead animal and smear it on the face of the initiate. Elliott described the custom as *"hunter's law with us."* He told of one man thus anointed, "his face glaring like an Indian chief's in all the splendor of war paint," who returned to his "young and lovely wife" without washing himself clean. This was an extraordinary moment: the bloody-faced man of honor wearing a badge of courage, returning home in triumph—with a strangely distorted "menstrual" flow from the head, symbolic of the ability to bring death rather than life into the world.[45]

The young initiate with blood on his head had played a game that definitely was not baseball. Such a man would have been puzzled by the great debate then raging in the North about the issue of "manly" versus "boyish" behavior among baseball players. A growing group of baseball enthusiasts had declared that the only manly way to play was to catch a ball on "the fly" rather than on "the bound." Early baseball rules had permitted a fielder to "put out" a hitter by catching the ball after it had bounced. To many in the North, a game that required catching a ball on "the fly" seemed more manly since it required greater skill.[46] But to a Southern man with blood on his head this debate could have made no sense. For a man of honor, manliness involved a demonstration of the ability to confront and to control death; it involved a demonstration of mastery over death. For Southern gentlemen, a boy did not become a man by catching either a bouncing or a flying ball.

Southern men achieved their feelings of pride and triumph in a realm far away from the world of balls. A hunter once stood with a companion, looking at the carcass of a bear he had just shot. He later recalled, "We felt more like great men then, than we ever have done since."[47] The South Carolinian Wade Hampton experienced the exhilaration of the kill when he was only five years old. He had been fearful of an aggressive drake. Then, under the beaming gaze of his elders, he proudly killed it with a toy sword.[48] The same feeling of triumph at a kill can be detected in the description of one hunter who delighted in eating the head of a newly killed deer. He baked it in a makeshift hole full of coals and then peeled off the skin. "First," he noted with relish, "there is some good picking on the jaws; then comes the tongue; and last, and daintiest of all, the brains, seasoned with red pepper and salt, and washed down with a tin mug of *cafe noir*, followed by a pipe. Such a repast leaves the hunter in the happiest frame."[49] The eating of the head no doubt produced "the happiest frame" because it fed more than the stomach of the hunter.

Because the meaning of death found in duels was related to the meaning of death found in hunts, many hunts resembled duels in several significant ways. Often, the hunter described the hunted as an animal that had issued a challenge. One of William Elliott's tales of hunting devilfish offers a good illustration. He wrote of a group of these winged fish that once came close to shorefront owned by his grandfather. They struggled to uproot the posts of a water fence "till they lashed the water into a foam with their powerful wings." Like any good man of honor, Elliott's grandfather objected to this intrusion into his personal space. "This bold invasion of his landmarks," Elliott wrote, "my grandfather determined to resent." He decided to hunt and kill these fish the next time they appeared. He preserved his honor by dispensing death to those who would challenge it.[50]

The hunter, like the duelist, often thought of his adversary as a worthy opponent. The greatest honor belonged to the man who confronted a noble foe. Hence, Elliott referred to a "devil fish" as a "gallant adversary." Similar statements appear in virtually all Southern descriptions of sporting hunts. It is extraordinary how many kind words Southern men reserved for wild turkeys. One Texas hunter tried but failed to catch a particular wild turkey for a period of more than three years. He even resorted to imitating the call of a female turkey. "But," he later reported, "the critter were so knowin'" that he always ran away. Finally, the hunter outsmarted the turkey by wearing his shoes backwards; the turkey (he believed) thought he had gone in the opposite direction.[51] Another Texas turkey hunter described the bird as "the most crafty game it will ever be your fortune to hunt."[52] Another waxed even more eloquent—turning the turkey into a beast truly worthy of the most honorable hunter. "The wild turkey," he wrote, "is to its barnyard kinsman what the racehorse is to the carthorse . . . his comb is a soldier's plume, his eye is full and hazel black, gleaming with something of a human look from his shapely head. . . . There is no pomposity or clumsiness about his air; on the contrary, his whole manners are those of an accomplished gallant and warrior."[53] Perhaps never before or since has the turkey been the object of such lavish praise.

Similar words of praise were granted to the other animals hunted for sport by Southern men of honor. Deer were confident, arrogant, wily, and swift; bulls were heroes; bears were ferocious and noble.[54] Southern men even extended their high praise to the fox.[55] They proudly told stories of cunning foxes that walked along fence rails in order to throw hunters off the scent, or of foxes that leaped over the edges of cliffs and into inaccessible caves in order to avoid being killed.[56] The body of the fox became greatly enlarged by the coat of words supplied by Southern men of honor. Others might look at a fox and see a tiny, relatively unthreatening creature. This perspective makes one immediately aware of the absurdity of chasing a small animal with packs of dogs and troops of men mounted on horseback with guns. The fox hunt only makes sense in the context of the world of honor. Men of honor created the myth of the wily and dangerous fox in order to turn it into a creature worthy of being hunted by gentlemen.

In the world of men of honor, animals spoke and thought in human language. Hunting stories were full of talking animals. Almost always, their speech was arrogant or boastful. This allowed the hunter to kill the animal and to be proud of having put it in a subordinate position. William Elliott, for example, told of waiting for a deer while hidden near a stream. The baying dogs were far in the distance and the deer was unaware of Elliott's presence. Elliott reported that he watched the deer glance in the direction of the dogs and then throw up its hind legs "with a sort of gambolling motion, as much as to say to his pursuers: '*That* for you, you wide-mouth'd curs! your throats are good, but as for your legs—*that* for you.'"[57] Hunters also recounted animal dreams and desires and imputed complex motives to the creatures they killed. The Southern naturalists James J. Audubon and John Bachman offered a description of foxhunting in which dogs flushed the fox and aroused it "perchance from a dreamy vision of fat hens, geese or turkeys."[58] Another hunter described a device that allowed him to imitate a female turkey in order to flush a male. He

FIGURE 12. "A Fox Surprised."

noted that once the call was given, the "cock . . . will rush to the spot with all the impetuosity of ungovernable lust and expected gratification."[59]

Men of honor avoided hunting creatures that were not arrogant, greedy, cunning, brave, lustful, heroic, ferocious, noble, or dangerous. Sometimes, in the midst of a hunt, the hunted animal might exhibit traits that did not merit death. If the animal seemed either insignificant or lovable it became difficult to achieve honor by killing it. Like a slave, such an animal might merit a kick or a paternal hand, but it would be denied the honorable death men gave to the equals they opposed in duels. During one hunt, for example, a ferocious bear did a great deal of damage to the dogs, knocking senseless the favorite dog of one of the hunters. In the end, the pack of dogs treed the bear. As the hunters moved in for the kill, however, the bear seemed to exhibit a less ferocious character. The narrator of the story looked up at the bear and thought that "the most urbane simplicity marked his countenance; he seemed of a character that would not have harmed a child, and if I had not seen him a few minutes before boxing the dogs with such vindictive vigor, I would have been willing to have climbed the tree, and put my arms around his neck." The hunter hesitated, unsure whether or not to kill. He stood frozen until another in his party reinterpreted the behavior of the bear. "Shoot him," a friend commanded. "Just see him making fun of us all." A moment later the bear was dead.[60]

Honorable hunters, like duelists, did not want to take unfair advantage of their worthy opponents. The animal had to be given a fair chance to avoid death. There was no pleasure gained nor honor earned in killing a helpless adversary. Only dishonorable hunters who earned their living from killing game, or poor people who hunted only to eat, would kill with quantity rather than quality in mind.[61] William Elliott wrote of a planter who hit a devilfish on the head and thereby stunned it, but felt it would be improper to take advantage of the fish while it lay in such a vulnerable position. Elliot reported that "while he had him *down, as it were, and off his guard,* [the planter] *did not repeat the blow.*"[62] Similarly, Southern men told many stories of fox hunts in which hunters protected treed foxes from dogs and released them so that they could be chased again.[63] Sometimes, men of honor objected to unfair techniques used in hunting foxes. The proper form of the fox hunt involved mounted men with guns and a pack of dogs. It seemed unfair to dig or to smoke foxes out of their holes. This kind of hunting looked more like production, in that it literally involved men with shovels and picks.[64]

Men of honor considered some animals unworthy of being hunted. These animals did not have the kind of characters that enhanced the reputation of their killers. For many Southern sport hunters (but by no means all of them), the opossum and the raccoon fell into this class. One such hunter, an overseer, objected when a stranger referred to an opossum as "a singular creature." He believed that the term "creature" or "critter" was too honorable for an opossum. The hunter informed his naive acquaintance that "a 'Possum, Sir, is not a critter, but a varmint."[65] Similarly, gathering shellfish off the coast of South Carolina was considered undignified work, suitable only for slaves. The death of a crustacean did not bring honor to a hunter. Men of honor did not regard the act of killing such animals as hunting at all. Like the digging of a fox out of his hole, it seemed more like production.[66]

Given all the words of praise that antebellum Southern men bestowed on the animals they deemed worthy of being hunted, one might get the erroneous impression that these men were about to create one of the first animal rights organizations. After all, who respected animals more than Southern men? Who devoted more words of praise to the nobility of bears, the beauty and speed of deer, or the intelligence of foxes? But all the complimentary language about animals did not foreshadow the rise of the ASPCA; it foreshadowed death. It should come as no surprise that the "humanitarian" concern for animal life had its roots in antebellum Northern culture, not in the South.[67] When William Elliott wrote respectfully about the animals he killed, Henry David Thoreau of Massachusetts responded with horror. Thoreau's reaction to Elliott's hunting tales is typical of the reaction of a man outside the culture of honor when confronted with the bloody face of the hunt. He could not understand why any man would hunt for "sport" rather than for "profit or subsistence." Thoreau pondered the issue in an 1861 journal entry. He included several long quotations from Elliott's *Carolina Sports*—descriptions of Elliott's delight at being an "ear-witness" to dogs tearing an animal to pieces, of shooting a wildcat in flight and having him fall fifty feet "into the very jaws of the dogs," and of slitting the throat of a deer. What was the "sport" of all this, Thoreau wondered. Elliott saw himself engaged in battle with wily and dangerous adversaries; he envisioned himself as master of the gateway that led to their death. Elliott thought of himself as a man of honor. Thoreau saw only unnecessary cruelty and murder.[68]

Another way in which the hunt resembled the duel is evidenced by the participants' great need to make their triumphs public. No honor could be bestowed on the man who failed to boast of his exploits. Modesty might have been seen as a virtue among some middle-class, urban men, but not among hunters and duelists.[69] Men of honor were always in fierce competition for glory. Southern hunters wanted to bring home the bodies of their victims in order to display their triumph to the community. On one fishing expedition, William Elliott killed a devilfish, only to see him slip off the harpoon and sink to the bottom. Elliott lamented, "We felt like mariners, who, after a hard conflict, had sunk a gallant adversary at sea—yet saved not a single trophy from the wreck to serve as a memorial of their exploit."[70] Later, the loss of the body of another devilfish prompted Elliott to note that he and his companions "considered our victory somewhat incomplete, because we had not carried off the bodies of the slain."[71] But usually Elliott did bring home the body. He described one hunt for wildcats that ended when "we dashed into town, our horns sounding a flourish as we approach—and our wildcats, flanked by the raccoon, showing forth, somewhat ostentatiously, from the front of the barouche [carriage]."[72]

Another way to brag about the hunt was to give away the meat. Elliott loved to eat the meat of the animals he killed, but he took greater pleasure in watching others do the eating. After describing a triumphant hunt during which he killed four deer, he waxed eloquent on this issue. "How pleasant to eat!" he wrote, but "how much pleasanter to give away! Ah, how such things do win their *hearts*—men's, and *women's* too! My young sporting friends, a word in your ear: the worst you can make of your game, is to eat it yourselves."[73] No clearer statement could be made illustrating the way the compulsion for honor produced a generous gentleman.

Southern hunters also loved to preserve and to display the dead bodies of their greatest kills. Colonel Ashe of South Carolina, for example, killed a large bear and had him preserved. An observer later reported that "the visitor is startled, on entering his country mansion, to find his [the bear's] effigy, erect and life-like, keeping sentry, as it were, in the hall."[74] Similarly, the proliferation of hunting stories in various antebellum magazines and newspapers is evidence of another form of public boasting. The form of these hunting stories was almost always the same. In one way or another, the author was saying to the reader, "I will tell you of a great achievement; it is probably better than anything you have done." Or, as one Opelousas snipe hunter put it at the start of his tale, "Can your sportsmen beat the following hunt. . . ."[75]

The desire to boast about a great kill also clarifies why Southern men preferred to hunt in groups and yet never thought of the hunt as a team sport.[76] Men hunting in groups competed with each other for honor and glory even as they seemed to cooperate. They always considered the cooperation to be superficial. Hunters never thought of a kill as a collective production. One dead animal always meant one triumphant hunter. The purpose of the group was to acknowledge the achievement, not to make it possible. Men who hunted together were not like members of a team who played baseball together. The language of antebellum baseball was the language of group production.[77] Some players might do better or worse than others. Some players might even emerge as "stars." But in the end it was always the "Knickerbockers"—the team—who won or lost the game.

The competition among men who hunted in groups appeared in different ways. Sometimes the men boasted openly. William Elliott once shot two bears with a single discharge. When another member of the group described the kill as a matter of luck, Elliott flew into a rage, cataloguing for all to hear his many other hunting feats. Was it luck, he screamed, that enabled him to kill two deer at a shot, five deer with five single shots, and thirty ducks at one fire?[78] Competition was also evident in the way hunters told stories to each other at the campsite before and after the hunt. Sometimes they struggled to tell the most improbable or funniest story. They always tried to best others in the group with their competitive banter.[79]

Southern hunting clubs often provided a setting for intense competition among hunters. These clubs existed all over the antebellum South. Often, the members constructed a clubhouse, organized regular meeting days, carefully selected the membership, elected officers, and held dinners to which members brought food in periodic rotation. Men in the clubs hunted together, played games together, and ate together. Some of the clubs stopped hunting as wildlife in the area became depleted, but they still continued to meet. The men loved to socialize, to eat and drink together, even if they could no longer kill animals. But whatever activity engaged the group, the members most of all loved to compete with each other in the quest for recognition and honor. The Camden Hunting Club of Georgia had a formal rule that ensured the public humiliation of a poor marksman. It used to fine members who did not hit or kill deer at a distance of less than forty yards when "the opportunity is fair."[80] One of the customs of the Hot and Hot Fish Club of All Saints Parish, South Carolina, was to have the president call in the members by raising a flag to signal the end of the hunt. Then the fishermen would display their catch and tell stories about their triumphs.[81] The St. Thomas Hunting Club of South Carolina had a provision for dividing venison killed by the members: "The Person who brings in the best Venison shall have the first choice, the next best the second choice & so on. The Goodness of the Venison in case of any dispute shall be settled by the President."[82] Club members also competed with each other when it came their turn to furnish or "find" dinner. At times, elaborate rules had to be instituted to suppress this part of the competition, as it had a tendency to get out of hand. The planter Thomas B. Chaplin of South Carolina, for example, took great pride in having brought to the club one day five times as much food as the men could eat.[83] Whenever a member produced a lavish feast, the others felt compelled to top the generosity. Such a custom could easily generate poverty along with honor.

The slave was a frequent character in descriptions and stories of Southern hunts. Male masters and male slaves often ventured into the woods together in search of animals to kill. In a sense, the woods became a space where the men of both races played together, away from the world of women. But the trip into the woods was never a trip from "culture" into "nature"; it was never a journey from slavery into freedom; it was never Huck and Jim away from a brutal world, alone yet together beneath the stars. Black and white men may have bonded in the woods, but never in a way that threatened bondage.

In fact, the hunt supported slavery. In the world of honor, men who killed animals earned the right to master slaves. And one of the central messages of hunting stories in the antebellum South was that only white men killed worthy animals. The behavior of the slave as recounted in these tales repeatedly demonstrated this point. Although the system of segregation meant that there was no mixing of the races *within* Northern baseball teams and games, the Southern hunting group frequently

included blacks as well as whites. But an integrated hunt was not an egalitarian hunt. A hunting party was usually organized in a rigid hierarchy.
Whites killed; blacks watched or acted in support roles. It is ironic that
the segregation of activities like Northern baseball carried a sublimated,
subversive, egalitarian message, since it implied that all people could
do it—separately. Segregation implied equality as well as inequality. But
the integrated hunt in the antebellum South never contained such a subversive message. The hunt demonstrated over and over again why some
men deserved to be masters and others deserved to be slaves. In this
way, stories of the hunt became an important part of the proslavery argument. The defense of Southern slavery did not simply appear in long,
formal essays and speeches. It achieved its most powerful and persuasive
form in discourses often only obliquely related to the explicit defense of
slavery.

Whites in the antebellum South generated virtually no descriptions of
the slave as a hunter. Southern hunting stories portrayed the slave as an
assistant or a witness—often a frightened witness—to a master's ability to
control death. William Elliott's descriptions of hunting in South Carolina
are typical.[84] Slaves rowed the boats that carried masters in pursuit of
devilfish. Slaves were the "drivers" who led dogs into the woods in order
to flush game. Repeatedly, he described slaves as paralyzed with fear at
critical moments of danger. In one tale, Elliott's son fell overboard and
landed briefly on the back of a devilfish. The white men in neighboring
boats immediately saw the danger, but the slaves at the oars seemed unable to act in order to prevent the impending death. As Elliott described
the scene, the slaves "when ordered to pull ahead, stood amazed or stu-
pefied, and dropping their oars and jaws, cried out, 'Great King! Mass
Tom overboard!' So intense was their curiosity to see how the affair
would end, that they entirely forgot how much might depend on their
own efforts. Could they have rowed and looked at the same time, it would
have been very well; but to turn their backs on such a pageant, every
incident of which they were keen on observing, was expecting too much
from African forethought and self-possession!"[85]

Elliott repeated a story with a similar point recounted to him by an "old
and trusted slave." One day many years before, a powerful devilfish had
grabbed the fishing line of the slave and began to pull him and his boat
toward the sea. All the slaves in the boat "threw themselves flat on their
faces, and gave themselves up for lost." According to Elliott, the "old and
trusted slave" later told him that "after lying a long time in this posture . . .
in expectation of death, I gained a little heart, and stealing a look over the
gunwale, *saw iron swim*—there was the anchor playing duck and drake
on the top of the water." Only slowly did he gain the courage to cut the
anchor loose. In Elliott's judgment, listening to this tale told by a slave

many years after the fact, "the earnestness of the old man, and the look of undissembled terror which he wore in telling the story, convince me that he spoke the truth."[86] The meaning Elliott attached to this story seems clear. The slaves became paralyzed with fear at a critical moment. They meekly awaited death. Even many years later, Elliott saw that the slave storyteller was still terrified. The slaves in this story were not masters of death, but its servants.

Elliott also told a story about whale hunting in which a man named Captain George decided to pursue whales in a skiff and needed two "boys" to row it for him. "'But, maussa,' said a slave named Pompey, 'I can't go close dat ting in maussa new boat anyhow. He tail strong as steam engine, and he knock the boat all to shivers.'" Elliott's purpose in recounting this exchange was to enhance the position of Captain George as a man who did not fear death. Captain George picked another "boy" to take the place of the frightened slave. Elliott tells us nothing about the bravery of this other "boy," but only about Pompey's fear.[87]

Elliott described his behavior during a shark attack with a similar point in mind. He had waded into waters off the South Carolina coast in order to fish. Behind him stood his slave Cain, holding his spear and a wicker basket of bait. Suddenly Cain emitted an "exclamation of terror" and Elliott turned to see a large shark blocking their escape to the shore. "My spear," he said, calmly and forcefully, to his petrified slave. "Keep close to me and shout when I do." Other sharks gathered nearby. "Repeating my order to Cain, and grasping my spear in both hands, I rushed upon the leading shark, and struck it down violently across his nose—shouting at the same time, at the top of my voice—while Cain, in a perfect agony of fear, gave a loud yell, and fell at full length in the water."[88] Then the sharks retreated—undoubtedly well aware (like the readers of this tale) that one of the men they had attacked was a master and the other was a slave.

III

Games of chance also flourished among the honorable men of the antebellum South. They most frequently bet on cards. They also gambled on dice, cockfights, horse races, and virtually anything else that involved competition. During the Civil War, the spirit of gaming was so intense among Confederate soldiers that when they lacked the usual opportunities for wagering, they placed bets on the swiftness of small boats with paper sails, and on the speed and fighting ability of lice. Southern men of honor wagered with a frequency and an intensity widely noted by visitors to the region. The forms of gambling varied over time and according to geography and social class, but the fact of gambling remained a constant. Although all Southern states passed laws against what they considered gambling excesses and abuses, and some Southern men objected on religious grounds, this opposition did little to reduce gambling in the society. Gambling was a serious form of play for these men.[89]

The best way to begin to appreciate the connections between gambling and honor is to examine closely the sharp contrast between a Southern gentleman's powerful love of gambling and his equally powerful hatred of professional gamblers. Consider the hatred of professionals. The original insult that prompted Henry Clay to challenge John Randolph to a duel was the charge that he was a "blackleg"—an unscrupulous professional gambler. Edmund Ruffin recounted an experience in his diary that illustrates a similar dislike. Once when he was in Washington, D.C., he was compelled to share a hotel room with a stranger. Ruffin reported that his roommate "did not come in until nearly daybreak this morning—& I hear from a friend who occupies the next room, that such has been his habit since he has been here, about a week—& that he infers he is a professional gambler. So I will take care to avoid the usual intimacy of compulsory room-mates."[90] Given such attitudes, it is no surprise that Southern states in the antebellum era frequently fined or banished professional gamblers.[91]

One of the most extreme attacks on professional gamblers in the South occurred in Vicksburg, Mississippi, in 1835. The citizens lynched five gamblers and exiled the rest. The incident began at a July 4 celebration involving members of a volunteer militia company and other townspeople. A rowdy and drunken professional gambler named Cabler insulted an officer and assaulted a volunteer while the latter two were trying to maintain order during the delivery of celebratory toasts. The gambler was ejected from the festivities. When members of the volunteer company moved to the center of town in order to perform some practice drills, they received word that Cabler was returning to kill one of the men who had been active in his expulsion. A group of townspeople chased and captured Cabler and discovered that he was carrying a loaded pistol, a large knife, and a dagger. They took him into the woods, tied him to a tree, whipped, tarred, and feathered him, and ordered his expulsion from the city.[92]

This incident triggered a more general and even more violent attack on all professional gamblers. Vicksburg citizens gathered that night, passed a resolution, and posted notices ordering all gamblers out of the city within twenty-four hours. The vast majority sensed the danger and immediately left. When the deadline had passed, several hundred townspeople began to move from house to house, searching for stragglers and burning abandoned gambling equipment. One house, however, contained a group of armed resisters. The mob surrounded it and the threatened gamblers fired into the crowd, killing a man described as "universally beloved and respected." The infuriated townspeople captured and hanged all five men who had resisted, "collected all the faro-tables into a pile, and burnt them." The dead gamblers dangled on display all night; they were cut down and buried in a ditch the next morning. The citizens of Vicksburg were proud of what they had done. They institutionalized their actions and formed themselves into the Anti-Gambling Society, "pledging their lives, fortunes, and sacred honours for the suppression of gambling, and the punishment and expulsion of gamblers."[93] This Vicksburg expulsion and lynching triggered an antigambling hysteria all along the Mississippi River. *Niles' Register* reported boatloads of displaced professional gamblers meandering up and down the Mississippi River in search of new homes.[94]

Why should men who so loved to gamble hate professional gamblers with such intensity? Part of the answer certainly involves the criminality of the latter group. In a city like Vicksburg gamblers were thought to be responsible for robbery and murder, and they repeatedly cheated "naive" young men, fleecing them by employing elaborate trickery and deceit. One historian has suggested that the Vicksburg lynchings symbolized the transition of a wild and lawless frontier town into a respectable city.[95] But the intensity of the hatred, and the breadth of its stretch over time and space in the South, suggests that the professional gambler touched a nerve in the culture. It was a sensitivity that reached from Edmund Ruffin's hotel bedroom in Washington to the shores of the Mississippi River. Although men of honor who gambled sometimes needed professionals to supply the equipment and setting for their games, they hated the professionals for mocking the values that gave meaning to their play. Professionals seemed to play a perverted form of their game. To understand the perceived perversion of the professionals, one must first understand why gambling seemed so attractive to gentlemen.

For Southern men of honor, gambling was closely related to dueling. The duel, in fact, can be seen as a form of gambling for extremely high stakes. An insulted man wagered his life as a way to demonstrate mastery over death. The duel was the type of gamble in which a man could achieve the highest honor because he assumed the greatest risk. All other gambling activities involved honor to the extent that their stakes approached the stakes of the duel. The best gamble was the gamble that risked everything. The historian T. H. Breen has noted the high-stakes gambling, especially on quarter-horse racing, that developed among the Virginia gentry in the late seventeenth and early eighteenth centuries. In their drive for honor, the great planters seemed to be willing to venture stakes of a size they would never have dreamed of risking in normal business transactions. The higher the stakes, the closer they came to risking everything.[96]

Quarter-horse racing eventually lost its dominant role as a sport among the Virginia gentry, but high-stakes gambling continued in other forms among Southern men of honor. Before Andrew Jackson was thirty years old he had risked all he owned on two separate occasions. Although he dabbled in games of dice as a youth and played cards throughout his life, his favorite gambling activity ultimately became the racing of Thoroughbred horses. For Jackson, the high stakes of the duel and the high stakes of racing were on a continuum. In 1806, the two activities literally merged when a dispute over the proper conduct of a horse race became a dispute on the dueling ground.[97] Many years later, Jackson advised his nephew that "you must risque to win." It was advice he had long followed both on and off the racetrack.[98]

Nineteenth-century men of honor felt compelled to risk everything in many different fields. They did it at tables while playing cards.[99] They did it at racetracks. They did it around cockpits. They did it on dueling grounds. And they did it in political contests and military battles. This compulsion was evident when Edmund Ruffin boarded a steamboat that approached Fort Sumter in the moments before the opening of the Civil War, hoping to be shot at because he "greatly coveted the distinction & *eclat.*" It was present when James Henry Hammond engaged in a dueling encounter as well as when he bred and raced Thoroughbred horses. It was apparent when James Johnston Pettigrew chose to face yellow fever in the South Carolina low country.[100] It showed up at Gettysburg and on other Civil War battlefields. When Confederate strategists repeatedly preferred to attack rather than to assume a more prudent defensive posture, they were only giving expression to another form of their powerful cultural impulse toward risk. It was a losing strategy—but it was a strategy few Southern gentlemen could resist.[101] The Confederacy may well have lost the Civil War as a result of lessons learned at Southern card tables and racetracks.

Gambling encounters among gentlemen also echoed some of the forms of dueling encounters. A gamble and a duel each involved a moment when a challenge to a contest was offered and accepted. This may have been done implicitly or informally when men sat down to play cards together, but a gambling challenge sometimes assumed a more formal shape in such activities as high-stakes Thoroughbred horse racing. In newspapers and sporting magazines, the owners of horses often issued challenges. One 1835 issue of the *American Turf Register and Sporting Magazine* contained the following challenge: "Have at ye, *Shark, Trifle, Monmouth, Mingo, Clara Howard, Henry, Archy,* and the rest! The editor of the Spirit of the Times is authorized to announce to the world in general, and the crack nags of the north in particular, that the owners of *Miss Medley* will be glad to run her against each or all of you, or any other horse in the United States, at Augusta, Geo. Who will first raize this *glaive* and do battle for the honour of his sire?"[102] An 1836 issue of the same magazine contained the following typical acceptance to a challenge: "In the Nashville Republican I see you propose to run a race: your mare Missletoe, &c. against any four year old raised in Tennessee, two mile heats, for $1,000 a side, half forfeit. I will meet you at Nashville, and run my bay filly, four years old, by imported Leviathan, dam by Archy, on the ninth day of June next, over the Nashville track, for $1,000 a side, half forfeit, and I will pay you $100 for your expenses coming there; or you can have the race for $2,000, if you prefer it. . . . I shall address this to you at Georgetown, Ken. and also publish it in the Nashville Republican, and send you a copy."[103] The form of this challenge and acceptance, even including the conditions of the match, was precisely the one that marked most duels. Men of honor thrust themselves forward, announcing their willingness to assume the risk of a contest.

Gambling, like dueling, involved issues of respect for the words of men. A bet was nothing more than a prediction of the future. In a betting contest, men of honor used language to describe a world that did not yet exist. Some time in the future, a betting man suggested, my horse will beat your horse. When the contest ended, some men would be shown to be liars: their words would be publicly demonstrated to be inconsistent with reality. Others would be shown to have told the truth: their words would become worthy of respect.[104] To be a man of good judgment was to be a man whose words became accepted as true. Each gambling contest was a battle over who was a liar. Therefore, each gambling contest bestowed honor or humiliation.

This concern for the respect accorded a man's word is evident in the public sporting correspondence of William J. Minor of Natchez, Mississippi, an enthusiast of Thoroughbred horse racing. Minor was a prolific correspondent of the antebellum sporting journal *Spirit of the Times*.[105] He offered his opinion on many topics. Sometimes he objected to letters sent by other writers full of "humbug, boasting, and puffing" about horses from their states or regions. In this way, he repeatedly sought to unmask his competitors. Minor also passionately defended or attacked the achievements of individual horses. One of his most virulent outbursts concerned his denigration of a Virginia horse named Boston. Minor wrote that Boston "lacked heart, and refused to exert himself when he became a little tired," and that he had a lung defect called "the tires." These comments became part of a two-year series of emotional letters from Minor and from many men who disagreed with him.[106] Minor demanded respect for his word on turf matters, and so did those with whom he argued. All these men sought the validation of their words through the victories of the horses they had praised in their letters and supported in their betting.

The connection between gambling and the respect accorded a man's word is also illustrated by an 1828 description of a bet on a horse race in Natchez, Mississippi. At the center of the incident, according to an eyewitness, was a pompous man, a "*ferocious* looking gentleman, with his overcoat thrown far back upon his shoulders—his arms suspended to his vest by his thumbs—his hat stuck upon the side of his head at an angle of about forty-five degrees—his boots fastened to a pair of spurs of about half a pound's weight, . . . and the whole man hung to a pair of enormous whiskers . . . in a word he was a '*Georgia-man,*' and a Major, *of course.*" He was a man who thrust himself forward not only through his appearance but also through his language. His bet became a part of his thrust. As the horses were brought onto the field this "Georgia man" arrogantly proposed a bet to the crowd: "Paul Pry [one of the horses] against the field." Who should take up the challenge but "a little Dutchman," who bet his horse, saddle, and bridle, or rather, as the narrator described it in a Dutch accent, his "horsh shattel and britel." Clearly, the pompous major was a perfect target for humiliation at the hands of the Dutchman. The first part of the humiliation came as Paul Pryor took the lead. The self-assured major asked the Dutchman if he would like to increase the bet. The Dutchman answered that he had no more to bet, but that he would bet his shirt if he believed that the ruffled shirtfront of the major was more than a "dickey"—that is, more than a false front. And "with great familiarity he applied his fingers to the Georgia-man's ruffle, that projected some four or five inches—and to his utter confusion, forth it came—zounds and death, it was a *dickey!*" The Georgia man's clothing had been shown to project a lie. The humiliation continued as a Yankee, "a raw-boned youth from the land of steady habits," joined in the laughter at the exposure of the major's false shirtfront. Another layer of humiliation was added when the major's horse failed to win the race. His prediction of the future had been shown to be as false as his shirt.

Later, as the eyewitness rode his horse home, he came upon the Dutchman "with an extra horse and the Major's coat thrown across the saddle" just as they passed the major walking on foot, "knee deep in the mud." The humiliation continued as the Dutchman offered the major a ride "in a tone of perfect good nature, but [with a] sarcastic twist of the mouth." The major cursed him and the Dutchman "started off with a brisk trot, and the Major was not a little annoyed by the splash from his horses heels." Then up came the Yankee on his horse, who shouted an insult and passed the major at full gallop, covering him with mud.[107] A bit of mud attached to every man who lost a bet.

But most gambling gentlemen tasted only briefly the sting of humiliation associated with losing a bet. By and large, gambling served to bind men of honor together rather than to split them apart. In fact, the meaning of a gambling exchange closely resembled dueling and gift exchanges in the way it helped define the community of gentlemen. Honorable men were supposed to gamble with their social equals, just as they were expected to confine their duels and reciprocal gift exchanges to social equals. Many antebellum Southern laws specifically excluded slaves and free blacks from gambling.[108] A large part of the reason for this exclusion certainly involved the desire of whites to reduce thievery. Since slaves could legally own no property, they could only gamble with the property of their masters. But this does not fully explain the laws that prohibited whites from gambling with free blacks, or blacks from gambling among themselves. Those laws resembled British laws that confined gambling to the nobility except during the twelve days of Christmas, or colonial laws that prohibited common people from gambling.[109] Gambling was supposed to be the preserve of the members of the dominant class because it allowed them to demonstrate the special virtue associated with that class: the willingness to assume risk.

Moreover, gambling implied an equality among the participants that would have threatened the social order if it had been permitted to cross racial lines. In a gambling contest men of honor played at domination; they played at who would be the master and who would be the slave. Two men matched their horses against each other. One won and the other lost. The winner demanded a payment from the loser. It was a small taste of domination for the winner; it was a small bit of mud kicked on the loser. But the inequality usually lasted only a moment. The loser paid the winner and the obligation was terminated. This analysis illuminates William J. Grayson's claim that "a gambling debt is a debt of honour, but a debt due a tradesman is not."[110] The gambling debt must be paid in order to bring the social relationship back to equality. A game that contained such meanings would make no sense when played between men who were not equal. What would be the thrill of briefly dominating a man you already dominated? Laws prohibited blacks and whites from gambling with each other because every gambling encounter was rooted in equality. In the beginning, two equal parties assumed the same risk; in the end, equilibrium was reestablished by payment of the debt. When the equilibrium was not restored, it was clear that the loser had become dishonored. This is what the Virginia planter Landon Carter meant when he lamented the excessive gambling losses of his son, who had become "every man's man but his own and his father's." "No affrican is so great a Slave," he believed, as the man who gambled away his financial independence.[111]

Gambling also resembled the duel (as well as Southern electoral politics) in the way its participants struggled to demonstrate their selflessness even as they passionately sought victory. This is a paradox at the heart of the gambling of Southern gentlemen. On the one hand, it was important for these men to win. When Andrew Jackson said "You must risque to win," he had little doubt that winning was the goal. A man of honor loved to display the symbols of victory. The monetary gains of a successful gamble were the material manifestations of the honor that had been bestowed. Although men could not display their monetary winnings the way they displayed the heads of animals they had hunted, they took pleasure in letting the world know about their great gambling victories.[112]

Yet at the same time, a gamble was about a lack of concern for victory and its material rewards. After all, gambling demonstrated a willingness to assume risk and the possibility of loss. It was a version of the way a dueling gentleman demonstrated his lack of interest in the material world by risking his life. The willingness to take such risks conveyed a lack of attachment to the material placed in jeopardy, whether it was a life or a sum of money. In fact, one of the character traits that was assumed to assure victory in these encounters was the lack of an overt attachment to victory. Victory came to those who did not seek it. Consider a description of one 1836 race at the Plaquemine Jockey Club in Louisiana. Storm was the favored horse, and he had just won the first heat. As the horses moved to the starting line for the second heat, an observer noted that "Storm, eyeing his competitors with the most ineffable contempt, came up champing his bit with all the haughtiness and proud bearing of one who displayed the victor in his tread—whilst Randolph and Mexican slid silently by with that meek and unassuming air, which is so characteristic of true merit." Needless to say, it was one of the meek and unassuming horses, Randolph, that was the victor. The contest ultimately was to be decided in a heat that pitted Mexican against Randolph. In this final confrontation, "Mexican, as usual, was perfectly cool, but Randolph bowing his neck and restlessly mouthing his bit, showed that he was very anxious to *be off.*" Mexican won the race, "fulfilling to the letter, the prediction of the *knowing ones.*"[113] Although the display of "cool" may have hidden a real desire to win, to lose composure was to face certain defeat. This was parallel to the way a proper duelist demonstrated a lack of concern for his life while having bullets shot at him, or the way many successful Southern political leaders displayed a lack of interest in their election before they won office, or the way masters exploited slave labor while they presented themselves as generous gift givers. Men who showed an interest in victory or gain, like the horses that chomped at the bit, were considered certain to fail. They ended like the blustering Georgia major—with mud splattered on their clothing.

One reason Southern gentlemen who gambled hated professional gamblers was that professional gamblers did not wish to risk everything. In fact, the goal of the professional was to minimize risk, even by cheating.[114] For a professional, the best bet was a sure bet—which was no bet at all for a Southern man of honor. The gambling of the professional was unrelated to the gambling of the duelist, the man of honor who risked everything as a demonstration of mastery. Moreover, professional gamblers hungered after monetary wealth; their play was more about greed than about honor. The professional looked on gambling as a business. Robert Bailey, an early-nineteenth-century gambler, nicely summarized the distinction between the "sportsman," who was a "high minded liberal gentleman, attached to amusements regardless of loss or gain; his motto is honor, his shield his judgment," and the professional, who engaged in "the *business* of general gaming, destitute of all honor and integrity" (emphasis added).[115] The Vicksburg citizens who hanged gamblers similarly criticized the greed, as well as the immorality, of the professionals, describing them as "destitute of all sense of moral obligation—unconnected with society by any of its ordinary ties, and intent only on the gratification of their avarice."[116]

Finally, since the goal of the professional was to make money, it was important for him to conduct his games with "strangers" rather than with equals whose position was identifiable in the social structure. He was not interested in permanent relations with the men with whom he gambled. Whereas the gambling of a man of honor was rooted in the constantly recurring equilibrium of the players, the professional gambler sought the disequilibrium associated with profit. The professional gambler was an itinerant because he removed money from the community. He constantly needed to find new sources for his income, or to live in a place such as New Orleans, where the new sources came to him. That is why professional gamblers flourished on the riverboats of the Mississippi or led lives that moved them from town to town.

This understanding of the way professional gamblers mocked the values of men of honor helps solve a peculiar puzzle associated with the 1835 hanging of gamblers in Vicksburg. At the very moment the citizens of Vicksburg executed and expelled gamblers, their neighbors in Hinds and Madison Counties lynched a group of whites and blacks suspected of plotting a slave rebellion. These simultaneous events seem connected, and yet neither contemporaries nor historians have been able to explain the linkage. An 1836 history and compilation of documents associated with the capture of "the great western land pirate" John A. Murrell, along with a description of Murrell's "Mystic Clan" and its relation to the Mississippi slave insurrection plot, also included a contemporary account of the hanging of the Vicksburg gamblers. Clearly, the compiler of this volume sensed a link between the events. Yet he noted that "the difficulty with the gamblers . . . was unconnected with the insurrection, except the high state of excitement that pervaded the whole southern country at that time, which had led the citizens to deal more rigorously with all offenders."[117] No modern historian has suggested any basis for a deeper relationship.[118]

But given the meaning of gambling in Southern culture, it becomes clear that all the white men hanged in Mississippi during early July 1835—those accused of plotting the slave insurrection as well as those accused of professional gambling—were viewed the same way by their accusers. First, like the gamblers of Vicksburg, the white men who were accused of plotting the slave insurrection were strangers in their communities. In the official description of the insurrection trials written by the "Committee of Safety," they were portrayed as relatively recent arrivals in the state, who had showed up with several newcomers from the North.[119] But more important than their shallow roots in the community was their position on the edge of the social structure. Nearly all the major plotters were identified as "steam doctors"—fraudulent practitioners of an alternative medical therapy. Moreover, they were all seen to have frequent conversations with plantation slaves, but little contact with their white neighbors. Joshua Cotton was "not liked by the citizens of Livingston, with whom he had no social intercourse." William Saunders's "deportment was such as to induce his employer to discharge him." The gentlemen who shared a boardinghouse room with A. L. Donovan asked him to leave. Ruel Blake "could claim few or none as friends."[120] Moreover, the white "slave insurrectionists" were portrayed as men unwilling to assume risk and as men primarily motivated by greed. They were linked to the mysterious "Mystic Clan" of "land pirates" who engaged in acts of thievery and murder by means of a vast conspiracy of stealth and fraud rather than open confrontation. "Steam doctors" were seen as lazy men who picked the pockets of their neighbors. Joshua Cotton was a man who had been "detected in many low tricks, and attempts to swindle." He confessed that his object in instigating rebellion among the slaves "was not for the purpose of liberating them, but for plunder." The neighbors of William Saunders often saw him "lurking about" in a suspicious manner. He had previously been sentenced to a Tennessee penitentiary for stealing. Albe Dean was seen "prowling about the plantations." Ruel Blake "had been a pirate."[121]

In other words, the gamblers of Vicksburg and the men accused of plotting a slave insurrection in Madison and Hinds Counties were the same type of men. They were strangers who sought money through stealth and trickery. They did not have to engage in plots together to represent the same threat to the core values and institutions of Southern society. When the members of the Livingston Committee of Safety described professional gamblers as "destitute of all sense of moral obligation—unconnected with society by any of its ordinary ties, and intent only on the gratification of their avarice," they could just as well have been describing the slave insurrectionists hanged by their neighbors.[122]

The distinction between the gambling engaged in by a professional and the gambling engaged in by a man of honor also helps explain why a risk taker like P. T. Barnum did not seem honorable in the eyes of Southern gentlemen. Barnum and other nineteenth-century entrepreneurs seemed as fond of risk as Andrew Jackson, William J. Minor, James Henry Hammond, Edmund Ruffin, and other gentlemen in the culture of honor. Barnum fully subscribed to Jackson's advice about risk. Early in his life he abandoned the security of a salaried position in order to assume the risks, and potentially greater rewards, of entrepreneurship.[123] Like Andrew Jackson, P. T. Barnum risked and lost all his money more than once during his career. What distinguished the gamble of the marketplace—the gamble of P. T. Barnum—from the gamble of gentlemen who bet on Thoroughbred horse races or dueled with each other? For one thing, the marketplace was a world of strangers— people with undetermined positions in the social structure. Barnum played with anyone; a man of honor gambled only with other men of honor. Moreover, entrepreneurs like Barnum assumed risk for the purpose of making money. Risk for such men was never an end in itself, but only a necessary means to the acquisition of money. Barnum sought to reduce risk whenever possible, which was consistent with his desire for wealth. For men of honor, the money that flowed to them from a successful gamble was not an end, but a symbol of honor earned by assuming risk and having one's word and judgment confirmed. Barnum would never gamble his life in a duel, for the duel was a gamble with no possibility of monetary gain. But the gamble of a gentleman involved honor to the extent that it approached the gamble of the duel. The perfect gamble for a man of honor allowed him to demonstrate his mastery of death; the perfect gamble for an entrepreneur allowed him to earn a living. Death was the subject when men of honor gambled; life was the subject when men of the market gambled.

The language spoken by antebellum Southern men of honor was dense with meaning. To pull noses was to comment on lies; to exchange gifts was to define community; to gamble on horses was to speak about death and about politics; and to duel was make statements about lies, gifts, gambling, politics, and death. Moreover, each of these conversations— and many others recounted in this book—was simultaneously also about slavery.

It is a humbling experience for a historian to attempt to map the complex associations characteristic of a language that has passed from the world. Such a project has no clear beginning or end point since language has a self-referential quality that precludes linear analysis. But I hope that I have established enough associations to have created an elementary primer of the language of honor. I hope that I have listened carefully to the men who once ruled a world.

NOTES

1. On dueling and other affairs of honor in the South, see Dickson D. Bruce, *Violence and Culture in the Antebellum South* (Austin: University of Texas Press, 1979); John Hope Franklin, *The Militant South* (New York: Beacon Press, 1956); Steven M. Stowe, "The 'Touchiness' of the Gentleman Planter: The Sense of Esteem and Continuity in the Antebellum South," *Psychohistory Review* 8 (winter 1979): 6–17; Steven M. Stowe, *Intimacy and Power in the Old South: Ritual in the Lives of the Planters* (Baltimore: Johns Hopkins University Press, 1987); William Oliver Stevens, *Pistols at Ten Paces: The Story of the Code of Honor in America* (Boston: Houghton Mifflin, 1940); Jack K. Williams, *Dueling in the Old South: Vignettes of Social History* (College Station: Texas A & M University Press, 1980); Elliott J. Gorn, "'Gouge and Bite, Pull Hair and Scratch': The Social Significance of Fighting in the Southern Backcountry," *American Historical Review* 90 (February 1985): 18–43; and Kenneth S. Greenberg, *Masters and Statesmen: The Political Culture of American Slavery* (Baltimore: Johns Hopkins University Press, 1985), 23–41.

2. Bertram Wyatt-Brown, *Southern Honor: Ethics and Behavior in the Old South* (Oxford: Oxford University Press, 1982), describes the system of honor with special reference to the Southern interior and southwestern slave states. But he believes that the values of honor were not confined to a class or region within the South. Edward L. Ayers, *Vengeance and Justice: Crime and Punishment in the Nineteenth-Century American South* (New York: Oxford University Press, 1984), also agrees that the language of honor was widely spoken all over the South.

3. Franklin, *Militant South*; Ayers, *Vengeance and Justice*; Stowe, *Intimacy and Power*; Wyatt-Brown, *Southern Honor*.

CHAPTER ONE
THE NOSE, THE LIE, AND THE DUEL

1. "Language" as used in this book does not mean vernacular language. It is closer to what Michel Foucault means by "discourse"—but I hesitate to use the term discourse because I do not accept many of Foucault's assumptions about language. Michel Foucault, *The Order of Things: An Archaeology of the Human Sciences* (New York: Vintage, 1973); see the discussion of "language" and "discourse" in John E. Toews, "Intellectual History after the Linguistic Turn: The Anatomy of Meaning and the Irreducibility of Experience," *American Historical Review* 92, no. 4 (October 1987): 889–93. See also *Modern European Intellectual History: Reappraisals and New Perspectives*, ed. Dominick LaCapra and Steven L. Klein (Ithaca, N.Y.: Cornell University Press, 1982), esp. 137–52.

2. The approach used here has been influenced by a number of works in intellectual history, linguistics, and ethnography. Of greatest importance are Clifford Geertz, *The Interpretation of Cultures* (New York: Basic Books, 1973); Clifford

Geertz, *Local Knowledge: Further Essays in Interpretive Anthropology* (New York: Basic Books, 1983); Clifford Geertz, *Works and Lives: The Anthropologist as Author* (Stanford, Calif.: Stanford University Press, 1988); James Clifford and George E. Marcus, *Writing Culture: The Poetics and Politics of Ethnography* (Berkeley and Los Angeles: University of California Press, 1986); John Higham and Paul K. Conkin, eds., *New Directions in American Intellectual History* (Baltimore: Johns Hopkins University Press, 1979); Joan Wallace Scott, *Gender and the Politics of History* (New York: Columbia University Press, 1988); Jonathan Culler, *The Pursuit of Signs: Semiotics, Literature, Deconstruction* (Ithaca, N.Y.: Cornell University Press, 1981); Jonathan Culler, *On Deconstruction: Theory and Criticism after Structuralism* (Ithaca, N.Y.: Cornell University Press, 1982); LaCapra and Klein, *Modern European Intellectual History*; and Dominick LaCapra, *Rethinking Intellectual History: Texts, Contexts, and Language* (Ithaca, N.Y.: Cornell University Press, 1983).

3. Neil Harris, *Humbug: The Art of P. T. Barnum* (Chicago: University of Chicago Press, 1973), 62–67.

4. *Charleston Courier*, January 21, 1843.

5. *Charleston Mercury*, January 20, 1843.

6. Ibid., February 1, 1843.

7. Ibid.

8. *Charleston Courier*, February 6, 1843.

9. Ibid., February 1, 1843.

10. Ibid., February 6, 1843.

11. Ibid.

12. *Charleston Mercury*, March 31, 1843.

13. *Charleston Courier*, February 1, 1843.

14. See especially the discussion of this issue in Drew Faust, *A Sacred Circle: The Dilemma of the Intellectual in the Old South, 1840–1860* (Baltimore: Johns Hopkins University Press, 1977).

15. For discussions of honor that emphasize similar values in other societies, see the essays in J. G. Peristiany, ed., *Honour and Shame: The Values of Mediterranean Society* (London: Weidenfeld and Nicolson, 1965); Christopher Boehm, *Blood Revenge: The Enactment and Management of Conflict in Montenegro and Other Tribal Societies* (Philadelphia: University of Pennsylvania Press, 1984); Stanley Brandes, *Metaphors of Masculinity: Sex and Status in Andalusian Folklore* (Philadelphia: University of Pennsylvania Press, 1980); Lila Abu-Lughod, *Veiled Sentiments: Honor and Poetry in a Bedouin Society* (Berkeley and Los Angeles: University of California Press, 1986); and Orlando Patterson, *Slavery and Social Death: A Comparative Study* (Cambridge, Mass.: Harvard University Press, 1982). Although there are similarities between the language of honor in the South and that used in many of these other societies, the vocabulary and the webs of associations differ enough so that the language would not immediately be transparent to a Southern white male who happened to visit.

16. On the significance of statesmanship in Southern culture, see Greenberg, *Masters and Statesmen*, 3–22.

17. Southern intellectuals could achieve honor only by entering the world of

statesmen. That may explain their attraction to the proslavery argument. See Faust, *Sacred Circle*, 112–31.

18. Greenberg, *Masters and Statesmen*; Williams, *Dueling in the Old South*, 1–12.

19. On the form of the ideal duel, see John Lyde Wilson, *The Code of Honor; or, Rules for the Government of Principals and Seconds in Duelling* (Charleston, S.C.: Thomas J. Eccles, 1838).

20. Quoted in Robert Baldick, *The Duel: A History of Dueling* (London: Chapman and Hall, 1965), 33. Baldick also notes that Touchstone in William Shakespeare's *As You Like It* lists the various causes of quarrels among gentlemen. He notes that one can avoid a fight for all causes except "the lie direct."

21. Quoted in Williams, *Dueling in the Old South*, 22–23.

22. For a full description of Barnum's career, see Harris, *Humbug*.

23. Quoted in ibid., 12–13.

24. In fact, Barnum himself opposed the duel and always felt that he was entering some strange and foreign land when he traveled in the South. For examples of Barnum's mockery of the duel, see P. T. Barnum, *Struggles and Triumphs; or, Forty Years' Recollections of P. T. Barnum*, ed. Carl Bode (1855; reprint, New York: Viking Penguin, 1981), 86, 138. On Barnum's lack of success in the South, see Harris, *Humbug*, 67. For a more extensive discussion of the way Barnum's attitude toward lies ultimately became widely shared in American middle-class culture, see Karen Halttunen, *Confidence Men and Painted Women: A Study of Middle-Class Culture in America, 1830–1870* (New Haven: Yale University Press, 1982).

25. For the idea that Southerners could engage in trade without fully adopting the bourgeois values associated with men of trade, see Eugene D. Genovese, *Roll, Jordan, Roll: The World the Slaves Made* (New York: Pantheon Books, 1974), and Elizabeth Fox-Genovese, *Within the Plantation Household: Black and White Women of the Old South* (Chapel Hill: University of North Carolina Press, 1988).

26. The lie was so central to the slave experience in the eyes of both masters and slaves that virtually every Southern primary and secondary source could be used in illustration. For specific examples, see Gilbert Osofsky, ed., *Puttin' On Ole Massa: The Slave Narratives of Henry Bibb, William Wells Brown, and Solomon Northrup* (New York: Harper and Row, 1969), and Deborah Gray White, *Ar'n't I a Woman? Female Slaves in the Plantation South* (New York: W. W. Norton, 1985).

27. Barnum, *Struggles and Triumphs*, 77–78.

28. Luckily, in this case, Witherspoon never issued the challenge. The record does not reveal the reasons. See J. Marion Sims, *The Story of My Life* (1884; reprint, New York: Da Capo Press, 1968), 100–102. The episode is a good example of the way humor can be used to establish a relationship of superiority. For examples of this in other cultures, see Brandes, *Metaphors of Masculinity*, 58, 115–28.

29. Sims, *Story of My Life*, 110–11.

30. Ibid., 73–77.

31. Benjamin Franklin, quoted in Stevens, *Pistols at Ten Paces*, 6.

32. Timothy Dwight, *The Folly, Guilt, and Mischiefs of Duelling: A Sermon*

Preached in the College Chapel at New Haven, on the Sabbath Preceding the Annual Commencement, September, 1804 (Hartford: Hudson and Goodwin, 1805), 9.

33. Lorenzo Sabine, *Notes on Duels and Duelling, Alphabetically Arranged, with a Preliminary Historical Essay* (Boston: Crosby, Nichol, 1856), 46. Simms's response is quoted on 317.

34. Evarts B. Greene, "The Code of Honor in Colonial and Revolutionary Times, with Special Reference to New England," in *Publications of The Colonial Society of Massachusetts* (Boston: Colonial Society of Massachusetts, 1927), 26:375, 387.

35. Gorn, " 'Gouge and Bite, Pull Hair and Scratch' "; Ayers, *Vengeance and Justice*, 9–10.

36. Gorn, " 'Gouge and Bite, Pull Hair and Scratch,' " 43.

37. See, for example, John W. Blassingame, ed., *Slave Testimony: Two Centuries of Letters, Speeches, Interviews, and Autobiographies* (Baton Rouge: Louisiana State University Press, 1977), 632.

38. "On Noses," *Russell's Magazine* 3, no. 6 (September 1958): 538.

39. Drew R. McCoy first brought the Rives-Gilmer dispute to my attention and then shared a draft of his own remarks on the affair; this material was subsequently published in Drew R. McCoy, *The Last of the Fathers: James Madison and the Republican Legacy* (Cambridge: Cambridge University Press, 1989).

40. The analogy extends to the way both men "care[d] not a whit" about the real nature of the object itself. Gilmer's honor would not have been offended if Rives had simply voted for the Force Bill. In fact, in his letters to Rives he makes it quite clear that their political differences alone would not have destroyed their friendship. The real grievance was that, because Gilmer had spoken for Rives, Rives's betrayal had led men to distrust Gilmer's word.

41. The relevant correspondence on which this and subsequent descriptions are based can be found in the *Richmond Enquirer*, July 26, 1833.

42. Ibid.

43. Quoted in *National Intelligencer*, May 13, 1833.

44. *Richmond Enquirer*, May 17, 1833; *National Intelligencer*, May 8, 1833.

45. *Richmond Enquirer*, May 17, 1833.

46. Ibid., May 14, 1833.

47. Quoted in Robert V. Remini, *Andrew Jackson and the Course of American Democracy, 1833–1845* (New York: Harper and Row, 1984), 3:61.

48. Ibid.

49. Ibid., 61–62.

50. Remini, *Andrew Jackson*, 61; *Richmond Enquirer*, May 14, 1833.

51. Peggy Eaton, *The Autobiography of Peggy Eaton* (New York: Charles Scribners Sons, 1932), 43–44.

52. Pertinax Placid, "A Tale of a Nose," *Southern Literary Messenger* 1, no. 8 (April 1835): 445–48.

53. Ibid., 447.

54. Ibid., 448.

55. Ibid.

CHAPTER TWO
MASKS AND SLAVERY

1. Sims, *Story of My Life,* 121. Because Sims wrote the description of this incident long after he moved from South Carolina, it should be kept in mind that the dialogue quoted here is certainly not precisely accurate. Sims probably created the dialogue as a way of conveying the meaning of conversations much less clearly remembered. But my analysis of this incident does not depend on the precision of Sims's memory.

2. Ibid., 122.

3. Ibid., 125.

4. See chapter 1.

5. Jefferson Davis, *The Rise and Fall of the Confederate Government* (New York: Thomas Yoseloff, 1958), 2:702; Mark E. Neely, Jr., Harold Holzer, and Gabor S. Boritt, *The Confederate Image: Prints of the Lost Cause* (Chapel Hill: University of North Carolina Press, 1987), 94.

6. Quoted in Howard T. Dimick, "The Capture of Jefferson Davis," *Journal of Mississippi History* 9, no. 4 (October 1947): 244.

7. United States War Department, *The War of the Rebellion: A Compilation of the Official Records of the Union and Confederate Armies,* ser. 1, vol. 49, part 2 (Washington, D.C.: Government Printing Office, 1897), 743. For an excellent discussion of Northern perceptions of Jefferson Davis's capture in his wife's clothing, see Nina Silber, "Intemperate Men, Spiteful Women, and Jefferson Davis," in *Divided Houses: Gender and the Civil War,* ed. Catherine Clinton and Nina Silber (New York: Oxford University Press, 1992), 283–305. See also Nina Silber, *The Romance of Reunion: Northerners and the South, 1865–1900* (Chapel Hill: University of North Carolina Press, 1993).

8. See, for example, *Harpers Weekly,* June 17, 1865, 373.

9. David Rankin Barbee, "The Capture of Jefferson Davis," *Tyler's Quarterly Historical and Genealogical Magazine* 29 (1948): 7, 39.

10. *New York Herald,* May 15, 1865.

11. Ibid., May 16, 1865.

12. Ibid., May 21, 1865.

13. A. H. Saxon, ed., *Selected Letters of P. T. Barnum* (New York: Columbia University Press, 1983), 132.

14. Harris, *Humbug,* 168–69; Neely, Holzer, and Boritt, *Confederate Image,* 93.

15. Neely, Holzer, and Boritt, *Confederate Image,* 95–96.

16. Ibid., 83, 85, 88.

17. See, for example, ibid., 87.

18. The fullest description is in Davis, *Rise and Fall,* 2:700–702. This is quoted at length in Varina Davis, *Jefferson Davis: Ex-President of the Confederate States of America, a Memoir, by His Wife* (New York: Belford, 1890), 631–46.

19. The statement that a host was "not at home" was a conventional way in which a servant might greet a visitor if the host did not wish to receive the visitor at that moment. But Randolph had departed from this convention in a clearly insulting way by personally greeting his unwanted visitor.

20. *Raleigh Register,* June 8, 1841.

21. Examples of this type of betrayal can be found in Blassingame, *Slave Testimony,* 114, 330–31, 431, 437, 439.

22. Examples of the broken promises of dying masters and the breakup of slave families contrary to the word of the master can be found in ibid., 415, 467, 520.

23. For some examples of sermons that seemed to receive a skeptical response from blacks, see George P. Rawick, ed., *The American Slave: A Composite Autobiography* (Westport, Conn.: Greenwood Publishing Co., 1972), 18:310; Lawrence W. Levine, *Black Culture and Black Consciousness: Afro-American Folk Thought from Slavery to Freedom* (Oxford: Oxford University Press, 1977), 44–45; and Blassingame, *Slave Testimony,* 420.

24. Blassingame, *Slave Testimony,* 423.

25. Frederick Douglass, *Narrative of the Life of Frederick Douglass, an American Slave* (1845; reprint, Garden City, N.Y.: Doubleday, 1963), 63; Harriet Jacobs, *Incidents in the Life of a Slave Girl, Written by Herself,* ed. Jean Fagin Yellin (Cambridge, Mass.: Harvard University Press, 1987), 128–32.

26. "Narrative of the Life of James Curry," in Blassingame, *Slave Testimony,* 140.

27. Henry Bibb, *Narrative of the Life and Adventures of Henry Bibb, an American Slave, Written by Himself,* in Osofsky, *Puttin' On Ole Massa,* 68.

28. This account of Douglass's confrontation with Covey is derived from Douglass, *Narrative of the Life,* 58–75, and Frederick Douglass, *My Bondage and My Freedom,* ed. William L. Andrews (1855; reprint, Urbana: University of Illinois Press, 1987), 128–53.

29. Douglass, *My Bondage and My Freedom,* 132.

30. Douglass, *Narrative of the Life,* 70.

31. Ibid., 74. Hegel described in more abstract terms this connection between risking life and attaining freedom; see G. W. F. Hegel, *The Phenomenology of Mind,* trans. J. B. Braillie (New York: Harper and Row, 1967), 228–40.

32. The double meaning in the word "lie" has also been noted by Adrienne Rich, *On Lies, Secrets, and Silence: Selected Prose, 1966–1978* (New York: W. W. Norton, 1979), 188. Double meanings often can be analyzed to reveal deep connections between seemingly unrelated elements in a culture.

33. Melton A. McLaurin, *Celia: A Slave* (Athens: University of Georgia Press, 1991). Celia was not typical in that she eventually resisted by killing her master.

34. For a full discussion of the nature of the Harriet Jacobs narrative, see Jacobs, *Incidents in the Life,* xiii–xxxiv. See also Fox-Genovese, *Within the Plantation Household,* 372–96.

35. Jacobs, *Incidents in the Life,* 27–42.

36. Elizabeth Fox-Genovese is skeptical that Jacobs successfully resisted Norcom. She believes that Jacobs simply did not want to reveal her rape to a middle-class Northern audience. This may be the case. Either way, it seems clear that Jacobs was not completely defenseless. Fox-Genovese, *Within the Plantation Household,* 392.

37. Jacobs, *Incidents in the Life,* 29.

38. Ibid., 53–57.

39. Ibid., 54.

40. Examples of this can be found in Blassingame, *Slave Testimony*, 503, 691, 706, and Osofsky, *Puttin' On Ole Massa*, 97, 115, 193, 251.

41. Blassingame, *Slave Testimony*, 138.

42. Rawick, *American Slave*, 18:262.

43. Blassingame, *Slave Testimony*, 301.

44. Genovese, *Roll, Jordan, Roll*, 40. For examples of how it felt to be a slave who could not testify, see the speech by Lewis Clarke, "Leaves from a Slave's Journal of Life," in Blassingame, *Slave Testimony*, 158; see also Rawick, *American Slave*, 18:122.

45. Helen Tunnicliff Catterall, ed., *Judicial Cases concerning American Slavery and the Negro* (1926; reprint, New York: Negro Universities Press, 1968), 1:311, 2:396.

46. Ibid., 2:183–84.

47. Ira Berlin, *Slaves without Masters: The Free Negro in the Antebellum South* (New York: Pantheon Books, 1975), 96.

48. See interview with John H. Hill in Blassingame, *Slave Testimony*, 427; see also 435.

49. Levine, *Black Culture and Black Consciousness*, 122. Other examples of masters commenting on the deceitful nature of their slaves can be found in Genovese, *Roll, Jordan, Roll*, 599–612.

50. Drew Gilpin Faust, *James Henry Hammond and the Old South: A Design for Mastery* (Baton Rouge: Louisiana State University Press, 1982), 69–104.

51. "Narrative of James Curry," 137.

52. Ibid., 138.

53. An excellent discussion of the issue of names in the master-slave relationship can be found in Genovese, *Roll, Jordan, Roll*, 443–50. See also Charles Joyner, *Down by the Riverside: A South Carolina Slave Community* (Urbana: University of Illinois Press, 1984), 217–22.

54. The full description of this incident can be found in "Narrative of the Life of William Wells Brown," in Osofsky, *Puttin' On Ole Massa*, 217–18. A similar story can be found in Faust, *James Henry Hammond*, 88.

55. Rawick, *American Slave*, 18:280.

56. Interview with David Holmes in Blassingame, *Slave Testimony*, 297.

57. John Dollard, *Caste and Class in a Southern Town* (1937; reprint, Garden City, N.Y.: Anchor Books, 1949), 309–10. The story is also told in Levine, *Black Culture and Black Consciousness*, 313.

58. This incident is described in the *New York Evangelist* and reprinted in Blassingame, *Slave Testimony*, 145–50. Other versions can be found in William G. Hawkins, *Lunsford Lane; or, Another Helper from North Carolina* (Boston: Crosby and Nichols, 1863), 137–61, and Lunsford Lane, "Narrative of Lunsford Lane," in *Five Slave Narratives*, ed. William Loren Katz (New York: Arno Press, 1969).

59. Blassingame, *Slave Testimony*, 149.

60. On paternalism, see Genovese, *Roll, Jordan, Roll*. For an illustration of the way slave-management techniques aimed at every aspect of plantation life, see James O. Breeden, ed., *Advice among Masters: The Ideal in Slave Management in the Old South* (Westport, Conn.: Greenwood Press, 1980).

61. Quoted in Levine, *Black Culture and Black Consciousness*, 122.

62. C. Vann Woodward, ed., *Mary Chesnut's Civil War* (New Haven: Yale University Press, 1981), 153.

63. Ibid., 113–14, 218.

64. Quoted in Ayers, *Vengeance and Justice*, 61.

65. Bertram Wyatt-Brown, "The Mask of Obedience: Male Slave Psychology in the Old South," *American Historical Review* 93, no. 5 (December 1988): 1228–52. See also Peter Kolchin, *American Slavery, 1619–1877* (New York: Hill and Wang, 1993), 133–68, for an excellent overview of the way American slavery created limited spaces for slave "semiautonomy." Kolchin and Wyatt-Brown both believe that the autonomy of slave society has been greatly exaggerated by recent scholars. But neither portrays a society where masters exercised total control over the lives of their slaves.

66. This seems true even for the unusually intrusive James Henry Hammond. Faust, *James Henry Hammond*, 69–104. The focus on the body can also be seen in various published essays on slave management. See Breeden, *Advice among Masters*.

67. Faust, *James Henry Hammond*, 93.

68. William Harper, "Memoir on Slavery," in *The Ideology of Slavery: Proslavery Thought in the Antebellum South, 1830–1860*, ed. Drew Gilpin Faust (Baton Rouge: Louisiana State University Press, 1981), 103.

CHAPTER THREE
GIFTS, STRANGERS, DUELS, AND HUMANITARIANISM

1. The two-volume work by Robert William Fogel and Stanley L. Engerman, *Time on the Cross: The Economics of American Negro Slavery* (Boston: Little, Brown, 1974), offers the classic modern statement of this position. The work of Fogel and Engerman has been the object of much criticism, but most critics concede that the planter class was deeply involved in a market economy.

2. Lewis Hyde, *The Gift: Imagination and the Erotic Life of Property* (New York: Vintage, 1979), makes a parallel point in relation to works of art. He sees the producers and consumers of art as involved in gift exchange even though many artists sell their paintings and many people pay fees to enter museums.

3. The classic study of the paradoxical nature of the gift is Marcel Mauss, *The Gift: Forms and Functions of Exchange in Archaic Societies*, trans. Ian Cunnison (New York: W. Norton, 1967).

4. Franz Boaz, *The Kwakiutl of Vancouver Island* (1909; reprint, New York: AMS Press, 1975). Hyde, *Gift*, 28–32, notes that the nineteenth-century potlatch was a corrupted version of an earlier system of gift exchange, yet this extreme form of exchange does reveal something common to most gift exchanges.

5. Thomas Hart Benton, *Thirty Years' View; or, A History of the Working of the American Government for Thirty Years, from 1820 to 1850* (New York: D. Appleton, 1854), 70–77, offers a full description of the duel. Benton's comments about Johnny can be found on 75. Randolph was very attached to his "body servant." In his will, not only did he award John his freedom (along with the award of freedom to all his slaves), but he also provided for a fifty-dollar lifetime annuity

"and as the only favor I have ever asked of any government, I do entreat the Assembly of Virginia to permit the said John and his family to remain in Virginia." Hugh A. Garland, *The Life of John Randolph of Roanoke* (New York: D. Appleton, 1853), 151.

6. Bernard Mayo, *Henry Clay: Spokesman of the West* (Boston: Houghton Mifflin, 1937), 519; Glyndon G. Van Deusen, *The Life of Henry Clay* (Boston: Little Brown, 1937), 86.

7. The nastiest public disputes occurred during the 1820 Missouri crisis and the debate over the bill for repairing the Cumberland Road in 1824. See Van Deusen, *Life of Henry Clay*, 140, 163–64. An insightful analysis of the Clay-Randolph duel can be found in Robert Dawidoff, *The Education of John Randolph* (New York: W. W. Norton, 1979), 255–59.

8. William Cabell Bruce, *John Randolph of Roanoke, 1773–1833* (New York: G. P. Putnam's Sons, 1922), 514–15; Benton, *Thirty Years' View*, 70.

9. Van Deusen, *The Life of Henry Clay*, 207; Benton, *Thirty Years' View*, 66–67.

10. Benton, *Thirty Years' View*, 65.

11. *Congressional Debates*, 19th Cong., 1st sess., 1825–26, 400–401; Bruce, *John Randolph of Roanoke*, 511–13; James F. Hopkins and Mary W. M. Hargreaves, eds., *The Papers of Henry Clay* (Lexington: University of Kentucky Press, 1973), 5:209n.

12. Hopkins and Hargreaves, *Papers of Henry Clay*, 5:208.

13. Benton, *Thirty Years' View*, 70. The Benton version of Jesup's description of his interview with Randolph is a longer version of the document published in Hopkins and Hargreaves, *Papers of Henry Clay*, 5:211.

14. Randolph referred to these instances only obliquely, carefully avoiding the mention of Kremer and Adams by name. Men of honor avoided the unnecessary or "promiscuous" use of other men's names.

15. Bruce, *John Randolph of Roanoke*, 514–15; Benton, *Thirty Years' View*, 70.

16. Benton, *Thirty Years' View*, 70.

17. Ibid., 71.

18. Ibid. Randolph made the same distinction in his letter of acceptance to the duel: "Mr. Randolph accepts the challenge of Mr. Clay; at the same time that he protests against the right of any minister of the Executive Government of the U.S. to hold him responsible for words spoken in debate as a Senator of Virginia; in crimination of such minister; or of the administration under which he shall have taken office." Hopkins and Hargreaves, *Papers of Henry Clay*, 5:211–12.

19. Bruce, *John Randolph of Roanoke*, 520.

20. Benton, *Thirty Years' View*, 74.

21. Ibid., 73.

22. Ibid., 76.

23. Ibid., 75–76.

24. Ibid., 76–77.

25. Hegel, *Phenomenology of Mind*, 228–40, offers the best theoretical description of the relationships among mastery, slavery, and the duel.

26. Hopkins and Hargreaves, *Papers of Henry Clay*, 5:254.

27. Ibid., 208.

28. Benton, *Thirty Years' View*, 74, 77.

29. Ibid., 77.

30. Patterson, *Slavery and Social Death*, 211–14, offers an excellent description of the way manumission can be understood as a gift exchange.

31. Edmund Kirke, *My Southern Friends* (New York: Carleton, 1863), 186–92, describes the Christmas distribution of basic supplies as gifts. But masters saw these distributions as gifts whenever they occurred.

32. Greenberg, *Masters and Statesmen*, 85–103; Genovese, *Roll, Jordan, Roll*, 75–87.

33. Theodore Rosengarten, *Tombee: Portrait of a Cotton Planter* (New York: William Morrow, 1986), 377, 416.

34. Edwin Adams Davis, ed., *Plantation Life in the Florida Parishes of Louisiana, 1836–1846, as Reflected in the Diary of Bennet H. Barrow* (New York: Columbia University Press, 1943), 82, 83, 85, 88.

35. Rosengarten, *Tombee*, 348.

36. Genovese, *Roll, Jordan, Roll*, 97–112.

37. Patterson, *Slavery and Social Death*, 217; Berlin, *Slaves without Masters*.

38. Randall M. Miller, ed., *"Dear Master": Letters of a Slave Family* (Ithaca, N.Y.: Cornell University Press, 1991), 41, 125.

39. W. E. B. DuBois, *Black Reconstruction in America: An Essay toward a History of the Part which Black Folk Played in the Attempt to Reconstruct Democracy in America* (1935; reprint, New York: Russell and Russell, 1966).

40. Dawidoff, *Education of John Randolph*, 48–67, offers a detailed analysis of Randolph's complex ideas on slavery as well as a description of his relations with the slave John.

41. Sometimes it is appropriate for historians to use works of literature to illustrate social relations. In this case, the "Frankie Mae" story describes a set of relations duplicated throughout the South over long periods of time. Jean Wheeler Smith, "Frankie Mae," in *Black-Eyed Susans: Classic Stories by and about Black Women*, ed. Mary Helen Washington (Garden City, N.Y.: Anchor Books, 1975).

42. Ibid., 6.

43. Ibid., 13.

44. Ibid., 15.

45. Hyde, *Gift*, 25–39, has an interesting discussion of the way gifts gain in value as they circulate through a community. This was sometimes true of gifts that circulated through the community of masters. But the gift a master gave to a slave did not gain in value; it simply died.

46. A similar story can be found in Captain Flack, *The Texan Rifle-Hunter; or, Field Sports on the Prairie* (London: John Maxwell, 1866), 210–11.

47. This entire account can be found in Porte Crayon [David Hunter Strother], *Virginia Illustrated: Containing a Visit to the Virginian Canaan, and the Adventures of Porte Crayon and His Cousins* (New York: Harper and Brothers, 1857), 149–56.

48. Greenberg, *Masters and Statesmen*, 23–41.

49. To think of political office-holding as a gift is not inconsistent with thinking of it as a duty. Some statesmen thought of office as a duty—a duty to give a gift to the people. Ibid., 3–22.

50. Carol Bleser, ed., *Secret and Sacred: The Diaries of James Henry Hammond, a Southern Slaveholder* (New York: Oxford University Press, 1988), 215.

51. Ibid., 271.

52. For these quotations, see Greenberg, *Masters and Statesmen* 8–11

53. Bleser, *Secret and Sacred*, 30.

54. Rhys Isaac, *The Transformation of Virginia, 1740–1790* (Chapel Hill: University of North Carolina Press, 1982), 70–71, describes the importance of hospitality for eighteenth-century Virginians. On Hammond's house and parties, see Bleser, *Secret and Sacred*, 36. Hospitality and treating are discussed in Wyatt-Brown, *Southern Honor*, 5, 337.

55. See, for example, Lewis E. Atherton, *The Southern Country Store, 1800–1860* (Baton Rouge: Louisiana State University Press, 1949), 27.

56. Bleser, *Secret and Sacred*, 55.

57. This entire episode is described in ibid., 89–90.

58. Hammond's diary entry on this matter is a bit confused. He says that the issue was a mere matter of business and yet he defends himself by suggesting that his signature had never been any more than a gift and that he expected "no benefit." See ibid.

59. Ibid., 76. See also 98–99 for a similar decision. The decision to withhold his signature also included market considerations. He did not want to assume additional risk in the current economic environment. But it is clear that he also understood the withholding of his signature as involving far more than market concerns.

60. Ibid., 170; see also 173. It is important to note that this transaction also had some market elements attached to it. Hammond apparently held some collateral from Hampton that had been given in exchange for his signature. He returned the collateral when Hampton returned the signature. For another example of the way a breakdown in gift relations signaled the start of a serious dispute, see Hammond's discussion of his conflict with his neighbor John Ransey, 108–14.

61. Ibid., 195. See 98–99 for a specific example that illustrates the generalization.

62. Davis, *Plantation Life*, 21–23.

63. Tony A. Freyer, "Law and the Antebellum Southern Economy: An Interpretation," in *Ambivalent Legacy: A Legal History of the South*, ed. David J. Bodenhamer and James W. Ely, Jr. (Jackson: University of Mississippi Press, 1984), 55.

64. Rhys Isaac, for example, notes that in eighteenth-century Virginia, passersby could help themselves to fruit from the orchards of the great planters; see *Transformation of Virginia*, 34.

65. Wyatt-Brown, *Southern Honor*, 331–35.

66. Frederick Law Olmsted, *A Journey in the Back Country, 1853–1854* (1860; reprint, New York: Shocken Books, 1970), 26. For an excellent discussion of travel and hospitality in the antebellum South, see Joe Gray Taylor, *Eating, Drinking, and Visiting in the South: An Informal History* (Baton Rouge: Louisiana State University Press, 1982).

67. Olmsted, *Journey in the Back Country*, 32.

68. Ibid., 401–3.

69. Ibid., 407.

70. The realm of hospitality seems to have been larger for the great planters of eighteenth-century Virginia. Isaac, *Transformation of Virginia*, 70–71.

71. Wilson, *Code of Honor*, 9, 10; Greenberg, *Masters and Statesmen*, 35.

72. James W. Ely, Jr., and David J. Bodenhamer, "Regionalism and the Legal History of the South," in Bodenhamer and Ely, *Ambivalent Legacy*, 13–14.

73. Rosengarten, *Tombee*, 484.

74. Samuel Gaillard Stoney, ed., "The Autobiography of William John Grayson," *South Carolina Historical and Genealogical Magazine*, 49, no. 1 (January 1948): 26–27. Grayson's entire autobiography was published as *Witness to Sorrow: The Antebellum Autobiography of William J. Grayson*, ed. Richard J. Calhoun (Columbia: University of South Carolina, 1990).

75. Stoney, "Autobiography of William John Grayson," 27.

76. Quoted in "Samuel Hoar's Expulsion from Charleston," *Old South Leaflets* (Boston: Directors of the Old South Work, 1845), 4.

77. See, for example, the various comments by the Virginian Edmund Ruffin in William Kauffman Scarborough, ed., *The Diary of Edmund Ruffin* (Baton Rouge: Louisiana State University Press, 1972), 1:19, 356, 464, 470.

78. Charles E. Whitehead, *Wild Sports in the South; or, the Camp-fires of the Everglades* (New York: Derby and Jackson, 1860), 68.

79. Olmsted, *Journey in the Back Country*, 409–10.

80. Rosengarten, *Tombee*, 398.

81. Flack, *Texan Rifle-Hunter*, 172.

82. Thomas L. Haskell, "Capitalism and the Origins of the Humanitarian Sensibility," part 2, *American Historical Review* 90, no. 3 (June 1985): 547–66.

83. George Fitzhugh, *Sociology for the South; or, The Failure of Free Society* (Richmond, Va.: A. Morris, 1854), reprinted in *Ante-bellum: Writings of George Fitzhugh and Hinton Rowan Helper on Slavery*, ed. Harvey Wish (New York: Capricorn Books, 1960), 65.

84. William J. Grayson, "The Hireling and the Slave," in *Slavery Defended: The Views of the Old South*, ed. Eric L. McKitrick (Englewood Cliffs, N.J.: Prentice-Hall, 1963), 58–59.

85. Edmund Ruffin, "The Political Economy of Slavery," in McKitrick, *Slavery Defended*, 79.

86. George Frederick Holmes, "Review of Uncle Tom's Cabin," in McKitrick, *Slavery Defended*, 106.

87. James Henry Hammond, "Letter to an English Abolitionist," in Faust, *Ideology of Slavery*, 193.

88. Ibid., 197. For a similar idea, see Grayson, "Hireling and the Slave," 61.

89. Some masters did have an expanded notion of responsibility rooted in a Christian missionary tradition. Just as the Christian tradition was in tension with the custom of dueling, it was also in tension with the local orientation of gift exchange. On the importance of the Christian tradition among Southern intellectuals, see Eugene D. Genovese, *The Slaveholders' Dilemma: Freedom and Progress in Southern Conservative Thought, 1820–1860* (Columbia: University of South Carolina Press, 1992).

CHAPTER FOUR
DEATH

1. Quoted in Adrienne Cole Phillips, "The Mississippi Press's Response to John Brown's Raid," *Journal of Mississippi History* 48, no. 2 (May 1986): 121.

2. Quoted in Cecil D. Eby, Jr., *"Porte Crayon": The Life of David Hunter Strother* (Chapel Hill: University of North Carolina Press, 1960), 105.

3. Steven A. Channing, *Crisis of Fear: Secession in South Carolina* (New York: Simon and Schuster, 1970), 24.

4. My claim is not that Southern white men had a unique understanding of death and the risks of life. Masters in many other slave societies (and others in some "free" societies) also judged men by the way they confronted death. The denial of "mere" life as a central value extended well beyond the limits of time and geography that bounded the antebellum South. My argument is only that no other culture elaborated these attitudes in precisely the same way with the same consequences. A central theme of every human culture, in some sense, may involve the way each conceives of its relation to death. But that does not diminish the significance of these attitudes as a central theme in Southern history. The classic work on the relationships among honor, slavery, and attitudes toward death is Patterson, *Slavery and Social Death*. See also Wendy Brown, *Manhood and Politics: A Feminist Reading in Political Theory* (Totowa, N.J.: Rowman and Littlefield, 1988); Brown argues that the willingness to risk death has been a central value in defining community among male political thinkers in Western culture.

5. Ruffin had always been a Southern nationalist, but events surrounding the Compromise of 1850 had pushed him to a higher level of active agitation. Betty L. Mitchell, *Edmund Ruffin: A Biography* (Bloomington: Indiana University Press, 1981), 70.

6. Scarborough, *Diary of Edmund Ruffin*, 1:350, 366–67.

7. Ibid., 382.

8. Ibid., 350.

9. Ibid., 367–68.

10. Ibid., 368.

11. The entire account, including sources for all the quotations, can be found in ibid., 369–71.

12. Ibid., 369–70.

13. Ibid., 370.

14. Ibid.

15. Ibid., 371.

16. Ibid.

17. On Wise's involvement as a second in the 1838 duel between Congressmen Jonathan Cilley and William J. Graves, see Greenberg, *Masters and Statesmen*, 28–31. For a description of Wise's involvement in other duels, see Barton H. Wise, *The Life of Henry A. Wise of Virginia, 1806–1876* (London: Macmillan, 1899), 40–41.

18. Wise, *Life of Henry A. Wise*, 246–47.

19. Ibid., 247.

20. Scarborough, *Diary of Edmund Ruffin*, 1:372.

21. Wise, *Life of Henry A. Wise*, 247.

22. On the martial spirit of the Southern master class, see Franklin, *Militant South*.

23. Robert Manson Meyers, ed., *The Children of Pride: A True Story of Georgia and the Civil War* (New Haven: Yale University Press, 1972), 1461–62, 723–24.

24. The typical modes of dying in the nineteenth century are described in Lewis O. Saum, "Death in the Popular Mind in Pre–Civil War America," in *Death in America*, ed. David E. Stannard (Philadelphia: University of Pennsylvania Press, 1975), 41–43. For a description of dying in antebellum Baltimore, see Kent Lancaster, "On the Drama of Dying in Early Nineteenth Century Baltimore," *Maryland Historical Magazine* 81, no. 2 (summer 1986): 103–16.

25. *Richmond Whig*, June 20, 1865, quoted in David F. Allmendinger, Jr., *Ruffin: Family and Reform in the Old South* (New York: Oxford University Press, 1990), 154.

26. The most complete secondary discussion of the death of Edmund Ruffin can be found in Allmendinger, *Ruffin*. See also Edmund Ruffin, Jr.'s description of the death of his father in a letter to his sons, in "Death of Edmund Ruffin," *Tyler's Quarterly Historical and Genealogical Magazine* 5, no. 3 (January 1924): 193–95, and Edmund Ruffin's justification for his suicide in Scarborough, *Diary of Edmund Ruffin*, 3:935–51.

27. Scarborough, *Diary of Edmund Ruffin*, 3:949.

28. Ibid., 937.

29. This description of Ruffin's death is consistent with that in Allmendinger, *Ruffin*, 152–85. But Allmendinger does not sufficiently recognize the central role played by "honor" in Edmund Ruffin's decision to kill himself. The quotation can be found in Scarborough, *Diary of Edmund Ruffin*, 3:942.

30. These quotations are scattered through several pages of Ruffin's description of his daughter's death. I have linked them here to highlight the point about a submissive death illustrating a submissive life. David F. Allmendinger, Jr., ed., *Incidents of My Life: Edmund Ruffin's Autobiographical Essays* (Charlottesville: Published for the Virginia Historical Society by the University of Virginia Press, 1990), 139, 140, 143, 149.

31. Ibid., 180, 181, 184, 186.

32. As a result of inconsistencies in the documents, there had been some confusion about the date of Ruffin's death. Recently, however, the issue has been resolved. See David F. Allmendinger, Jr., and William K. Scarborough, "The Days Ruffin Died," *Virginia Magazine of History and Biography* 97 (January 1989): 75–96.

33. "Death of Edmund Ruffin," 193.

34. *The Death and Funeral Ceremonies of John Caldwell Calhoun* (Columbia, S.C.: A. S. Johnston, 1850), 52.

35. See the dramatic description of Calhoun's last speech as well as the other events surrounding his death in Margaret L. Coit, *John C. Calhoun: American Portrait* (Boston: Houghton Mifflin, 1950), 490–511.

36. Quoted in ibid., 497.

37. *Death and Funeral Ceremonies*, 6.

38. Ibid., 10.

39. Ibid., 53.

40. *Niles' Weekly Register*, August 8, 1835, 407–8.

41. Faust, *James Henry Hammond*, 370–79.

42. Bleser, *Secret and Sacred*, 299–302.

43. Ibid., 301–2.

44. It is important to remember that the borders of the category "men of honor" are not precise. Robert E. Lee, for example, was a gentleman in the tradition of honor who also embodied a style of Christian gentility. His death reveals both elements. See the descriptions of Lee's death in A. L. Long, *Memoirs of Robert E. Lee: His Military and Personal History, Embracing a Large Amount of Material Hitherto Unpublished* . . . (Secaucus, N.J.: Blue and the Gray Press, 1983), 472–73. On the mixture of the Christian and honor traditions in the Old South, see Bertram Wyatt-Brown, "God and Honor in the Old South," *Southern Review* 25, no. 2 (April 1989): 283–96.

45. Robert Manson Meyers, ed., *A Georgian at Princeton* (New York: Harcourt Brace Jovanovich, 1976), 5.

46. Another example of a master's description of the slavish death of a slave can be found in "The Night Funeral of a Slave," *DeBow's Review* 20 (February 1956): 218–21. Here, the faithful slave's last words were reported by his owner as "Master, meet me in heaven."

47. Virginia Ingraham Burr, ed., *The Secret Eye: The Journal of Ella Gertrude Clanton Thomas, 1848–1889* (Chapel Hill: University of North Carolina Press, 1990), 435–36. Numerous examples of the way Baltimore women died in the early nineteenth century can be found in Lancaster, "On the Drama of Dying." Repeatedly, they died happy and resigned. Catherine Clinton, *The Plantation Mistress: Women's World in the Plantation South* (New York: Pantheon Books, 1982), 154–59, describes the death of several plantation mistresses.

48. Davis, *Plantation Life*, 431–40.

49. It would be an exaggeration to suggest that no Southern whites saw bravery in the behavior of Nat Turner and the other rebels. But such comments were rare, and they make up a decidedly minor part of white descriptions of the revolt. See Stephen B. Oates, *The Fires of Jubilee: Nat Turner's Fierce Rebellion* (New York: New American Library, 1975), 111, 112. *The Constitutional Whig*, August 29, 1831, refers to one rebel "who might have been a hero, judging from the magnanimity with which he bears his suffering." Reprinted in *The Southampton Slave Revolt of 1831: A Compilation of Source Material*, ed. Henry Irving Tragle (Amherst: University of Massachusetts Press, 1971), 52.

50. Tragle, *Southampton Slave Revolt of 1831*, is an excellent collection of many of the important documents of the rebellion. Also see the introductory essay in Kenneth S. Greenberg, ed., *The Confessions of Nat Turner and Related Documents* (Boston: St. Martin's Press, 1996).

51. *Richmond Enquirer*, August 30 and September 27, 1831, reprinted in Tragle, *Southampton Slave Revolt of 1831*, 44, 100.

52. *Richmond Compiler*, September 3, 1831, reprinted in Tragle, *Southampton Slave Revolt of 1831*, 60.

53. *Richmond Constitutional Whig*, September 3, 1831, reprinted in Tragle, *Southampton Slave Revolt of 1831*, 70.

54. *Richmond Constitutional Whig*, September 3 and 26, 1831, reprinted in Tragle, *Southampton Slave Revolt of 1831*, 70, 92.

55. On the issue of whose voice speaks in the *Confessions*, see Henry Irving Tragle, "Styron and His Sources," reprinted in Tragle, *Southampton Slave Revolt of 1831*, 406–9.

56. Thomas R. Gray, *The Confessions of Nat Turner*, reprinted in Tragle, *Southampton Slave Revolt of 1831*, 308.

57. *Richmond Compiler*, September 3, 1831, reprinted in Tragle, *Southampton Slave Revolt of 1831*, 60.

58. *Constitutional Whig*, September 3 and 26, 1831, reprinted in Tragle, *Southampton Slave Revolt of 1831*, 70, 93.

59. Thomas Roderick Dew, "Abolition of Negro Slavery," in Faust, *Ideology of Slavery*, 68.

60. Levine, *Black Culture and Black Consciousness*, 69–70, 74–78.

61. Robert N. Elliott, "The Nat Turner Insurrection as Reported in the North Carolina Press," *North Carolina Historical Review* 38 (January 1961): 16.

62. Tragle, *Southampton Slave Revolt of 1831*, 275.

63. Ibid., 432.

64. William Gilmore Simms, "The Morals of Slavery," in *The Pro-slavery Argument as Maintained by the Most Distinguished Writers of the Southern States*, ed. Chancellor Harper, Governor Hammond, Dr. Simms, and Professor Dew (Charleston, S.C.: Walker and Richards, 1852), 223–24.

65. Greenberg, *Masters and Statesmen*, 99.

66. Harper, "Memoir on Slavery."

67. Hammond, "Letter to an English Abolitionist," 178. See also Simms, "Morals of Slavery," 223–24.

68. *Constitutional Whig*, September 3 and 17, 1831, reprinted in Tragle, *Southampton Slave Revolt of 1831*, 94, 70.

69. *Petersberg Intelligencer*, August 26, 1831; *Constitutional Whig*, August 29, 1831; Gray, *Confessions of Nat Turner*, all reprinted in Tragle, *Southampton Slave Revolt of 1831*, 40, 55, 304.

70. This report was published in the *Norfolk Herald* and cited in F. Roy Johnson, *The Nat Turner Story* (Murfreesboro, N.C.: Johnson, 1970), 166.

71. *Richmond Enquirer*, November 4, 1831; *Petersburg Intelligencer*, November 4, 1831, reprinted in Tragle, *Southampton Slave Revolt of 1831*, 133, 135–36; see also other reports of Turner's capture on 135–39.

72. Gray, *Confessions of Nat Turner*, 303, 316.

73. Laurence Greene, *The Raid: A Biography of Harpers Ferry* (New York: Henry Holt, 1953), 205. It was also reported that Wise had received a letter from P. T. Barnum, requesting Brown's clothing and pike. Phillips, "Mississippi Press's Response," 129.

74. Truman Nelson, *The Old Man: John Brown and Harper's Ferry* (New York: Holt, Rinehart, and Winston, 1973).

75. Elliott, "Nat Turner Insurrection," 6.

76. *Richmond Compiler,* September 3, 1831, reprinted in Tragle, *Southampton Slave Revolt of 1831,* 62; Oates, *Fires of Jubilee,* 111.

77. For indications of the extent of decapitation, see Oates, *Fires of Jubilee,* 113; *Constitutional Whig,* August 29 and September 3, 1831, reprinted in Tragle, *Southampton Slave Revolt of 1831,* 52, 69; Johnson, *Nat Turner Story,* 135, 197; see also 199–200.

78. Johnson, *Nat Turner Story,* 199–200; William Sidney Drewry, *The Southampton Insurrection* (Washington, D.C.: Neale, 1900), 102.

79. Gray, *Confessions of Nat Turner,* 317.

80. Eby, *"Porte Crayon,"* 105, 108.

81. *Constitutional Whig,* August 29, 1831.

82. *Norfolk Herald,* November 14, 1831, reprinted in Tragle, *Southampton Slave Revolt of 1831,* 140.

83. On Dew's background and for information on the influence of his proslavery essay, see Faust, *Ideology of Slavery,* 21–23, and Larry E. Tise, *Proslavery: A History of the Defense of Slavery in America, 1701–1840* (Athens: University of Georgia Press, 1987), 70–74.

84. Harper et al., *Pro-slavery Argument,* 287–490.

85. Tise, *Proslavery,* 70–74. See also Tise's discussion of the way historians have thought about the Dew essay, 388–89 n. 40.

86. Thomas R. Dew, "Professor Dew on Slavery," in Harper et al., *Pro-slavery Argument,* 312.

87. Ibid., 297.

88. Ibid., 301.

89. Ibid., 313.

90. Ibid., 318–22.

91. Dew is less explicit about the link between slavery as a substitute for death in criminal cases, but it seems implied by his argument. Ibid., 323–24.

92. Ibid., 324–26.

93. Ibid., 332–33.

94. Ibid., 338.

95. Ibid., 344.

96. Ibid., 392–410.

97. William Sumner Jenkins, *Pro-Slavery Thought in the Old South* (Chapel Hill: University of North Carolina Press, 1935), 118–19.

98. Harper, "Memoir on Slavery," 86.

99. Grayson, "Hireling and the Slave," 62.

100. Ruffin, "Political Economy of Slavery," 73.

101. Dew, "Professor Dew on Slavery," 306.

102. Thornton Stringfellow, "The Bible Argument; or, Slavery in the Light of Divine Revelation," in *Cotton Is King, and Pro-slavery Arguments,* ed. E. N. Elliott (Augusta, Ga.: Pritchard, Abbott, and Loomis, 1860), 489.

103. Thomas Virgil Peterson, *Ham and Japheth: The Mythic World of Whites in the Antebellum South* (Metuchen, N.J.: Scarecrow Press, 1978), 5.

104. Iveson L. Brookes, *A Defense of the South* (Hamburg, S.C.: Republican Office, 1850), 23.

105. *African Servitude: When, Why, and by Whom Instituted: By Whom, and How Long, Shall It Be Maintained?* (New York: Davies and Kent, 1860), reprinted in Peterson, *Ham and Japheth*, 146.

106. Samuel Cartwright, "The Prognathous Species of Mankind," in McKitrick, *Slavery Defended*, 143–44.

107. Samuel A. Cartwright, "Slavery in the Light of Ethnology," in Elliott, *Cotton Is King*, 713–14.

108. Harper, "Memoir on Slavery," 129.

109. Robert F. Durden, *The Gray and the Black: The Confederate Debate on Emancipation* (Baton Rouge: Louisiana State University Press, 1972), 50.

110. Josiah C. Nott, "Climates of the South in Their Relations to White Labor," in *The Cause of the South: Selections from Debow's Review, 1846–1867*, ed. Paul F. Paskoff and Daniel J. Wilson (Baton Rouge: Louisiana State University Press, 1982), 60–61. The Nott essay was originally published in the After War series in *DeBow's Review* 1 (February 1866): 166–73. See also Genovese, *Slaveholders' Dilemma*, 61.

111. Chancellor Harper, "Slavery in the Light of Social Ethics," in Elliott, *Cotton Is King*, 581.

112. James Henry Hammond, "Slavery in the Light of Political Science," in Elliott, *Cotton Is King*, 658–61.

113. Fitzhugh, *Sociology for the South*; George Fitzhugh, *Cannibals All! or, Slaves without Masters!* (1857; reprint, ed. C. Vann Woodward, Cambridge, Mass.: Harvard University Press, 1988), 17.

114. Simms, "Morals of Slavery," 215.

115. Elliott, *Cotton Is King*, vii.

116. *New Orleans Bee*, March 16, 1861, reprinted in Durden, *Gray and the Black*, 10.

117. Greenberg, *Masters and Statesmen*, 85–103.

CHAPTER FIVE
BASEBALL, HUNTING, AND GAMBLING

1. John Rickards Betts, *America's Sporting Heritage: 1850–1950* (Reading, Mass.: Addison-Wesley, 1974), 380 n. 11.

2. Charles A. Peverelly, *Book of American Pastimes* (n.p., 1866), 337.

3. Ibid., 337–38.

4. Harold Seymour, *Baseball: The Early Years* (New York: Oxford University Press, 1960), 8–9.

5. Ibid., 9–12.

6. Albert G. Spalding, *America's National Game: Historic Facts concerning the Beginning, Evolution, Development, and Popularity of Base Ball* (New York: American Sports Publishing, 1911), 95.

7. Ibid., xii, 2.

8. Ibid., 3–9.

9. Seymour, *Baseball*, 5, 7; Warren Goldstein, *Playing for Keeps: A History of Early Baseball* (Ithaca, N.Y.: Cornell University Press, 1989), 12–13.

10. These early baseball clubs were not like modern professional teams. They were amateur social clubs of young gentlemen or working-class men.

11. Goldstein, *Playing for Keeps*, 10; Seymour, *Baseball*, 6.

12. Goldstein, *Playing for Keeps*, 12; Seymour, *Baseball*, 24. On the spread of baseball in New York and other northern cities, see Steven M. Gelber, "'Their Hands Are All out Playing': Business and Amateur Baseball, 1845–1917," *Journal of Sport History* 11, no. 1 (spring 1984): 10.

13. Goldstein, *Playing for Keeps*, 4–5. For a description of the spread of baseball in postwar Chicago, see Stephen Freedman, "The Baseball Fad in Chicago, 1865–1870: An Exploration of the Role of Sport in the Nineteenth-Century City," *Journal of Sport History* 5, no. 2 (summer 1978): 42–60.

14. Seymour, *Baseball*, 34, 52.

15. Goldstein, *Playing for Keeps*, 4–5, 73.

16. Ed Folsom, "The Manly and Healthy Game: Walt Whitman and the Development of American Baseball," *Arete: The Journal of Sport Literature* 2, no. 1 (fall 1984): 46–47.

17. Seymour, *Baseball*, 52.

18. Folsom, "Manly and Healthy Game," 50; David Quentin Voigt, *American Baseball: From Gentleman's Sport to the Commissioner System* (Norman: University of Oklahoma Press, 1966), 11–12.

19. Dale A. Somers, *The Rise of Sport in New Orleans, 1850–1900* (Baton Rouge: Louisiana State University Press, 1972), 48–51.

20. Spalding, *America's National Game*, 95.

21. Bell Irvin Wiley, *The Life of Johnny Reb: The Common Soldier of the Confederacy* (Baton Rouge: Louisiana State University Press, 1943), 159.

22. Wells Twombly, *Two Hundred Years of Sport in America: A Pageant of a Nation at Play* (New York: McGraw-Hill, 1976), 70–71.

23. Betts, *America's Sporting Heritage*, 89; Lawrence W. Fielding, "War and Trifles: Sport in the Shadows of Civil War Army Life," *Journal of Sport History* 4, no. 2 (summer 1977): 160.

24. Rawick, *American Slave*, 3:101.

25. Ken Leitner was interviewed in 1937 at the age of eighty-five. This puts his birthdate at 1852.

26. Or—to put it a bit more precisely—they did not run when they were chased. They might occasionally engage in a footrace, but that was quite different from the act of running *away* from a ball.

27. For a collection of these advertisements for the eighteenth century, see Lathan A. Windley, comp., *Runaway Slave Advertisements: A Documentary History from the 1730s to 1790* (Westport, Conn.: Greenwood Press, 1983). Virtually every advertisement begins with the phrase "run away."

28. Greenberg, *Masters and Statesmen*.

29. Steven M. Gelber, "Working at Play: The Culture of the Work Place and the Rise of Baseball," *Journal of Social History* 16 (June 1983): 3–20.

30. Seymour, *Baseball*, 15, 16.

31. Goldstein, *Playing for Keeps*, 24–25.

32. Ibid., 25–26.

33. See, for example, Gelber, " 'Their Hands Are All out Playing,' " 5–27.

34. Goldstein, *Playing for Keeps*, 14; Spalding, *America's National Game*, 6. Even in 1866, Peverelly noted with approval the relatively short length of a baseball game. Peverelly, *Book of American Pastimes*, 337.

35. Private drinking seems to have been a part of the life of nineteenth-century baseball clubs. See Goldstein, *Playing for Keeps*, 80.

36. Freedman, "Baseball Fad in Chicago," 44–45.

37. Goldstein, *Playing for Keeps*, 22–23.

38. Ibid., 20–27.

39. On the popularity of the hunt in the antebellum South, see Clarence Gohdes, ed., *Hunting in the Old South: Original Narratives of the Hunters* (Baton Rouge: Louisiana State University Press, 1967). See also Dickson D. Bruce, Jr., "Hunting: Dimensions of Antebellum Southern Culture," *Mississippi Quarterly* 30 (1977): 259.

40. "A Hunting Article," *Southern Literary Messenger* 17, no. 1 (January 1851): 47.

41. "Duck Shooting in Georgia," *American Turf Register and Sporting Magazine* 6, no. 10 (June 1835): 509.

42. For a fuller discussion of the importance of Southern oratory in the culture of honor, see Greenberg, *Masters and Statesmen*, 12–15.

43. Bruce, "Hunting," suggests that the primary purpose of the hunt was not to kill animals. Stuart A. Marks, *Southern Hunting in Black and White: Nature and Ritual in a Carolina Community* (Princeton: Princeton University Press, 1991), 18–38, discusses many features of the antebellum Southern hunt in addition to its connection to death.

44. William Elliott, *Carolina Sports by Land and Water; Including Incidents of Devil Fishing, Wild-Cat, Deer, and Bear Hunting, Etc.* (New York: Derby and Jackson, 1859), 43.

45. Ibid., 174.

46. Goldstein, *Playing for Keeps*, 49.

47. "Hunting Article," 47.

48. Wyatt-Brown, *Southern Honor*, 157, retells the story of Wade Hampton and the drake.

49. Flack, *Texan Rifle-Hunter*, 92.

50. Elliott, *Carolina Sports by Land and Water*, 17.

51. Gohdes, *Hunting in the Old South*, 12.

52. Ibid., 23.

53. Whitehead, *Wild Sports in the South*, 16.

54. See, for example, the descriptions of the character of animals in Elliott, *Carolina Sports by Land and Water*, 207; *American Turf Register* 5 (April 1834): 397–99, reprinted in Gohdes, *Hunting in the Old South*, 78–79; and Whitehead, *Wild Sports in the South*, 50.

55. See, for example, *Southern Quarterly Review* 13 (April 1848): 414–19.

56. Ibid., 423–25.

57. Elliott, *Carolina Sports by Land and Water*, 207.

58. Quoted in *Southern Quarterly Review* 13 (April 1848): 421.

59. "Field Sports," *American Turf Register and Sporting Magazine* 7, no. 7 (March 1836): 323. For a similar description of lustful and noble male turkeys responding to the hunter's imitation of a female, see Captain Flack, *A Hunter's Experiences in the Southern States of America* (London; Longmans Green, 1866), 239–47

60. Whitehead, *Wild Sports in the South,* 50.

61. Somers, *Rise of Sport in New Orleans,* 38.

62. Elliott, *Carolina Sports by Land and Water,* 82–83; quotation on 83.

63. *Southern Quarterly Review* 13 (April 1848): 421, 423–24; "The Chase in North Carolina!!" *American Turf Register and Sporting Magazine* 5, no. 9 (May 1834): 473.

64. *Southern Quarterly Review* 13 (April 1848): 414.

65. Phillip Henry Gosse, *Letters from Alabama* (London, 1859), 226–34, reprinted in Gohdes, *Hunting in the Old South,* 87–93; quotation on 93.

66. Rosengarten, *Tombee,* 131.

67. On the rise of the humanitarian interest in animals, see James Turner, *Reckoning with the Beast: Animals, Pain, and Humanity in the Victorian Mind* (Baltimore: Johns Hopkins University Press, 1980).

68. Thoreau's journal entry can be found in Bradford Torrey, ed., *The Writings of Henry David Thoreau: Journal, August 1, 1860–November 3, 1861* (Boston: Houghton Mifflin, 1906), 20:315–19.

69. Goldstein, *Playing for Keeps,* 76.

70. Elliott, *Carolina Sports by Land and Water,* 33.

71. Ibid., 73.

72. Ibid., 169.

73. Ibid., 191.

74. Ibid., 262.

75. "Snipe Shooting in Opelousas," *American Turf Register and Sporting Magazine* 5, no. 9 (May 1834): 477.

76. On the desire of Southern planters to hunt in groups, see Rosengarten, *Tombee,* 128.

77. Gelber, "'Their Hands Are All out Playing,'" 5–27.

78. Elliott, *Carolina Sports by Land and Water,* 222–23.

79. See, for example, Flack, *Hunter's Experiences,* 115, and Gohdes, *Hunting in the Old South,* 31–63.

80. Gohdes, *Hunting in the Old South,* xiii. See Bruce, "Hunting," 261, for another example of a rule that a hunter missing a shot "within 40 yards" had to buy "a dozen champagne for the group."

81. Richard B. Harwell, ed., "The Hot and Hot Fish Club of All Saints Parish," *South Carolina Historical and Genealogical Magazine* 48 (1947): 42.

82. J. H. Easterby, ed., "The St. Thomas Hunting Club, 1785–1801," *South Carolina Historical and Genealogical Magazine* 46, no. 3 (July 1945): 124.

83. Stoney, "Autobiography of William John Grayson," 37, describes how the hunting club in Beaufort, South Carolina, punished members who brought more (or less) than the required amount of food. Rosengarten, *Tombee,* 395.

84. Elliott does include one story of a brave slave in his collection. "May"

harpoons a devilfish, jumps on its back, and kills it. But this story is so unusual that it stands as an exception that calls a reader's attention to the more typical pattern. Elliott, *Carolina Sports by Land and Water*, 17–18.

85. Ibid., 79–80.

86. Ibid., 102–3.

87. Ibid., 118.

88. Ibid., 142.

89. Wyatt-Brown, *Southern Honor*, 339–50; Wiley, *Life of Johnny Reb*, 38–39; John M. Findlay, *People of Chance: Gambling in American Society from Jamestown to Las Vegas* (New York: Oxford University Press, 1986), 10–78; Ann Fabian, *Card Sharps, Dream Books, and Bucket Shops: Gambling in Nineteenth-Century America* (Ithaca, N.Y.: Cornell University Press, 1990), 1–58.

90. Scarborough, *Diary of Edmund Ruffin*, 1:158.

91. Wyatt-Brown, *Southern Honor*, 346.

92. *Niles' Register*, August 1, 1835, 381–82; H. R. Howard, *The History of Virgil A. Stewart* (New York: Harper and Brothers, 1836), 263–68.

93. Howard, *History of Virgil A. Stewart*, 266–68.

94. *Niles' Register*, August 8, 1835, 393, 401.

95. Findlay, *People of Chance*, 47.

96. T. H. Breen, "Horses and Gentlemen: The Cultural Significance of Gambling among the Gentry of Virginia," *William and Mary Quarterly*, 3d ser., 34, no. 1 (April 1977): 239–57. On the issue of high-stakes betting, see 252–53.

97. This was the famous duel fought between Jackson and Charles Dickinson as a result of a dispute over a race between Jackson's horse, Truxton, and Ploughboy. The duel was an extension of the competition of the race. John Spencer Bassett, *The Correspondence of Andrew Jackson* (Washington, D.C.: Carnegie Institution, 1926), 1:122–40. On Jackson's general love of gambling, see Findlay, *People of Chance*, 38–40; Barbara Stern Kupfer, "A Presidential Patron of the Sport of Kings," *Tennessee Historical Quarterly* 29, no. 3 (fall 1970): 243–55; and John Dizikes, *Sportsmen and Gamesmen* (Boston: Houghton Mifflin, 1981), 3–44.

98. Bassett, *Correspondence of Andrew Jackson*, 4:475.

99. For numerous examples of gambling for extremely high stakes over cards on Mississippi River boats, see George H. Devol, *Forty Years a Gambler on the Mississippi* (Cincinnati: Devol and Haines, 1887).

100. Scarborough, *Diary of Edmund Ruffin*, 1:582; Faust, *James Henry Hammond*, 50–57, 158–59; Clyde N. Wilson, *Carolina Cavalier: The Life and Mind of James Johnston Pettigrew* (Athens: University of Georgia Press, 1990), 82–83.

101. Grady McWhiney and Perry D. Jamieson, *Attack and Die: Civil War Military Tactics and the Southern Heritage* (University, Ala.: University of Alabama Press, 1982), most carefully documents the Southern tendency to take the offensive during the Civil War. The authors attribute this tendency to the Celtic heritage of Southerners. My concern is less with any heritage than with the powerful cultural forces that kept alive the tradition of taking the offensive.

102. *American Turf Register and Sporting Magazine* 7, no. 1 (September 1835): 30.

103. *American Turf Register and Sporting Magazine* 7, no. 9 (May 1836): 425.

104. See, for example, the language in *American Turf Register and Sporting Magazine* 7, no. 10 (June 1836): 462–63.

105. Mark A. Keller, "Horse Racing Madness in the Old South—The Sporting Epistles of William J. Minor of Natchez (1837–1860)," *Journal of Mississippi History* 47, no. 3 (August 1985): 165. Keller has discovered seventy-three letters written by William J. Minor and published in the *Spirit of the Times* between 1837 and 1860.

106. Ibid., 173–75.

107. Laura D. S. Harrell, "Horse Racing in the Old Natchez District," *Journal of Mississippi History* 12, no. 3 (July 1951): 136–37.

108. Interesting legal cases involving the exclusion of slaves and free blacks from gambling can be found in Catterall, *Judicial Cases*, 1:318, 443; 2:362, 419, 466; 3:120, 121, 218, 247.

109. Findlay, *People of Chance*, 17, 22; Breen, "Horses and Gentlemen," 250–51.

110. William J. Grayson, "The Character of a Gentleman," *Southern Quarterly Review* 7 (January 1853): 59; Wyatt-Brown, *Southern Honor*, 345.

111. Quoted in Findlay, *People of Chance*, 27–28.

112. On the materialism of seventeenth-century Virginia gentry, see Breen, "Horses and Gentlemen," 246. The same analysis could be applied to almost any nineteenth-century Southern gentleman gambler.

113. *American Turf Register and Sporting Magazine* 7, no. 10 (June 1836): 462–63.

114. See, for example, the gambling stories in Devol, *Forty Years a Gambler*.

115. Robert Bailey, *The Life and Adventures of Robert Bailey* (Richmond, Va.: J. and G. Cochran, 1822), 66–67. See also Findlay, *People of Chance*, 48.

116. The Vicksburg report is reprinted in Howard, *History of Virgil A. Stewart*, 264.

117. Ibid., 263.

118. Edwin A. Miles, "Mississippi Slave Insurrection Scare of 1835," *Journal of Negro History* 42, no. 1 (January 1957): 48–60; Laurence Shore, "Making Mississippi Safe for Slavery: The Insurrectionary Panic of 1835," in *Class, Conflict, and Consensus: Antebellum Southern Community Studies*, ed. Orville Vernon Burton and Robert C. McMath, Jr. (Westport, Conn.: Greenwood Press, 1992), 96–127.

119. Howard, *History of Virgil A. Stewart*, 238–59.

120. Ibid., 239, 244, 248, 252.

121. Ibid., 239, 242, 244, 245, 246, 252.

122. Vicksburg report reprinted in ibid., 264.

123. Barnum, *Struggles and Triumphs*, 64.

INDEX

Pages with illustrations are listed in boldface.
Titles are not given unless necessary to identify or differentiate a person.

White Junior (character), 67, 69, 73
white Southern men. *See* Men of honor
Whitman, Walt, "Song of Myself," 120
wild turkey hunting, 127–28, 129
Wilson, John Lyde, 82
Wise, Henry A., 159n.17; on John
  Brown's death, 90–91
Witherspoon episode, 12–13
women, 3, 32; black or slave women, 33,
  37; death and dying of, 94, 98,

161n.47; men dressed as, 25, **27**, **30**,
151n.7; as powerless, 29–30; slave mistresses, 37, 38, 49
words: of honor, 12, 139–40, 145–46; of
  slaves, 11, 37, 39–40
Wyatt-Brown, Bertram, 48, 161n.44;
  Southern Honor, xiv; "The Mask of
  Obedience," 154n.65

Yeadon, Richard, 4–6, 9